Economic Regulatory Policies

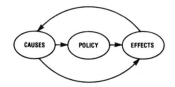

Policy Studies Organization Series

Economic Regulatory Policies

Edited by
James E. Anderson
University of Houston

Lexington Books
D.C. Heath and Company
Lexington, Massachusetts
Toronto   London

41010

Library of Congress Cataloging in Publication Data

Main entry under title:

Economic regulatory policies.

Includes index.
1. Trade regulation—United States—Addresses, essays, lectures.
2. United States—Economic policy—1971- —Addresses, essays,
lectures. I. Anderson, James E.
KF1600.A75E3   382.1'0973   75-32870
ISBN 0-669-00366-2

Published simultaneously in Canada

Printed in the United States of America

International Standard Book Number: 0-669-00366-2

Library of Congress Catalog Card Number: 75-32870

Contents

41010

List of Tables

Introduction

One of the major tasks of governments in the United States is the control, direction, or support of private economic activity. Congress, for example, devotes much of its time to the consideration of economic regulatory legislation, and scores of national administrative agencies are involved in its implementation. During the process of implementation agencies help give shape to the content and direction of public policy. The courts may also become importantly involved in the formation of public economic policy.

Although governments in the United States have always intervened in the economy, whether as regulators, promoters, or operators, most existent regulatory legislation and programs are products of the twentieth century. Many factors have contributed to the expansion of government economic activity: the increasing complexity and interdependency of our economy and society; the need for government to adjust or resolve group conflicts; the ethical desire to protect the economically weak against some of the actions and predations of the economically strong; the desire of some groups to protect or promote their interests through the regulation of competing groups, as in the case of the railroads and motor carriers; the needs and demands created by crises such as recession, inflation, and war; and changed attitudes toward the proper role of government vis-à-vis the economy. Moreover, the constitutional power of government to act in the economic arena has been expanded by interpretation and usage in response to felt needs.

In recent decades both liberals and conservatives have advocated and supported the expansion of government economic activity, albeit perhaps for different purposes or beneficiaries. As Professor Theodore Lowi has argued, liberals and conservatives once could readily be distinguished on the basis of liberals' willingness to expand governmental action to bring about deliberate social and economic change and conservatives' customary opposition to such endeavors. The principle of positive government has now been firmly established for decades and the question requiring response has been transformed from one of ''shall government act'' to ''on whose behalf shall government act.'' Thus liberals are likely to support legislation and programs of benefit to labor and low income groups while conservatives are more apt to advocate those of benefit to business and upper income groups. Given this condition, the factors mentioned in the preceding paragraph, and the usually strong support of particular programs by their beneficiaries, the economic role of government seems more likely to expand than to contract in the foreseeable future (which is the best kind of future with which to deal). If a few programs disappear (such as "fair trade," i.e., resale price maintenance), others are likely to expand, as in the cases of energy and environmental protection.

A common set of categories classifies public economic programs under the headings of promotion, regulation, and government ownership. In this framework, promotion involves governmental activity designed to stimulate, encourage, or assist private economic activity, regulation pertains to its restriction or control, and government ownership to the actual conduct of business activity by public authorities. While not lacking in usefulness, these categories are not mutually exclusive. All government economic activity involves an element of control (or regulation) in that it is designed to encourage desired actions and discourage or prohibit undesired actions. Thus, government could encourage industrial plant modernization by subsidy (promotion) in the form of tax credits, as it now does, or by regulation requiring that industrial plants meet certain standards of modernization (with penalties for noncompliance), or by taking substandard plants into government ownership. If the latter two methods seem a bit "farfetched," it is because promotion has become the accepted method for encouraging or achieving industrial plant modernization in our society. (Yet, the case of rail passenger service and Amtrak indicates the government enterprise alternative is not totally unlikely.) Moreover, what is viewed as promotion from the perspective of one group may be perceived as regulation or restriction by another. Thus, minimum wage legislation is promotional for employees but regulatory for employers to the extent it prevents them from paying wages as low as they would prefer or the "market" would permit. The Tennessee Valley Authority has benefited the users of electricity in its area while limiting the opportunities of private utility companies and providing "yardstick regulation" of their rates. In putting together this symposium on economic regulatory policies this broader view of regulation has been followed.

Perhaps the major economic policy development in the post-World War II era has been explicit assumption of responsibility by the national government for the maintenance of economic stability or, as stated in the Employment Act of 1946, the maintenance of "maximum employment, production, and purchasing power." Whereas inflation and recession once were thought to be beyond the control of government and man-made laws, governments and presidents are now clearly expected to deal, and deal successfully, with these problems. Notwithstanding the importance of this function, and its intensely political nature (e.g., witness the struggles of the Nixon and Ford administrations), political scientists have, with few exceptions, little examined the formation of macro-economic policy. Norman Thomas, after briefly reviewing the efforts of political scientists and economists, presents a research agenda for the study of macro-economic policy formation. The expansion of "uncontrollable" expenditure items in the national budget, and the implications of this trend for fiscal policy-making are the concern of John Gist. Conventional wisdom, which is supported by experience, has it that taxes can be lowered more easily than raised. From Gist's discussion one may conclude that it will also be much easier to increase than to decrease expenditures. The effect of these developments is to limit the usefulness of discretionary fiscal policy as an anti-inflationary instrument. A major recent event in macro-economic policy activity was the institution of direct price and wage controls in 1971 by the Nixon Administration, which acted on authority granted by the Economic Stabilization Act of 1970. Markley Roberts looks at these controls from the perspective of an AFL-CIO economist and finds them wanting. Undoubtedly, not everyone will agree with Roberts' analysis. Although almost everyone has an interest in preventing inflation, the ways in which this can be attempted are not neutral in impact, as he demonstrates.

The national government has been concerned with directly supporting agricultural prices and incomes since the late 1920s. The Agricultural Adjustment Acts, parity, flexible versus rigid price supports, the Brannan plan, the soil bank, and "a free market for agriculture" have been some of the symbols and focal points for controversy in this issue area. Until the middle 1960s, the question of what forms and level of price supports, if any, there should be was a continuing feature of the national policy agenda. The "farm problem" was perceived essentially as a problem of low prices and incomes caused by surplus production. In the 1970s, however, because of changed domestic and international conditions, the farm has begun to be redefined as one of too little rather than too much production. Richard Fraenkel and Don Hadwiger survey some of the literature and findings relating to the agricultural policy process on the United States and provide some comparisons with the less developed countries. Some recent changes in U.S. agricultural price support policies, and the shift of agricultural policy-making from the subsystem to the macro-political arena, are the subjects of Garth Youngberg's essay. In the future the "politics of hunger" and the "food problem" are likely to be significant features of the agricultural policy process.

During the last decade a substantial volume of consumer protection legislation has been enacted by Congress on such matters as automobile safety, truth-in-lending, fair packaging, meat inspection, and consumer product safety. The consumer protection movement, or more simply "consumerism," has become a force of considerable political potency. In the business community, consumerism has often been viewed as a problem or nuisance complicating the conduct of business activity. Opposition to consumer legislation has been growing and, through 1975, the opponents have been able to block legislation creating a Consumer Protection Agency. Mark Nadel scrutinizes the consumer movement and finds some cracks developing in the coalition. Charles Hagan provides a comparative treatment of national policies relating to the sale of cigarettes within the context of their impact on health. To what extent should government protect people against a health hazard which they apparently enjoy?

Three areas of economic regulation (in the conventional sense of restriction or limitation) are dealt with in Section IV. Daniel Fiorino discusses the experience of the Federal Power Commission in its efforts to regulate the field price of natural gas. William Jenkins, in turn, is concerned with the development and application of national policy toward banking mergers. Both Fiorino and Jenkins provide not only a good view of substantive policy in their subject areas but also insightful treatments of the role of the courts, especially the United States Supreme Court, in policy formation. In the area of labor-management relations the trend has been for national policy to become more and more detailed. This, however, does not resolve confusion and disagreement over the meaning of statutory provisions. Charles Bulmer and John Carmichael discuss the problems confronting the National Labor Relations Board in enforcing the statutory obligations of employers to bargain in "good faith" with employers. Much has been written and said about the possession by administrative agencies of too much discretionary power. How would you, the reader, proceed to limit agency discretion in this instance?

Governments in the United States have always provided a variety of forms of support and assistance for the business community generally or for particular segments thereof. (For example, the second statute enacted by Congress under the Constitution provided for a protective tariff.) Business groups, while deploring regulation, have not often hesitated to seek governmental aid for particular problems. The Department of Commerce is one symbol of their success. Although we like to distinguish between public and private spheres of activity in the economy, in actuality it is often difficult if not impossible to draw a clear line between the two. Lloyd Musolf examines some trends in recent years which have contributed to the mingling of public and private economic activity and the addition of more "mix" to our mixed economy. James Dunn looks at the possibility of public ownership of the U.S. railroads from a comparative vantage point. The experience of other industrial nations indicates that public ownership is not a panacea for the ills of the railroad industry. Regardless of who owns the railroads, he contends, large public subsidies will be needed and called for to keep the railroads running. One way or another, the government is going to be more deeply involved in this industry. Patent policy, one of the nation's oldest business promotional policies, is treated by Larry Baum. He finds that in the formation and implementation of patent policy, the diffuse general interest, because of official support and presentation, often prevails over more specific, intense interests favoring lenient patent standards. This is an aspect of policy formation which deserves more study by both political scientists and those of more activist orientation. Moreover, his essay shows how inquiry into an area of policy viewed as rather unexciting by most persons can yield useful insight into the policy process.

There has never been a shortage of critics of business regulatory programs. Liberals and conservatives, business spokesmen and business critics, the informed and the less informed, all have found defects and objectionable qualities in particular programs. In recent years something of a movement for deregulation of some industries and activities has developed and has developed support from various sources including the Ford Administration. Deregulation of natural gas prices is advocated as necessary to increase gas supplies by encouraging exploration through higher prices. (The industry, of course, has opposed rate regulation since it was imposed in the early 1950s.) Deregulation of railroad and airlines is seen as necessary to open these industries to competition, thereby increasing their operating efficiency and responsiveness to public needs. Whether the current movement (which term may impose too much unity on rather diverse actors, motives, and events) will result in the abandonment of many regulatory programs is questionable. We have a general systemic bias in favor of regulation, and each regulatory program has its supporters and beneficiaries. Thus calls for deregulation of the railroads do not excite wide enthusiasm within the industry, the railroads generally having learned to live with and indeed like regulation because of the benefits it confers.

George Daly and David Brady, and Alan Stone, provide a pair of challenging and insightful commentaries on economic regulation. From a perch labeled the free market, Daly and Brady survey the rationale for and the shortcomings of economic regulation. It is hard to quarrel with their ultimate conclusions that deregulation is likely to be both gradual in nature and limited in extent. Is not dissatisfaction with the operation and results of the market a major cause of government intervention in the economy? Alan Stone also looks askance at regulation. Dealing in some detail with the Federal Trade Commission and trade regulation, he contends that much regulation fails to have the intended impact because of the discretion which the regulated possess and which they can use to frustrate regulation. He examines some alternatives to the existing system of regulation and concludes that more consideration should be given to public ownership as a means for making industry more responsive to public values.

Political scientists have not shown vast interest in economic regulatory policies, in either their teaching or research. Thus, the general textbooks written by political scientists on government and the economy are either out of print or out of date. A perusal of the content of political science journals during the past decade or so will indicate no substantial renewal of interest in this area. This is notwithstanding the growing interest in the discipline in policy studies, policy analysis, policy theory, and related concerns. (Of course, what some political scientists now do as "policy analysis" looks much the same as what they did previously under a different rubric.) Why, it can be asked, are such issue areas as foreign policy, civil rights and liberties, and urban policies, but not economic policies, seemingly appropriate concerns for political scientists. Are not economic policies too important to be left to lawyers and economists. Or, should such language seem too belligerent, do not political scientists have something to contribute here? Most of the authors in this volume are political scientists and the products of their efforts indicate that the answer should be yes.

Hopefully, which describes the feelings of missionaries, racetrack habitues, and editors of symposia such as this, this volume will both disseminate useful information on the substance and formation of economic regulatory policies and kindle further interest in their study and analysis. If we take public policies as the focus of our efforts, we can learn not only about the substance and impact of public policies, and the development and nature of public problems, but also about the governmental processes that have long been regarded as proper concerns for political scientists.

Economic Regulatory Policies

Part I
Economic Stability

1

Political Science and the Study of Macro-Economic Policy-Making

Norman C. Thomas

In the last decade the formulation of macro-economic policy has assumed increasing importance as the nation has grappled with chronic inflation and, in the past year, with the most severe recession since World War II. Political scientist Thomas E. Cronin believes that presidents now devote more attention to managing the economy than to all other aspects of domestic policy. The president's task is to develop a set of policies that will maintain prosperity, which is defined ideally as full employment and price stability, and to persuade Congress to adopt those policies.

There are three basic means by which the federal government may affect the performance of the economy, monetary policy, fiscal policy, and incomes policy. Monetary policy, which is exercised by the autonomous Federal Reserve Board, involves expansion or contraction of the supply of money and credit. Fiscal policy refers to the impact of governmental expenditures and revenues. Incomes policy primarily entails mandatory wage and price controls and advisory wage-price guidelines. Macro-economic policy consists of the substantive mix of monetary, fiscal, and incomes policies.

Economists have written at length concerning the optimum strategy for achieving the goal of high employment without inflation and policymakers do not want for advice nor do they lack alternative policy options although there is no readily apparent remedy for the current ills of the economy. Most economists, however, are in agreement concerning the nature of the policy problem as reflected in the Phillips curve:

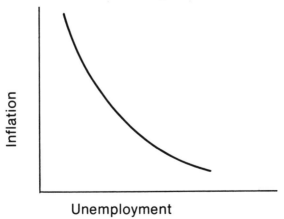

Unemployment

I am indebted to my colleagues Henry J. Anna and Andrew K. Semmel for their helpful criticisms and suggestions.

Inflation and unemployment are inversely related. For a given rate of inflation there is a given level of unemployment. It is possible to reduce unemployment by tolerating more inflation and vice versa. The short-run question facing economic policymakers is what set of monetary and fiscal measures produces the politically optimum balance between inflation and unemployment? It should be recognized, however, that the location of the Phillips curve is not permanent. It reflects the current structure of the economy and existing governmental programs. The long-run policy question is how to move the curve to the left. The situation confronting macro-economic policymakers in 1975 was one in which the Phillips curve moved sharply to the right in part as a result of high prices for foreign oil and other imported commodities and as a partial consequence of other structural changes.

Although economists have studied the macro-economic policy problem at length, their analyses have been concerned almost entirely with its substantive aspects. They have paid little attention to the processes by which the policy choices are made.[1] Indeed, it would be surprising if they had done so for their professional orientation does not lie in the direction of process, but rather it focuses on, and quantifies, the dimensions of choice—the costs, the benefits, and the alternative ways to achieve a given result.[2] Political science, on the other hand, has a basic orientation toward the process of decision. Political scientists are deeply concerned, among other things, with the how and the why of governmental policy choice.

Put another way, economists focus on policy output and outcomes because they deal with objective utilities. That is, economics lends itself to more precision since the basic concepts and units of analysis that it employs—profits, revenues, physical plant, production, etc.—are readily measurable. Yet, economists are not able easily to account for or assess the subjective utilities or values that policymakers assign to possible outcomes. Political science is better able to deal with subjective utilities. Political scientists employ concepts and analytical units such as power, influence, interests, and access that, although they are difficult to measure, are designed to facilitate analysis of the processes whereby society allocates values.

In spite of the increasing salience of macro-economic policy, however, political scientists have largely neglected the study of the process by which it is made. The most notable exceptions to this observation are Pierce's study of fiscal policy formation, Reagan's examination of the Federal Reserve System, and Flash's analysis of the Council of Economic Advisers.[3] Of course, neither Pierce, whose research concentrated on the Johnson administration nor Reagan, whose study carried through the Eisenhower administration, provide any analysis of the critical developments of the past five years. Nor does either of them explore the relationship between monetary and fiscal policy or consider the role of incomes policy since their studies had more limited parameters than macro-economic policy. Flash came closer to examining the full ambit of macro-economic policy-making in his analysis of the CEA, but his research carried only through 1964 and his focus was on the advisory role of economists rather than the dynamics of policy formation.

The limited concern political scientists have shown for macro-economic policy contrasts sharply with the extensive range of process studies in the national security, budgeting, and domestic policy areas. These inquiries have produced conceptual frameworks and empirical findings that have led to increased awareness of the factors shaping policy, an understanding of the relationship between substance and process, and the capacity to evaluate the operation of policy processes using such criteria as representativeness, efficiency, and leadership effectiveness. While it is debatable whether process studies have resulted in improvements in policy-making, they have certainly increased understanding and sparked controversy over the interpretation of the findings and the analytical approaches employed.[4] It is the thesis of this chapter that macro-economic policy affords an opportunity for the conduct of similar investigations. The utility and applicability of differing approaches to the study of policy processes can be further tested thereby and information on the subject and the understanding of policy-making increased substantially.

It is in the realm of national security policy that process studies have been most extensive and provocative. Intensive case studies of major decisions[5] and extensive analysis of policy-making machinery[6] have provided descriptive and prescriptive models which could profitably be applied to the study of macro-economic policy. The most useful of these is the bureaucratic politics model developed originally by Hilsman, Huntington, Neustadt, and Schilling[7] and amplified and elaborated more recently by Allison and Halperin.[8] More prescriptive and less sweeping is George's multiple advocacy.[9] These conceptual approaches suggest means of imparting coherence and central purpose to national security policy through organizational strategies that take account of political and bureaucratic realities. Even with the benefit of an extensive body of literature, however, political science has not produced a viable solution to "the foreign affairs organizational problem."[10] It has, however, reached a point where it can systematically analyze the policy process and offer useful criticism and advice concerning it to Congress and the president. In the area of macro-economic policy, we have hardly begun to develop an empirical base on which to attempt such functions.

Studies of domestic policy areas have proceeded along somewhat different lines. Following the path suggested initially in Freeman's study of a small agency, the Bureau of Indian Affairs in the Department of the Interior, scholars have analyzed policy subgovernments of subsystems built around individual agencies or related sets of programs.[11] In addition, we have an abundance of case studies of individual legislative and administrative policy decisions. This research has employed several models of the domestic policy process including group theory, elite theory, systems theory, and the classical institutional model based on the Constitution.[12] These approaches, when applied eclecticly and flexibly, provide a basis for explaining domestic policy-making. The analysis of domestic policy processes, however, has not been as prescriptively oriented as the study of national security policy.

Studies of the budgetary process have resulted in the development of systematic explanatory theories that have considerable relevance for the study of macro-economic policy. The principal contributions derive from the work of Wildavsky, Fenno, and Schick. Wildavsky's conception of budgeting as an incremental process in which "the base is as important as the rate of increase"[13] and agencies devise various strategies to protect and increase the base is fundamental to any understanding of one of the key aspects of macro-economic policy formation. However, Wildavsky does not examine the relationship between spending and efforts to manage the economy. Fenno's contribution is an intensive examination of the appropriations process in Congress. Conceiving of the House Appropriations Committee as a political system having identifiable internal parts existing in an identifiable external environment, Fenno explains its decisions in terms of efforts of committee members to stabilize internal and external relationships over time.[14] Manley employed a related approach in his study of the House Ways and Means Committee,[15] a key unit in the macro-economic policy process. The Fenno-Manley approach could be used to study other congressional committees involved in making economic policy. Allen Schick argues that budgeting, and by implication other aspects of economic policy making, should be studied from a systemic as well as a process perspective.[16]

In the remainder of this chapter I shall suggest a research agenda for the study of macro-economic policy formation. My proposals draw upon approaches used in other policy process studies and assume that it will take considerable time and the effort of many persons before we reach a level of understanding comparable to that achieved in other policy areas.

The most immediate and important item on the agenda is to develop an empirical base sufficient to permit the evaluation of the process in order that changes may be recommended and alternative organizational structures and processes formulated. This should involve three distinct research thrusts; case studies of major policy decisions and actions, analysis of the policy arena, and intensive examination of the central macro-economic decision-making process within the presidency. Some relevant work has been accomplished along these lines, but much remains to be done.

The most useful case studies are those that go beyond mere empirical description and are undertaken in the context of an appropriate conceptual framework. Available case studies of macro-economic policy-making carry through the Johnson administration,[17] but of these, only Pierce's study of the 1967 income tax surcharge employs an approach that raises and answers theoretical questions concerning the nature of the policy process and provides a comprehensive overview of how the process operated. The major shifts in economic policy made during the Nixon and Ford administrations have yet to be examined.

In addition to case studies, the arena within which macro-economic policy is made should be thoroughly investigated. The functions and objectives of the various organizational participants, in the bureaucracy, Congress, and outside of government, the relationships between the participants, and decision-making processes, both routine and crisis, provide multiple research opportunities. Again, Pierce comes closest to accomplishing this task, but he explicitly excluded monetary policy and did not examine any of the major organizational participants in depth or the public-private sector interactions. Nor were there any agencies in existence during the period of his study that were responsible for incomes policy, e.g., the Cost of Living Council.

We need intensive studies of the major organizational participants in the macro-economic policy arena. Flash's study of the CEA and Reagan's analysis of the Federal Reserve System require considerable updating and the macro-economic policy roles of the Treasury, the Office of Management and Budget, and the councils created to monitor or enforce wage and price controls and guidelines have yet to be examined. Furthermore, the organized private interests, e.g., the AFL-CIO, the American Banking Association, etc., and several relevant congressional committees that operate in the arena require study from the perspective of their impact on macro-economic policy. As specific organizational studies are completed it will then be possible to develop a comprehensive overview of the policy-making process.

Particularly close attention to economic decision-making in the presidency is essential because of the president's unique constitutional position. Of all the participants in the policy arena he alone is potentially able to provide cohesion and purpose. Analysis of presidential decision-making in this area should increase our understanding of the constraints that prevent him from accomplishing this objective. It is important to ascertain the ways in which presidential economic policy-making differs from other policy-making if we are to suggest how the process might be improved. Pierce provides a starting point for these inquiries with his description of economic forecasting by the "troika" comprised of economists from the CEA, the Treasury, and OMB. Flash's analysis of the CEA members' impact on policy as a knowledge/power relationship with the president furnishes a useful approach to the study of an agency involved in the process. What remains undone, however, is substantial. Specifically, we need to examine alternative sources of economic advice available to the president, the processes by which the president chooses and selects from among economic advisers, and the means by which presidential decisions involving fiscal policy are coordinated with monetary decisions of the autonomous Federal Reserve Board and with congressional actions.

In undertaking this research agenda four of the major conceptual approaches can be readily adapted from studies of other policy-making processes; rational process, organizational process and bureaucratic politics models, and a modified systems model. The first three models are appropriate because macro-economic policy making clearly involves activity at the levels incorporated in the three analytical "cuts" of rational process, organizational process, and bureaucratic politics.

Most economics who have written in the area implicitly employ the rational process model.[18] That is, they conceive of the federal government acting on the economy through various policy tools in order to achieve specific measurable objectives. The government, as a unitary actor, chooses rationally in selecting a set of policies appropriate to the achievement of the current goal. The choice is regarded as a rational act based on information and forecasts. Such an approach is quite necessary in explaining economic policy, but as in the case of national security policy it is incomplete.

Macro-economic policy is also the output of an organizational process within the federal government. The organizational process model employs the governmental organization, e.g., the Treasury, the Federal Reserve Board, the CEA, etc., as its analytical unit and views policy as the product of routines designed to protect and enhance organizational interests. In this context, policy-making involves intra-governmental competition between organizational components. The choices of organizational leaders are constrained by several factors including the organization's goals, mission, budget, and capabilities. Although some studies have taken organizational interests into account (especially those that focus on the Federal Reserve Board) such considerations tend to be ignored for the most part. The macro-economic policy process clearly involves intense organizational competition, the ramifications of which must be analyzed if we are to understand and explain the process more to our satisfaction.

Bureaucratic politics involves a third conceptual model which regards policy as the result of bargaining between individual actors engaged in struggles for personal power. It focuses on individual officials who share power unequally and who act "according to various conceptions of national, organizational, and personal goals."[19] This approach, which Allison calls the governmental politics model, should also be employed in studying macro-economic policy-making, for the policy stands of the key individuals involved quite obviously reflect their personal experiences, career patterns, and positions in the bureaucracy.[20]

The bureaucratic politics view of macro-economic policy decisions as the result of bargaining between individuals, acting independently or in concert with others, has been the implicit model employed by journalists in their accounts of the macro-economic policy process,[21] but it has not been a major feature of process studies by political scientists. Its principal drawbacks are that it requires extensive amounts of information obtainable only through interviews and the reports of participant observers, it is difficult to avoid falling victim to the tendency of process participants to assign excessive weight to idiosyncratic personality variables, and it tends to overstate the degree of decentralization in the policy process.[22]

A fourth major approach that has been employed in studying policy-making processes that could be applied advantageously in analyzing macro-economic policy-making is a modified systems model. Generally it entails conceiving of policy as the product of a political subsystem. Much of what is now done in economic forecasting on the basis of econometric models makes implicit use of a systemic model; however, the economists who conduct such activity are unconcerned with the policy conversion process. If we are to understand and explain the policy conversion process it will be necessary to identify the principal participants, examine their relationships with each other and the external environment of the policy subsystem in which they operate in terms of their expectations and perceptions, and to analyze the feedback that results from changing economic conditions caused in part by their policy decisions. Pierce suggests a systemic conception of the fiscal policy process, but does not carry it through his study. Even though the systemic approach has its limitations—a static character and a lack of explanatory leverage—we sorely need the taxonomic advantages that it offers[23] so we can compare the macro-economic policy subsystem with other policy systems. We should be able to be more explicit about similarities and differences in these policy systems so that we can have confidence that our explanations and suggestions carry the weight of systematic inquiry.

The task of developing alternative macro-economic policy-making processes is compounded not only by the absence of a substantial body of systematic analysis, but also by the unique characteristics of the policy arena. The independence of the Federal Reserve Board and its special relationship to the banking industry resemble the pattern found in regulatory agencies, but the powers of the "Fed" are far more sweeping in their potential impact than those of any other regulatory bodies. The dependence of top policymakers, who for the most part are laymen, or advisers who are experts, either economists or financial specialists, creates a situation in which the problems of democratic control and responsibility associated with professionalism and technocracy are as serious as those encountered in any other area. And, the negative political consequences of the decisions reached are as apt to be swift and as far reaching as any except those that involve peace and war.

There is, then, a macro-economic policy organizational problem of considerable importance that warrants serious and extended study. This chapter has attempted to identify the problem and suggest where and how students of the policy process might begin to analyze it. There is both a fruitful field for investigation and a substantial challenge that could result in highly relevant and useful practical results.

Notes

1. See, for example, Walter W. Heller, *New Dimensions of Political Economy* (New York: W.W. Norton & Co., 1967); Herbert Stein, *The Fiscal Revolution in America* (Chicago: University of Chicago Press, 1969); and Arthur M. Okun, *The Political Economy of Prospertiy* (New York: W.W. Norton & Co., 1970).

2. Okun, *Political Economy*, p. 3.

3. Lawrence C. Pierce, *The Politics of Fiscal Policy Formation* (Pacific Palisades: Goodyear Publishing Co., 1971); Michael D. Reagan, "The Political Structure of the Federal Reserve System," *American Political Science Review* 55 (March 1961): 64-76; and Edward S. Flash, *Economic Advice and Presidential Leadership* (New York: Columbia University Press, 1965), and his "Macro-Economics for Macro-Policy," *The Annals of the American Academy of Political and Social Science* (March 1971): 46-56.

4. See the extensive review and evaluation of foreign policy process studies in I.M. Destler, *Presidents, Bureaucrats, and Foreign Policy: The Politics of Organizational Reform* (Princeton: Princeton University Press, 1975).

5. Most notable are Graham T. Allison, *Essence of Decision: Explaining the Cuban Missile Crisis* (Boston: Little, Brown & Co., 1971); Richard E. Neustadt, *Alliance Politics* (New York: Columbia University Press, 1970); and Glenn D. Paige, *The Korean Decision: June 24-30, 1950* (New York: The Free Press, 1968).

6. See, for example, Keith C. Clark and Laurence J. Legere (eds.), *The President and the Management of National Security: A Report by the Institute for Defense Analysis* (New York: Praeger Publishers, 1969); and Destler, *Presidents, Bureaucrats*, Destler describes thirteen major studies of the foreign policy process conducted since 1945.

7. Roger Hilsman, *To Move a Nation: The Politics of Foreign Policy in the Administration of John F. Kennedy* (New York: Doubleday & Co., 1967); Samuel P. Huntington, *The Common Defense: Strategic Programs in National Defense* (New York: Columbia University Press, 1961); Richard E. Neustadt, *Presidental Power* (New York: John Wiley & Sons, 1960); and Warner R. Schilling, "The H-Bomb Decision: How to Decide Without Actually Choosing," *Political Science Quarterly* 76 (March 1961), and his "The Politics of National Defense: Fiscal 1950," in Schilling, P.Y. Hammond, and G.H. Snyder (eds.), *Strategy, Politics, and Defense Budgets* (New York: Columbia University Press, 1962).

8. Allison, *Essence of Decision*; Morton H. Halperin, with Priscilla Clapp and Arnold Kanter, *Bureaucratic Politics and Foreign Policy* (Washington: The Brookings Institution, 1974); and Allison and Halperin, "Bureaucratic Politics: A Paradigm and Some Policy Implications," *World Politics* 24 (Supplement 1972): 40-79.

9. Alexander L. George, "The Case for Multiple Advocacy in Making Foreign Policy," *American Political Science Review* 66 (September 1972): 751-785.

10. The phrase is Destler's, *Presidents, Bureaucrats*, p. 83.

11. See J. Lieper Freeman, *The Political Process: Executive Bureau-Legislative Committee Relations* (New York: Random House, 1965); Theodore J. Lowi, *The End of Liberalism: Ideology, Policy, and the Crisis of Public Authority* (New York: W.W. Norton & Co., 1969), Chapter 4; Harold L. Wolman, *Politics of Federal Housing* (New York: Dodd, Mead & Co., Inc., 1971); and Norman C. Thomas, *Education in National Politics* (New York: David McKay Co., 1975).

12. See the summaries in James E. Anderson, *Public Policy-Making* (New York: Praeger Publishers, 1975), Chapter 1; and Peter Woll, *Public Policy* (Cambridge: Winthrop Publishers, 1974), Chapter 2.

13. Aaron Wildavsky, *The Politics of the Budgetary Process*, revised edition (Boston: Little, Brown & Co., 1974), p. xix.

14. Richard F. Fenno, Jr., *The Power of the Purse: Appropriations Politics in Congress* (Boston: Little, Brown, and Co., 1966), p. xviii.

15. John F. Manley, *The Politics of Finance* (Boston: Little, Brown & Co., 1971).

16. Allen Schick, "The Road to PPB: The Stages of Budget Reform,"

Public Administration Review 26 (December 1966): 243-258; "Systems Politics and Systems Budgeting," *Public Administration Review* 29 (March/April 1969): 137-151; and "A Death in the Bureaucracy: The Demise of Federal PPB," *Public Administration Review* 33 (March/April 1973): 146-156.

17. See Heller, *New Dimensions*; Okun, *Political Economy*; and Pierce, *Politics of Fiscal Policy Formation*.

18. An exception is Sherman Maisel, *Managing the Dollar* (New York: W. W. Norton & Co., 1973).

19. Allison, *Essence of Decision*, p. 144.

20. Halperin, *Bureaucratic Politics*, pp. 84-85.

21. See the periodic descriptive accounts in *National Journal Reports* and *Congressional Quarterly*.

22. The principal criticisms of the bureaucratic politics model include; Robert J. Art, "Bureaucratic Politics and American Foreign Policy: A Critique," *Policy Sciences* 4 (1973): 467-490; Amos Perlmutter, "The Presidential Political Center and Foreign Policy: A Critique of the Revisionist and Bureaucratic-Political Orientations," *World Politics* 26 (October 1974): 87-106; and Stephen Krasner, "Are Bureaucrats Important?" *Foreign Policy* 7 (Summer 1972): 159-179.

23. See J. David Singer, *A General Systems Taxonomy for Political Science* (New York: General Learning Press, 1971).

2

Budget Control and Fiscal Policy-Making

John R. Gist

Introduction

In his message on the fiscal year (FY) 1975 budget, President Nixon projected that in four years, by FY 1979, outlays for existing and proposed programs would total $391 billion.[1] Less than two years later, in a speech delivered October 6, 1975, his successor challenged Congress to reduce FY 1977 outlays by $28 billion in order to hold total outlays for that year *down* to $395 billion.[2] In other words, even with practically no new spending initiatives in FY 1976 and 1977 and a proposed $28 billion *reduction* in expenditures, President Nixon's projection for 1979 will have been exceeded by 1977.

This example illustrates one of the fundamental obstacles confronted by presidential administrations and Congresses in the fiscal policy-making process—the inability to contain the growth of federal budget outlays. The dramatic budgetary expansion over the past few years is primarily the result of growth in existing programs, most notably the various entitlement programs such as Social Security, Medicare and Medicaid, public assistance, veterans' benefits, civilian and military retirement payments, etc., outlays for which are uncontrollable in the regular appropriations process. The mandatory outlays for these programs have grown much faster than the rest of the budget, thus reducing policymakers' discretion over aggregate spending and creating severe problems for stabilization policy.

This chapter examines the problem of control over federal budget outlays and discusses its effects on fiscal policy-making. It begins with a discussion of the meaning of "uncontrollability," the measurement of its growth over time and the way it affects the budgetary functions of stabilization and allocation. It then addresses the questions of why uncontrollables exist, why they have grown so dramatically in response to recent economic conditions, and what efforts have been made to cope with them. Finally, the prospects for spending reductions and the likely effects of the 1974 Congressional Budget Reform Act are examined.

Uncontrollability, Allocation, and Stabilization

The budgetary phenomenon with the rather unfelicitous title of "uncontrollability" refers to the inability of the administration or the Congress to

13

change budget outlay or appropriation totals within the budget cycle—i.e., without basic legislative changes. According to the budget document for FY 1976, "Outlays are considered to be relatively uncontrollable in any one year when Government decisions in that year can neither increase nor decrease them without changing existing substantive law."[3] A recent study distinguished between the technical definition of uncontrollable used in the budget and an analytical meaning relating to the ". . . feasibility of changing federal expenditures both in the short run, when many other consideration also limit changes, and in the long run, when a much broader range of spending options can be considered."[4]

The measurement of the extent of uncontrollability depends in part on one's purpose and time perspective. For an analysis of the amount of control available each year in the regular appropriations process alone, the focus on new budget authority each year is most appropriate. Weidenbaum has measured this by totaling four overlapping categories of budget authority—trust funds, permanent and indefinite appropriations, fixed charges, and ongoing projects.[5] In earlier research I have used Weidenbaum's first three categories only, and have shown that the percentage of new budget authority that is uncontrollable has increased nearly monotonically since FY 1961 to roughly 60 percent of the budget.[6] Although that analysis underestimated somewhat the size of controllables by excluding certain fixed charges in the budget,[a] its finding that uncontrollables have increased monotonically is corroborated by data on budget outlays from the FY 1976 budget, which will be examined below.

It is true, of course, that all spending is in principle controllable by Congress, at least in the long run;[7] but the long-run view requires that one take not only a multi-year perspective on the budget, but also adopt a broader conception of the budgetary process at a single point in time by including all legislative authorizations that affect budget outlays. This conception of the budgetary process has not been the one traditionally adopted by the Congress, although recent reforms may change this.

If one is concerned with fiscal policy, as we are here, it is more appropriate to focus on outlays. Only a portion of total new budget authority is ever spent in the year it is granted; but total outlays in a fiscal year consist of all money spent that year regardless of when the budget authority was granted. Because fiscal impact is best measured by the amount of money actually spent in a given year, the discussion and data employed here will stress outlays.

A useful distinction is made among the three functions of the public budget—the *allocation* of total output between private and public goods and among public goods; the *distribution* of wealth and income among the

---

[a] The only fixed charges included were military retirement pay, veterans' payments public assistance, and the Commodity Credit Corporation.

population; and the *stabilization* of the economy through high employment and price stability.[8] The phenomenon of uncontrollability has, in the past, usually been analyzed as a problem of allocation. Weidenbaum was concerned with the built-in resistance it creates to altering budgetary priorities.[9] Subsequent research has demonstrated the significance of this phenomenon for budgetary theory. For example, Wanat has found that Congress treats "mandatory" requests differently from "programmatic" ones.[10] I have argued elsewhere that incrementalism does not explain budgetary outcomes because uncontrollables minimize the availability to Congress of the incremental budgeting strategies on which the theory is based.[11] But the theory of incrementalism is fundamentally a theory about allocation. Incrementalism describes and explains how budgeters decide how much to allocate to activity X or agency Y and what simplifying rules are applied in doing so. Expenditure aggregates are not the primary concern of this theory, although aggregates are expected to increase slowly from year to year as a consequence of the multitude of smaller allocative decisions.

Recently, more recognition has been given to uncontrollability as an impediment to fiscal policy-making. For example, in his State of the Union address in January, 1975, President Ford warned that the

. . . size and growth of the Federal budget has taken on a life of its own. . . . When these (uncontrollable) programs are enacted, there is no dollar amount set. No one knows what they will cost. All we know is that whatever they cost last year, they will cost more next year.

It is a question of simple arithmetic. Unless we check the excessive growth of Federal expenditures or impose on ourselves matching increases in taxes, we will continue to run huge inflationary deficits in the Federal budget.[12]

An excellent scholarly treatment of uncontrollability as a fiscal policy problem appears in the annual Brookings study of the FY 1976 budget.[13] Although the authors of that study are critical of the view that budget outlays are necessarily uncontrollable in the long run, they conclude that for fiscal policy purposes, the amount of spending that is controllable in the short run is even *less* than that suggested by the official budgetary estimates of controllable outlays.[14]

To introduce an analysis of the fiscal problems created by diminishing control over budget outlays, we will begin by examining the trend in the reduction of budget control. Table 2-1 records the trend in controllable and uncontrollable outlays relative to total spending for the eleven-year period from FY 1967 through FY 1977. During this time, uncontrollable outlays increased by 224.2 percent, from $93.7 billion to $260.7 billion. In the same period, total outlays increased by 149.0 percent, from $158.3 billion to $394.2 billion. And if one looks only at the increase in controllable outlays,

Table 2-1
Trend in Uncontrollable Percentage of Total Outlays, FY 1967-77

Fiscal Year	Total Outlays ($ billions)	Controllable Outlays ($ billions)	Relatively Uncontrollable Outlays ($ billions)	Uncontrollable % of Total Outlays
1967	$158.3	$64.6	$ 93.7	59.2%
1968	178.8	71.6	107.2	59.9
1969	184.5	68.1	116.4	63.1
1970	196.6	70.9	125.7	64.0
1971	211.4	71.0	140.4	66.4
1972	231.9	78.4	153.5	66.2
1973	246.5	73.5	173.0	70.2
1974	268.4	73.9	194.5	72.5
1975	324.6	87.1	237.5	73.2
1976 (est.)	373.5	101.0	272.5	73.0
1977 (est.)	394.2	90.4	303.8	77.1

Source: *The Budget of the United States Government, Fiscal Year 1977*. Figures for 1976 and 1977 are estimates as of January, 1976, and are therefore probably less accurate for 1977 than for 1976.

they grew by only 39.9 percent, from $64.6 billion to $90.4 billion. The trend in the last column of table 2-1 shows a nearly monotonic rise in uncontrollable outlays as a percentage of total outlays. And the largest increments in uncontrollable outlays occur simultaneously with the largest deficits in the period, one of which is the largest in our history, in war or peace time.

While fiscal policymakers are more interested in aggregates than increments, a brief look at the annual increments in total controllable and uncontrollable outlays will help illustrate further the problems the latter have created for fiscal policy-making. While the increments in total outlays have been substantial, the increments in uncontrollable outlays have equalled or surpassed the total increments five of ten times since FY 1967. These data are displayed in table 2-2. The implications and questions these data raise for both budgetary allocation and stabilization policy are closely related and theoretically as well as practically significant.

In terms of allocation among different programs, the practical question is, if the increment in *total* outlays is insufficient to cover the incremental costs of uncontrollables, then how are the latter to be "financed"? Where is the money to come from? Could the administration "finance" the extra cost by running a higher deficit? Here allocation problems spill over into stabilization policy. The administration and the Congress do have the option of increasing the deficit; however, since the data reported here are either actual outlays or administration estimates, they presumably already represent the largest deficit tolerable to the administration, indeed, perhaps

Table 2-2
Annual Increments in Total, Uncontrollable and Controllable Outlays, FY 1967-77

Fiscal Year Interval	Increment in Total Outlays ($ billions)	Increment in Uncontrollable Outlays ($ billions)	Increment in Controllable Outlays ($ billions)
1967-68	$20.5	$13.5	$7.0
1968-69	5.7	9.2	−3.5
1969-70	12.1	9.3	2.8
1970-71	14.8	14.7	.1
1971-72	20.5	13.1	7.4
1972-73	14.6	19.5	−4.9
1973-74	21.9	21.5	.4
1974-75	56.2	43.0	13.2
1975-76 (est.)	48.9	35.0	13.9
1976-77 (est.)	20.7	31.3	−10.6

Source: *The Budget of the United States Government, Fiscal Year 1977.*

larger than was tolerable. We can only conclude that the budgets submitted for these years anticipated that increments in uncontrollables would be paid for at the expense of the budget *base*. The last column of table 2-2, which indicates the amount of the annual increment that is controllable, shows that in two cases there were virtually no increments to allocate and in two cases there were in fact *decrements*, i.e., reductions in controllables. Indeed, note that controllable outlays actually declined between 1968 and 1971.

It is apparent then that stabilization requirements have created budgetary allocation problems. Limits on total expenditures and the deficit have, in certain years, caused reductions in programs in the budget *base*. The theoretically important consequence of this fact is that the dictum of incrementalism that the budget is reviewed only from the base up is in need of some revision. The base has, because of the exigencies of stabilization, become a subject of scrutiny for allocation purposes, contrary to conventional wisdom. This problem was noted in the budget document for FY 1976: "One consequence (on uncontrollability) has been that necessary fiscal policy adjustments have been increasingly concentrated on a small and diminishing portion of total outlays—that part which was most readily 'controllable'."[15] This problem is likely to continue as long as the economy suffers from "stagflation," which will be discussed below.

I have shown what uncontrollability means, the extent of its effect on outlays, and suggested some implications for budgetary allocation and stabilization policy. I turn now to an examination of some other basic questions. First, the question of why uncontrollables exist in the first place will be explored. Then, after very briefly reviewing some fundamental precepts of modern fiscal policy, I will suggest the reasons for the abnormal growth which has emerged as such a serious fiscal policy problem and discuss previous efforts to cope with the problem.

Reasons for Uncontrollability and its Growth

Why does the phenomenon of uncontrollability exist? What reasons are there for any portions of the budget to be beyond annual appropriations review? In order to try to explain the existence of uncontrollables, it is helpful to make the distinction that Weidenbaum does between "naturally" and "artificially" uncontrollable appropriations.[16] Some appropriations represent implicit contracts between government and citizens, such as interest payments or Social Security, and thus may be regarded as "naturally" uncontrollable. But there are many uncontrollable appropriations which do not fit that description, such as revenue sharing, public assistance, food stamps, etc. I have investigated this question elsewhere,[17] and offered two alternative explanations to account for the incidence of uncontrollables. The first explanation views uncontrollables as the outcome of strategies by the authorization committees of Congress to bypass the Appropriations Committees. The other explanation starts with Wildavsky's argument that the calculations that the Appropriations Committee members make every year are extremely burdensome, and that they must adopt aids to calculation to reduce their burden.[18] One very useful aid would be to make appropriations uncontrollable so that the burden is shifted from the Appropriations Committee to some other committee. Since the two explanations posited different behavior on the part of the Appropriations Committee members, one anticipating their opposition and the other their consent, the debate and recorded votes on various uncontrollables constituted the data used in trying to determine if either was valid. The results were mixed—there was some evidence to support each explanation, although the most surprising finding was that uncontrollables generally evoked little or no debate on the *issue of spending control*.[19] The one fairly consistent justification given for funding a program through some uncontrollable mechanism was that it would *reduce the uncertainty* of the recipients of the funds about the vagaries of the congressional appropriations process.[20] Put differently, the justification was to take these programs out of politics (in the pejorative sense of the word). Of course, from a normative perspective, this justification defies the argument that the establishment of spending priorities belongs in the realm of values and thus should remain part of the political process. In fact, however, to say that the programs are "removed from politics" only means that they are removed from the politics of the Appropriations Committees and instead subjected to the politics of a substantive committee. In sum, to argue that uncontrollables will reduce uncertainty as to appropriations (read "Appropriations Committee behavior") is to say the obvious. It begs the theoretical question of why coalitions have been formed to do this for some programs and not for others.

Apart from the more theoretical and extremely interesting question of why uncontrollability occurs, there is the more empirical question of why uncontrollables recently have expreienced such an incredible rate of growth. A short review of modern fiscal theory will serve as an introduction to the suggested reasons.

Modern fiscal theory is usually dated from the publication forty years ago of John Maynard Keynes' *General Theory of Employment, Interest and Money*,[21] although it may be more correct simply to date it from the 1930s. In any case, since the Great Depression, and especially since the Second World War, economists and public officials have increasingly recognized and accepted the essential role of the governmental sector in promoting economic stability. But the "new economics" of countercyclical fiscal policy was not publicly embraced by any presidential administration until the 1960s. Even John Kennedy, who is regarded as the first president to sell successfully the merits of countercyclical fiscal policy to the Congress and the public,[22] campaigned in 1960 as a fiscal conservative and relied on the shibboleth of the balanced budget.[23] But in January of 1963, Kennedy proposed the tax cut which came to be regarded as "the crown jewel of the new, liberal economics."[24] The tax cut he proposed, which was finally enacted in 1964 was

the first major stimulative measure adopted in the postwar era at a time when the economy was neither in, nor threatened imminently by, recession. And, unlike U.S. tax reductions in the 1920's, late 1940's, and 1954, the 1964 action was taken in a budgetary situation marked by the twin facts that the federal budget was in deficit and federal expenditures were rising.[25]

While the budget itself has always served a stabilization function, there has unquestionably been a shift in emphasis in its presentation, so that the first consideration of the impact of the budget now is in terms of its fiscal objectives rather than in terms of allocation.

The theory of modern fiscal policy is itself fairly straightforward. For any given level of productive capacity, there is a level of aggregate demand that is consistent with full employment. Since government spending is a component of total demand, and taxes affect the consumer component of total demand, changes in government spending and taxes can help achieve full employment by their effect on aggregate demand. Since the enactment of the Employment Act of 1946, the federal government has accepted the responsibility to use fiscal policy to maintain high employment. The instruments of fiscal policy by which it can achieve this objective are commonly known as the *automatic* and *discretionary stabilizers*. Automatic stabilizers are instruments which have their effect without requiring legislative action. They include the progressive income tax and outlays for unemployment compensation and Social Security, all of which operate to increase relative purchasing power in contractionary periods and to decrease relative purchasing power during expansionary periods, thus cushioning fluctuations in either direction. These tools are supplemented by discretionary stabilizers, which include expenditures and tax rates.

The size of the total budget deficit or surplus, however, registers the effects of both sets of stabilizers, so that the deficit does not indicate how much stimulus is being added to the economy by the discretionary acts of the government. In other words, a deficit can be produced during a recession by a decline in revenues and increases in unemployment compensation, which are both due to automatic stabilizers, as well as by tax reduction, which is discretionary. The total deficit does not enable us to distinguish the effects of automatic from those of discretionary stabilizers, and so economists have developed the concept of the *full employment surplus* (deficit), which is defined as the surplus (deficit) that would occur at current expenditures and tax rates if the economy were at full employment. By controlling, in effect, for the influence of autonomous changes in the economy, which is what the use of the full employment concept does, changes in the size of the full employment surplus from year to year measure the influence of discretionary policy.

The general prescriptions of discretionary fiscal policy are relatively simple—when demand is insufficient to clear available output from the market, the government should increase spending or reduce taxes (or both) in order to increase aggregate demand; and when aggregate demand is excessive and inflation threatens, government spending should be decreased or taxes increased (or both).

The problem with applying these prescriptions to the fiscal crisis of the 1970s has been that we experienced severe recession and severe inflation simultaneously, and fiscal theory provides no unambiguous cues for dealing with "stagflation," i.e., inflationary recession. If government should increase expenditures or reduce taxes in order to combat recession, it is likely to add excessively to total demand and thus aggravate inflation. Tax increases or expenditure reductions to combat inflation will remove purchasing power and hence contribute to the recession. Tax reduction combined with expenditure reductions of the same size, such as proposed by President Ford in October of 1975, would be more neutral, but would be likely to combat inflation more than recession, since the government would spend the entire $28 billion, whereas taxpayers are likely to save some of it. But if expenditure reductions were to come primarily from transfer payment programs, which is what the administration had advocated in the past, then the net effect would be even more neutral, since transfer recipients' spending patterns are likely to be more similar to taxpayers' patterns than to the government's. However, the ability of the administration to obtain reductions in uncontrollable transfer programs is precisely what is at issue. It has generally been thought, until recent years, that the political aspects of the spending process were less dilatory than those of the taxing process,[26] and that therefore expenditures were a more flexible tool of fiscal policy because of the shorter time lag in their implementation. Expenditures are no longer as flexible. The rapid growth in uncontrollables has made expenditure reductions even more difficult than tax increases. This growth has been a response partly to the operation of the automatic stabilizers during inflationary recession, and partly to congressional actions. While uncontrollables cannot be altered in the annual appropriations process, they have been altered in the substantive committees that have jurisdiction over them.

Since 1970, for example, Congress, upon the recommendations of its tax writing committees, enacted three increases in Social Security benefits (totaling 47 percent increase in benefits).[27] In 1974 Congress enacted a cost-of-living escalator into the Social Security Act, which increases benefits by the percentage of the increase in the Consumer Price Index.[28] Other federal entitlement programs—food stamps and child nutrition programs, civil service and military retirement benefits, Supplemental Security Income—also incorporate cost-of-living escalator clauses.

Therefore these programs are particularly sensitive to inflation,[29] which has in the recent past exceeded 10 percent on an annual basis. Unemployment compensation would normally decline during inflation, but unemployment of 8 to 9 percent has sent its costs skyrocketing to nearly $20 billion per year. At the same time, outlays for Supplemental Security Income, Social Security and food stamps are also sensitive to recessionary declines in national income. Thus we can see that the automatic stabilizers, which are supposed to cushion economic fluctuations have actually acted to *accentuate* fluctuations when inflation and recession occur together. All expenditures have increased, with Social Security, food stamp, and SSI outlays increasing in response to both pressures. But federal revenues are not similarly affected—they increase in response to inflation but decline in response to recession, thus tending to remain fairly stable.[30] The extremely rapid growth in uncontrollables is at once a cause and a consequence of stagflation, and the circularity of the process makes it difficult to know where to look for their origin in order to cope with it. A review of recent efforts to contain the growth of uncontrollables for fiscal policy purposes reveals nearly universal failure.

The first notable effort to curb spending occurred in June of 1968, when, after nearly a year of conflict, negotiation and compromise between the administration and the Congress, Congress finally passed the Revenue and Expenditure Control Act, which imposed a surcharge of 10 percent on personal and corporate income taxes.[31] As its price for the enactment of the surcharge the Congress, for the first time in history, legislated a spending ceiling of $180.1 billion, which necessitated a $6 billion reduction in FY 1969 budget outlays. However, the bill as passed specifically excepted outlays which the president deemed necessary for Vietnam operations, for interest, veterans' benefits and services and payments from the Social Security trust funds which would exceed the amounts estimated in the budget.[32] Later in the year, in a series of appropriations bills, the Congress also exempted certain appropriations, including funds for FBI personnel, public assistance, the Commodity Credit Corporation, school assistance in federally affected areas and vocational education.[33] Most of the items on these lists of exemptions and exceptions are uncontrollables. While the administration and Congress succeeded in cutting $8.4 billion from outlays, as Fisher notes, the unanticipated growth in uncontrollables forced spending through the "ceiling": "The total increase in exempted and excepted areas came to $6.9 billion. As a result, the net reduction represented only $1.5 billion, and budget outlays totaled $184.6 billion instead of the "ceiling" of $180.1 billion."[34]

The failure of this first congressional spending ceiling did not deter the Congress from trying again in 1969. A "ceiling" of $191.9 billion on FY 1970 outlays was established in a supplemental appropriation bill, but two escape clauses were added. One provided that if any congressional action or inaction affected outlays, the spending limitation was to be adjusted accordingly, and the other provided that the president should adjust the amount of the overall limitation if necessary to allow for unanticipated growth in certain uncontrollables. Adjustments were allowed up to $2 billion.[35] By the end of FY 1970, however, uncontrollables had forced outlays well beyond the $193.9 billion maximum "ceiling," and this was acknowledged in an outlay ceiling of $197.9 for FY 1970 passed in a supplemental appropriation bill in 1970.[36]

The same bill also incorporated another ceiling, this one on FY 1971 outlays. The ceiling for FY 1971 was set at $200.8 billion, but the provisions regarding congressional action and adjustments for uncontrollables were retained. However, a cushion of $4.5 billion was allowed for uncontrollables, raising the actual "ceiling" to $205.3 billion. Once again, uncontrollables were impervious to the "ceiling" and caused outlays to increase to $211.4 billion by the end of the fiscal year.

The Congress did not pass an expenditure ceiling for FY 1972 because, according to Louis Fisher, the previous ceilings had given the Nixon Administration additional authority to impound funds.[37] But an expenditure ceiling was proposed by President Nixon in 1972. He requested congressional enactment of a $250 billion spending ceiling for FY 1973 as well as a provision granting the president statutory authority to reduce outlays for any program he chose, including uncontrollables, in order to limit federal spending to that amount. This proposal represented a request for an unprecedented delegation of budgetary discretion to the president, a proposal not at all in keeping with the House of Representatives' traditional jealousy of its spending prerogatives.[38] Surprisingly, the House passed the bill but the Senate amended it to provide exemptions for uncontrollables and to reduce presidential discretion.[39] Ultimately, both the spending limitation and delegation of authority were deleted in conference committee. Subsequently, the president, despite an increase of $8.7 billion in outlays for Social Security, Medicare, veterans' payments and interest, succeeded, by means of a series of controversial impoundments and vetoes, in holding outlays to $264.5 billion.

Future Prospects for Controlling Outlays

Given these instances of congressional inability to control outlays for entitlement programs, what are the prospects for future efforts? First, it is clear that Congress has not tried to enact a firm ceiling on outlays. The three it did enact provided escape clauses that defeated their primary purpose. Second, from the brief history recounted above, what one notices is that the only time spending was held below the desired ceiling was when there was wholesale vetoing and impoundment. Impoundment is made more difficult, however, by the new Congressional Budget Reform and Impoundment Act of 1974. Under the new procedures, a deferral, or temporary withholding of funds, can be accomplished by the president alone (after informing the Congress) unless either house passes an ' "impoundment resolution" any time after the president's message. An impoundment resolution forces the president to release the funds. A rescission, or permanent withholding of funds, requires an affirmative vote of both houses of Congress on a "recission bill" within forty-five days of the president's message.

It has not yet been demonstrated that a real spending ceiling will not work because one has not been tried as yet. Theoretically this is what the

Congress will be doing under the provisions of the 1974 act, which represents Congress' most comprehensive effort to reform its own budgetary process. Although it deals with a variety of subjects, its main objective is to make Congress, for the first time, take a comprehensive view of the budget before passing any single appropriation bill. Congress is to do this by passing at least two concurrent resolutions on the budget, setting forth total outlays and new budget authority, outlays and budget authority by functional category, the amount of the surplus or deficit, the level of federal revenues and the appropriate level of the public debt. The final concurrent resolution must specify the amount of the discrepancy (if any) between the spending required by various appropriations, entitlements, etc., and what is contained in the concurrent resolution. The figures must be reconciled by legislative action by September 25 of each year.

Section IV of the act deals specifically with "backdoor spending," entitlement programs, and other forms of uncontrollable spending. The purpose of this section is to subject all "new spending authority"—i.e., all contract authority, borrowing authority and entitlements enacted *after* the provision in the Budget Reform Act—to the annual budget reconciliation process. But certain provisions of Section IV restricting its applicability raise questions as to how effective it will be in controlling outlays.

For example, although Section IV subjects all *new* contract authority or borrowing authority to the appropriations process, it does not affect that which was in effect when the legislation was enacted. Thus, for example, federal housing loans, provided under contract authority, will be unaffected. In addition, existing entitlements are exempted from the section as are all Social Security trust funds, the revenue sharing trust fund and all trust funds that are 90 percent self-financed. Permanent appropriations, which comprised approximately 13 percent of new budget authority in FY 1975 and 1976, are barely discussed at all, except to say that the Appropriations Committees should study them. These restrictions raise serious questions as to whether the act will be effective in containing uncontrollables. Furthermore, since final reconciliation does not preclude increases in the ceiling, it is still possible that ceilings will have little practical effect in reducing outlays.

If the foregoing analysis is correct, the prospects for a reduction in federal outlays for FY 1977 of the order of magnitude proposed by president Ford—$28 billion—seem remote. Whether it can be done depends in large part upon whether changes are made in current legislation. It is literally true, as Blechman and his colleagues have argued, that we are not committed to any future spending in the long run, even for such things as Social Security.[40] The obvious problem with this, of course, is that Congress generally takes a short-run view. And even if changes in legislation are seriously considered, it may still take a great deal of time to get them enacted, especially because of the strong opposition which such proposals would stir up.

If we assume no major changes in legislation for entitlements, what strategies might guide policymakers in their search for reductions of $28 billion in outlays? Clearly, the fact that 75 percent of outlays are uncontrollable, at least in the short run, means that attention is likely to be focused on the $88.7 billion, or 25.3 percent which can be controlled. Controllables are more expendable in the short run. But controllable dollars are not distributed randomly across the budget—they are highly concentrated in the defense sector, primarily, of course, in the Department of Defense. Over 70 percent of all FY 1976 defense outlays are controllable, and of all controllable outlays listed in the 1976 budget, over two-thirds are credited to the national defense area. This does not include outlays for NASA and atomic energy defense activities. Thus their large size suggests that defense outlays would be a logical focus of attention because their size provides the largest opportunities for savings.[41]

It is unquestionably true that not all defense dollars are equally controllable in the short run. Personnel, and Operation and Maintenance costs, being more immediate and continuous, are inherently more difficult to reduce in the short run than are Procurement and RDT&E, which usually involve longer-term commitments which are more easily stretched out, deferred or canceled. There seems to be some disagreement among scholars as to the *degree* of control over defense outlays. One study estimates that even with substantial policy shifts, short-term reductions in outlays would approach $10 billion at the most.[42] But a noted scholar of defense budgets, while not specifying a dollar figure, seems to be more optimistic:

Appropriations for Military Personnel categories are almost uniquely determined by previous troop strength decisions. Military Procurement and Construction category accounts, on the other hand, are quite vulnerable. Also, it is not difficult to stretch out production schedules or to keep a project in the Research and Development stage for an extra year. Similarly, military construction projects can often be stretched out or delayed.[43]

The apparent vulnerability of defense outlays due to their controllability and size had not eluded the attention of the Department of Defense itself. Assistant Secretary of Defense (Comptroller) Robert C. Moot remarked in an address to the Naval War College:

In a time of budgeting stringency or economic necessity, one must control what can be controlled and make cuts there regardless of the fact that huge increases in the uncontrollable area are of lesser priority. It simply takes too long and is too difficult to make the changes . . . Since defense is 65 percent of the controllable portion of the budget, defense still must bear the brunt of short-term reductions even if it means that some military readiness must be sacrificed.[49]

To assert that defense is vulnerable to fiscal policy exigencies is not to say that it will necessarily decline. In the first place, there is still the one-third of controllables that lie in the domestic sector, although almost the entire total of $29.1 billion controllable domestic dollars would have to be cut in order to meet the President's objective. In the second place, the administration, if not the Congress, has staunchly supported the defense budget against cutbacks and in fact proposed a substantial increase in FY 1976. It is unlikely that defense will bear the brunt of reductions, as the quotation above suggests it will.

Yet the administration has apparently reached the conclusion that proposing reductions in specific domestic programs simply does not work.[45] A possible alternative then, but one that is generally regarded as unpalatable because of its inefficiency, is a general, across-the-board reduction in outlays of about 7 percent. Such an alternative is generally shunned because it punishes the good programs along with the bad, but it is likely to be more acceptable politically when everyone has to suffer. And there is evidence to suggest that this is the approach the administration will take. As the president himself has stated: "Spending discipline by the Federal Government must be applied across the board. It cannot be isolated to one area, such as social programs, nor can we completely insulate any area such as defense. All must be restrained."[46]

Conclusion

Although across-the-board reductions are inequitable, they may appear to be more equitable, and hence more attractive, than any alternative in the short run. They may *in fact* be more equitable than any other *simple* (i.e., easily calculated) alternative. But whatever techniques are applied in the short run, it is apparent that the most effective way to slow the growth in uncontrollables and at the same time reduce the governmental percentage of total GNP (another administration goal) is economic recovery. Bringing an end to inflationary recession should dampen the multiplicative effect the automatic stabilizers have had on certain entitlement programs, and a rapid expansion in GNP may help reduce the relative size of the governmental component. Such a solution is easily recommended, and although it is not likely to be achieved easily, it seems to be the only real long-term solution.

Notes

1. *The Budget of the United States Government, Fiscal Year 1976* (Washington: U. S. Government Printing Office, 1975), p. 9.

2. *New York Times*, October 7, 1975, p. 24.

3. *The Budget, Fiscal Year 1976*, p. 29.

4. Barry M. Blechman, Edward M. Gramlich, and Robert W. Hartman, *Setting National Priorities: The 1976 Budget* (Washington: The Brookings Institution, 1975), p. 191. Another recent study which focuses on the problem of uncontrollability is Martha Derthick, *Uncontrollable Spending for Social Services Grants* (Washington: The Brookings Institution, 1975).

5. Murray Weidenbaum, "Institutional Obstacles to Reallocating Government Expenditures," in *Public Expenditures and Policy Analysis*, Robert Haveman and Julius Margolis, eds. (Chicago: Markham Publishing Company, 1970), pp. 232-45.

6. John R. Gist, *Mandatory Expenditures, the Defense Sector and the Theory of Budgetary Incrementalism* (Beverly Hills, California: Sage Professional Papers in American Politics, 2, 04-020, 1974), p. 10.

7. Blechman et al., *Setting National Priorities*, p. 213.

8. Richard Musgrave, *The Theory of Public Finance* (New York: McGraw-Hill, 1959), Chapter 1.

9. Weidenbaum, "Institutional Obstacles," pp. 232-33.

10. John Wanat, "Bases of Budgetary Incrementalism," *American Political Science Review* 68 (September 1974): 1221-28.

11. Gist, "Mandatory Expenditures," pp. 6-11.

12. *Weekly Compilation of Presidential Documents* 11 (January 20, 1975): 47.

13. Blechman et al., *Setting National Priorities*, pp. 197-210.

14. Ibid., pp. 203-207.

15. *The Budget, Fiscal Year 1976*, p. 49.

16. Weidenbaum, "Institutional Obstacles," p. 243.

17. John R. Gist, *Uncontrollable Federal Spending and the Theory of Budgetary Incrementalism*, Ph.D. dissertation, Washington University, 1973, Chapter 6.

18. Aaron Wildavsky, *The Politics of the Budgetary Process* (Boston: Little, Brown and Company, 1974), Chapter 2.

19. Gist, *Uncontrollable Federal Spending*, p. 234.

20. Ibid., p. 247.

21. John Maynard Keynes, *The General Theory of Employment, Interest and Money* (New York: Harcourt, Brace and Company, 1936).

22. Walter Heller, *New Dimensions of Political Economy* (Cambridge: Harvard University Press, 1966), pp. 35-41.

23. Herbert Stein, *The Fiscal Revolution in America* (Chicago: The University of Chicago Press, 1969), Ch. 5.

24. Ibid., p. 214.

25. Arthur Okun, *The Political Economy of Prosperity* (Washington: The Brookings Institution, 1970), p. 47.

26. See, for example, James M. Buchanan, *The Public Finances* (Homewood, Illinois: Richard D. Irwin, Inc., 1965), pp. 95-96.

27. Blechman et al., *Setting National Priorities*, p. 66.

28. Ibid., p. 59.

29. Sometimes overly sensitive. See ibid., p. 60.

30. Ibid., p. 52.

31. An excellent case study of the enactment of this legislation is found in Lawrence C. Pierce, *The Politics of Fiscal Policy Formation* (Pacific Palisades, California: Goodyear Publishing Company, 1971), Chapter 7.

32. PL 90-364, 90th Congress, June 28, 1968.

33. For a summary of these appropriations acts, see the volume *Appropriations, Budget Estimates, etc.,* Senate Document 112, 90th Congress, 2nd Session, p. 1363.

34. Louis Fisher, *President and Congress: Power and Policy* (New York: The Free Press, 1972), p. 108.

35. *Second Supplemental Appropriation Act, 1969*, PL 91-47, 91st Congress, July 22, 1969.

36. *Second Supplemental Appropriation Act, 1970*, PL 91-305, 91st Congress, July 6, 1970.

37. Louis Fisher, *Presidential Spending Power* (Princeton: Princeton University Press, 1975), p. 153.

38. The source here is Richard F. Fenno, *The Power of the Purse: Appropriations Politics in Congress* (Boston: Little, Brown and Company, 1966).

39. U.S., *Congressional Record*, 92nd Congress, 2nd Session (1972), CXVIII, pp. 34633-36 and 35924-54.

40. Blechman et al., *Setting National Priorities*, p. 213.

41. It is worth noting here that these same criteria of controllability and size are also the first two cited by James D. Barber in his study of municipal boards of finance. See his *Power in Committees* (Chicago: Rand McNally, 1966), p. 38.

42. Blechman et al., *Setting National Priorities*, p. 204.

43. John P. Crecine and Gregory W. Fischer, "On Resource Allocation Processes in the U.S. Department of Defense," in *Political Science Annual, 1973*, Cornelius Cotter, ed. (Indianapolis: Bobbs-Merrill, 1973), p. 218.

44. Robert C. Moot, "Defense Spending: Myths and Realities," *Naval War College Review* 23 (December 1970): 9.

45. See the remarks of Sidney L. Jones, assistant Treasury secretary for economic policy in *National Journal* 7 (November 15, 1975): 1569.

46. *New York Times*, October 7, 1975, p. 24. Also, assistant Treasury Secretary Jones is quoted as saying: "To say we can pinpoint programs to get the budget back under control—we can't. . . . So we have to slow down the momentum through an across-the-board cut." *National Journal* 7 (November 15, 1975): 1569.

3 Wage-Price Controls and Income Distribution

Markley Roberts

All economic policies have income distribution effects—effects on economic and social justice.[1] In addition to private economic decision-making and technological change, income distribution is affected by political decisions on government tax and spending policies, money supply, credit, and interest rate policies, manpower development and employment policies, social insurance and social welfare transfer payments, and (less obviously, perhaps), by public policies toward education, recreation, cultural opportunities, public safety, and environmental protection. With this broad view in mind, it is obvious that economic controls on wages, prices, profits, and other forms of income will inevitably have direct impact on income distribution. Efforts to freeze an existing income distribution sanctify the status quo. Laissez-faire policies favor rewards to the powerful. And economic controls planned by legislators to achieve certain goals—such as fighting or restraining inflation—can be implemented and administered in ways that counteract the intentions of the legislators.

A sense of justice, equity, or fairness is essential to public acceptance of economic controls (or any other public policy). Ordinary people may have trouble defining justice, but they sense and complain when it is absent or inadequate. Political and economic considerations, therefore, are necessarily and inextricably tied together in dealing with anti-inflation programs. The enduring human concern for equity or fairness is the rock on which European income policies have foundered,[2] and it is the rock on which U.S. wage-price policies foundered in the mid-1960s and again in the early 1970s.

There are a variety of theories purporting to explain the setting of wages. The theories generally adopt a marginal productivity approach or a bargaining approach or some combination,[3] but there is also a too-much-neglected view of wage-setting as a reflection of social valuation of the work performed.[4] No final single judgment among these theories is likely, but, for the purposes of this discussion, it is important to note that wage-setting is subject to a variety of built-in restraints. In companies where workers are not represented by trade unions, wages and salaries are set unilaterally by employers who are happy to apply wage restraint. Where workers are represented by unions, wages and salaries are set through a process of collective bargaining with the employer, with the effective

31

restraint of employer resistance, except in localized instances of very tight labor markets for specific skills. Wage-setting is also subject to the time-lags and advance notice that are part of the bargaining process. By contrast, price-setting has no such built-in restraints, except for changes in economic conditions. And in a number of key industries, a few major corporations so dominate their industries that they set prices with little, if any, effective competition.

Furthermore, the U.S. economy is big and complex with many different markets, industries, and occupations—each with many specific and different conditions and problems that have to be dealt with. Some industries have wage inequities or substandard wages. In many industries, technology is changing jobs, job content and skill requirements, and displacing workers and jobs. The rising cost of living eats into workers' buying power. These issues are real and urgent to both workers and employers and they require workable solutions. It is the genius of the American institution of free labor-management collective bargaining to find pragmatic, workable solutions—not by using mechanical formulas but by going through a give-and-take process that strengthens the contending parties' sense of participation in reaching a fair, equitable, workable agreement. There is no single "magic number"—not productivity change, not the Consumer Price Index, not a combination of these, nor any other "magic number"—that can be used as a key to setting workers' wages and salaries. The U.S. economy is too big and complex.

In the early 1960s, the President's Council of Economic Advisers (*1962 Economic Report*) started promoting a so-called wage-price guidepost policy, a system of indirect, indicative controls. Average increases in wages and fringe benefits were supposed to be limited voluntarily to the trend rate of rising private output per man-hour in the previous five years—a rate that was soon nailed down to 3.2 percent. But the "voluntary guidepost" for prices was developed from a vague theoretical tautology without any policy implications. The price level would remain stable if prices of rapidly-rising productivity industries would decline, while prices of other industries would remain stable or increase, depending on their productivity increase in relation to the national average. In fact, the Consumer Price Index rose only 1.3 percent a year from 1960 to 1965, but after-tax profits rose an average 12 percent a year.

From 1960 to 1965 the rise in real worker compensation per man-hour (2.9 percent a year) lagged considerably behind the increase in productivity (3.6 percent a year in the private economy). When the textbook theory of "voluntary guidepost" policy was translated into action in the real world, it turned out to be a sophisticated, largely one-sided pressure to hold down wage increases. The planners forgot that wages and salaries are not merely a cost to employers and a factor in the price of goods and services. Wages and salaries are also income to workers and the biggest source of consumer buying power.

So the "voluntary guidepost" policy contained a precise percentage guideline for increases in workers' wages and fringe benefits. But there was no effective guideline for prices, profits, dividends, executive compensation and other forms of income. This was obviously unfair and the guidepost policy broke down in 1966 when airline mechanics won a 4.9 percent package from the then highly profitable major airlines.

Early in 1966, as Vietnam War spending started to increase pressures on the American economy, the AFL-CIO declared:

If the President determines that there is a national emergency that warrants extraordinary stabilization measures—with even-handed restraints on all costs, prices, profits, dividends, rents, corporate executive compensation (salaries, bonuses, and stock options), as well as employees' wages and salaries, he will have the support of the AFL-CIO. But rigid application of a single 'magic number', based on one economic factor alone, cannot be a workable or fair means of wage determination in a country of continental size, with thousands of different markets, industries and occupations. We are prepared to sacrifice—as much as anyone else, for as long as anyone else—so long as there is equality of sacrifice.[5]

This is still the position of the AFL-CIO.

It is interesting to note that the chairman of the Phase 2 Price Commission expressed similar ideas in his lessons-from-controls summary. "In order for controls to succeed, they will have to be supported by the public," C. Jackson Grayson, Jr. declared. "Controls will work only if the public chooses to make them work. . . . Americans are willing to sacrifice a great deal as long as they feel everyone is sacrificing equally. As soon as they feel some are carrying less than their share of the burden they withdraw their support."[6]

The Nixon New Economic Plan inaugurating the first direct peacetime economic controls August 15, 1971, was attacked by the AFL-CIO as a "system of unfair and inequitable government control of wages, for the benefit of business profits."[7] This judgment was supported by the stock market, often regarded as a good indicator of business expectations. The stock market reflected expectations that the wage-price freeze would improve the relative share of corporate profits at the expense of wages and this expectation persisted after the freeze; furthermore, current proposals for control of corporate profits were "a tacit admission that price controls would not be entirely effective."[8]

In May 1972 the Joint Economic Committee of Congress declared, "The control program is a vehicle for economic injustice." The committee pointed out that controls, guidelines, and other anti-inflation policies were "directly designed to influence or control income distribution." The committee went on to say, "It should be frankly recognized that a program to control wages and prices is, by definition, a program to control the distribution of real income. The distributional effects are the heart of the program. The current program appears to lock in and put the stamp of approval on many existing inequities."[9]

Labor opposition to the controls program stemmed not only from concern about relative shares distribution of income (including special concern for low-wage workers), but also from the crippling effect of controls on collective bargaining, a wage-setting procedure which is a fundamental article of faith for union leaders. The "nullification of contracts" by the control program drew far more outraged protest from labor leaders about the "sanctity of contracts" than it did from business, thus further supporting union suspicions that business leaders expected a differential impact on profits and wages.

Union representatives believed their darkest suspicions were confirmed in 1974 when Arnold Weber, director of the Pay Board in 1971 and 1972, was quoted by *Business Week* as saying "Business had been leaning on Shultz and McCracken to do something about the economy, especially wages. The idea of the freeze and Phase 2 was to zap labor and we did."[10] Weber later denied the "zap" quote, but union leaders remained convinced that the quotation accurately reflected a pro-business, anti-labor approach to controls. This experience with a pro-business administration of controls strengthened the union view that blank-check "inflation-fighting" controls authority should not be given to the president, that controls legislation can be administered in ways quite different from the original intent of Congress.

In fact, no effective price control system was ever set up, no effective profit controls were ever put into operation throughout the period of phases and freezes. Corporate after-tax profits went up 21 percent in 1971, 16 percent in 1972, 27 percent in 1973, and 18 percent in 1974. In contrast to these impressive corporate profits gains, hourly earnings of private, nonagricultural workers went up only 7.1 percent in 1971, 6.5 percent in 1972, 6.4 percent in 1973, and 8 percent in 1974. If hourly earnings are measured in constant dollars, workers' hourly earnings' buying power rose only 2.7 percent in 1971, 3.1 percent in 1972, 0.1 percent in 1973, and in 1974 actually dropped 2.6 percent. The decline in buying power of earnings reflected, in part, consumer price increases of 4.2 percent in 1971, 3.2 percent in 1972, 6.2 percent in 1973 and 12.2 percent in 1974.[11]

There are no simple, easy answers for a democracy seeking simultaneously full employment, price stability, and free political and economic institutions, including free collective bargaining. But the existence of complex problems and the difficulty of their solution does not relieve us from the obligation to pursue these goals within a context of fairness and equity and maximum participation in decision-making. Fairness and equity may be difficult to define precisely, but their absence makes economic controls impossible to maintain. Furthermore, in a democracy there is no alternative to bargaining—collective bargaining is institutionalized in labor-management relations and political bargaining institutionalized in the democratic political process by which we determine political, economic, and social policy. The bargaining process does not produce final solutions, but it helps satisfy the human need to participate freely and effectively in the decision-making of the institutions that shape our lives.

Notes

1. Income distribution theory seems to be always in an "unsatisfactory" condition. In 1946, William Fellner and Bernard F. Haley, (eds.), *Readings in the Theory of Income Distribution* (Homewood, Illinois: Richard D. Irwin), reprinted 1951, p. vii, declared that "The present state of the theory of income distribution is generally considered unsatisfactory, and it is rightly so considered." Twenty-five years later, Martin Bronfenbrenner, *Income Distribution Theory* (Chicago: Aldine-Atherton, 1971), p. 386, said that "'Everyone' bewails the unsatisfactory state of distribution theory." Bronfenbrenner's final chapter, "Guidelines, Guideposts, and Incomes Policies," surveys incomes policy issues.

2. See Lloyd Ulman and Robert J. Flanagan, *Wage Restraint: A Study of Incomes Policies in Western Europe* (Berkeley, Calif.: University of California Press, 1971); and Walter Galenson (ed.), *Incomes Policy: What Can We Learn from Europe?* (Ithaca, N.Y.: New York State School of Industrial and Labor Relations, Cornell University, 1973).

3. For example, see Edward B. Jakubauskas and Neil A. Polumba, *Manpower Economics* (Reading, Mass.: Addison-Wesley, 1973), pp. 78-89. See also John T. Dunlop (ed.), *The Theory of Wage Determination*, (London: Macmillan, 1957); and Daniel J.B. Mitchell, "Union Wage Policies: The Ross-Dunlop Debate Reopened," *Industrial Relations* 11, 1 (February 1972): 46-61.

4. For example, see Barbara Wootton, *The Social Foundations of Wage Policy* (London: Allen & Unwin, 1955); also, Martin Rein and Petter Marris, "Equality, Inflation and Wage Control," *Challenge* 18, 1 (March/April 1975): 42-50.

5. AFL-CIO Executive Council Statement, February 21, 1966. Daniel J.B. Mitchell, "The Future of American Wage Controls," *California Management Review* 17, 1 (Fall 1974): 50, notes that "In all countries where income policy is under consideration, organized labor always demands that all forms of income be covered, not just wages." Mitchell, Phase 2 Pay Board Chief Economist, concludes (p. 57) "Paradoxically, although

economists tend to concentrate on the wage aspects of incomes policy, the price side is the more complicated to regulate," but he fails to discuss regulation of profits.

6. C. Jackson Grayson, Jr., *Confessions of a Price Controller* (Homewood, Ill.: Dow Jones-Irwin, 1974), p. 234.

7. AFL-CIO Executive Council Statement, March 22, 1972.

8. Sol S. Shalit and Uri Ben-Zion, "The Expected Impact of the Wage-Price Freeze on Relative Shares," *American Economic Review* 64, 6 (December 1974): 904-914.

9. Joint Economic Committee, U.S. Congress, *Price and Wage Controls: An Interim Report*, May 22, 1972, p. 17.

10. *Business Week*, April 27, 1974, p. 108.

11. For a review of the 1971-74 controls program see John T. Dunlop, "Statement of Dr. John T. Dunlop, Director, Cost of Living Council, Before the Subcommittee on Production and Stabilization of the Senate Committee on Banking, Housing and Urban Affairs, February 6, 1974" (multilith). For a business view, see U.S. Chamber of Commerce, *Wage and Price Controls: A Failure in History, Theory and Practice* (Washington, D.C., 1975).

**Part II
Agriculture**

4

The Agricultural Policy Process

Don F. Hadwiger and Richard Fraenkel

Introduction

Our chapter briefly reviews the recent history of the agricultural policy process, and the development of agricultural institutions and technology, with a view towards the interaction of these elements. We define "institutions" broadly, to include political and legal ground rules under which production takes place, as well as arrangements among producers providing for cooperation or competition.[1] We deal primarily with the United States, although we note similarities with other countries, and emphasize the importance of this interaction for the less developed countries (LDCs).

In a sense, both technology and institutions may be considered as the outputs of the agricultural policy process, because the political system is the ultimate arbiter of benefits, and more concretely, because the small-sized operating units in agriculture, unlike in most other industries, have obliged farmers to make demands on the policy process to develop new technologies and to control market conditions.

In the American case, the knowledge basis for the technological revolution in agriculture was produced largely by the land grant colleges.[2] Ground rules and arrangements were made, through public policy, to stabilize and maintain prices on major farm commodities. A wide range of other specialized services and protective arrangements was provided to the U.S. agricultural population.[3]

An agricultural population is never homogeneous. In 1900, 39 percent of those working on U.S. farms were wage earners rather than "farmers."[4] In 1969, the "bottom half" of all farmers produced only 5 percent and the "top" 20 percent of all farmers produced 76 percent of the total amount of farm products sold.[5] Changes in the institutional and technological environment of agriculture may affect the welfare of each group in the rural population differently. Price support programs (with benefits based on gross sales) have long been considered an example of institutional bias toward large producers.[6] Research programs leading to development of large-scale machinery have lowered the per unit costs of production for large farmers, but have tended to squeeze out small farmers who cannot afford this equipment and who continue to face the old, higher costs.[7]

39

Group Formation

In certain ways the group structure in U.S. agriculture is diverse. Its membership and financial base have been achieved through unique combinations of benefits (and frequently by controlling benefits provided by a particular federal agency). Farm groups have been able to ally with both business and labor, with right-wing, middle, and left-wing groups. Farmers have organized not only interest groups but important political movements and third parties.

In other important ways the structure has been quite narrow. Although farm groups have had encompassing social programs these groups invariably have found their membership (and leadership) within the ranks of middle or large commercial farmers, and the catalytic goals were those addressed to the economic problems of commercial farmers.[8] The impact of economic discrimination and price instability (often exacerbated by bad weather) provided the issues on which these groups achieved political significance.

The importance of economic problems in the formation of groups outside the United States is highlighted in case studies by Seymour Martin Lipset and Suzanne Berger. In both cases (specialized vegetable producers in Brittany and Saskatchewan wheat farmers respectively) groups were formed with the aim of trying through institutional changes to control market price fluctuations and to moderate the consequences of these fluctuations upon farm incomes.[9]

A large number of organizations have been formed in the United States to represent small farmers, sharecroppers, and farm workers. Thirty-one of them were in existence since 1920.[10] These groups, however, were hardly visible as influences upon institutional change. Reasons may include the alertness of commercial farmer groups (prompted by representatives of plantation agriculture) in perceiving these other agricultural interests as being in conflict with their own. Commercial farm groups were partly[11] or fully[12] responsible for termination of the New Deal's Farm Security Administration, whose programs were designed for poor farmers, and also for ending the Bureau of Agricultural Economics, which sought a clearer analysis of, and alternatives for, the existing distribution of benefits from agriculture.[13] The principle of scaling commercial program benefits toward smaller farmers was rejected with the Brannan Plan.[14] Farm groups joined in support of labor legislation on the condition that benefits were not extended to farm workers. Minor exceptions to this conflict posture toward other agricultural interests include program goals of the National Farmers Union during most years.

Rural values were another impediment to poor farmers and farm workers. Farmers held to the work ethic,[15] which offered to each participant the prospect for accumulation of some wealth in this highly speculative occupation.[16] This may explain why "higher prices" were, and are, the most popular economic palliative even among farmers with little to sell.

Another factor to be considered in the case of American agriculture, which is not likely to be present in many of the developing countries, was the "exit" option available to some unsuccessful farmers and to farm youth.[17]

Group Strategies

The strategies chosen by groups to influence policy outputs are in response to opportunities for access to decisionmakers at the "political" and "administrative" levels of a political system. These opportunitis for access vary according to the national political system. In the above-mentioned cases of Brittany and Saskatchewan, farmers organized a national lobby group and a mass political party.[18] The decentralized American system, on the other hand, provides opportunities to influence local administration as well as national policy.

U.S. commercial farm interests have pursued the following three strategies which together secured them a great deal of control over agricultural institutions:

1. One strategy was a national coalition of commodity interests, centering in the congressional agriculture committees, which asserted functional jurisdiction over agriculture policy and administration. Members of the congressional agriculture committees usually have had specific commodity interests,[19] as have the subcommittees and the major subdivisions in federal program agencies. There were many conflicts to be resolved between and within commodities, in developing and continually reworking a variety of commodity programs, and this task was shared by the Secretary of Agriculture, the full congressional committees, and the general farm organizations.

This farm coalition was formed in the 1920s, during which period it passed credit and regulatory laws but failed to enact the first major commodity proposal, due to presidential vetoes.[20] Programs for many commodities were enacted and revised during the Roosevelt and Truman administrations, and meanwhile the commodity coalition defeated several alternatives proposed by the administration, such as the Brannan Plan.[21] An impasse then occurred during the 1950s,[22] due to conflict with the American Farm Bureau Federation and Secretary of Agriculture Ezra Benson; but the coalition again successfully asserted itself under Secretary Orville Freeman. Since then, new political forces and economic conditions may have severely challenged the coalition strategy.

2. A second strategy has been to channel farmer voting into support for commodity programs in presidential and in two-party congressional elections. This strategy was successful despite smaller farmer numbers and typically low (but varying) turnout.[23] In the absence of consistent ideological and group ties, the free-swinging "farm vote" was particularly persuasive in behalf of supported commodity prices.

3. A third strategy has been so-called administrative "cooptation." U.S. farm bureaucracies have relatively little autonomy not only because congressional leaders have served as "permanent secretaries of agriculture,"[24] but also because administrative structures have permitted—were even designed to provide for—clientele involvement in administration. The Extension Service achieved its character virtually as part of a farm organization. The price support programs have been administered locally by farmer committees, which have provided a recruitment pool for agency executives. Economist Alex McCalla noted, in reference to the land grant college research establishment, "we have identified very closely with our perceived clientele so that often, after a couple of generations, we . . . come to perceive their sanction of our activities as necessary and desirable."[25]

Policy and cooptation strategies were mutually supportive, as was demonstrated by Philip Selznick in the case of the Tennessee Valley Authority, which accepted the Farm Bureau and land grant colleges into its local decision structure in order to neutralize the congressional farm bloc and also to adjust to its political situation locally.[26]

Through these mutually supportive strategies, U.S. commercial farmers have attained extraordinary control over institutional and technological change. There seems no paradox in the conclusion that the institutional and technological biases which they continually implanted did contribute in large measure to the decline of farmer numbers.

Commercial farmer control of agricultural policy has not, however, gone unchallenged. The U.S. Department of Agriculture, though largely subject to the coalition and in many respects decentralized, has often sought such wider clienteles and missions, as were generated by its political leadership or its own planning agencies and outstanding personnel.

The "new" Department of Agriculture, which came into existence in the 1930s, incorporated the earlier functions of science and education with a host of new functions—including price supports for commercial farmers, and major programs for soil conservation, rural electrification, farm worker relief and resettlement, and food assistance to needy families.

Mechanisms to coordinate these programs around new missions of food production and rural welfare were developed both at the grassroots level and in Washington. At the grassroots was a system of community-wide "land use" committees which were to be the vehicle for citizen coordination of all major agricultural programs. In Washington, the Bureau of Agricultural Economics was developed as an agency of great competence which could plan and coordinate developmental programs around a set of broad goals. These planning and coordinating mechanisms were soon terminated by the commercial farmer coalition, and much of Secretary Wallace's new department was eroded away.

Subsequent secretaries of agriculture tried and were usually frustrated in efforts to develop comprehensive departmental missions. Recently, the USDA has received largely uninvited support from nonfarm interests leading to new rural development programs—particularly for housing and community facilities, nutrition programs, food stamps and school lunches. These social welfare programs account for about two-thirds of the current USDA budget.

Several noncommercial interests have effectively challenged the farm coalition, beginning with the civil rights movement of the 1960s whose Poor People's Crusade camped for several weeks on the mall outside the office of the secretary of agriculture, demanding food and jobs. A nascent consumer movement activated by muckraking studies of agricultural and food policy and by increasing food prices has sought policies for cheaper, safer food. A "hunger lobby" has effectively supported a $4.5 billion food stamp program; environmentalists have raised ecological questions; townspeople in nonmetropolitan America have become an effective constituency seeking rural development; and collective bargaining for hired farm labor has been achieved through the efforts of unions and other groups. Assistant Secretary of Agriculture Don Paarlberg has referred to these new activities as "the new farm policy agenda." These interests, he said "have been placed on the agenda over the protests of the agricultural establishment. The agricultural establishment has, in large measure, lost control of the agricultural policy agenda."[27]

Meanwhile, the agricultural coalition has become more fluid, having suffered from the decline in farmer votes, the rise of consumer voting power, and congressional reforms which somewhat reduced the power of senior congressmen. Also, the congressional agricultural committees seemed to be less commodity oriented since cotton has become less significant in southern agriculture, and since wheat and feed grains are no longer so continuously dependent upon federal price support and surplus removal programs. As farm size has grown and as many agricultural functions have been taken over by large agribusiness firms, a number of USDA farmer services, such as agricultural production research and extension education, have seemed of less importance to commercial farmers, and of more importance to other clienteles.

Meanwhile, much power within the coalition seems to have shifted to the "liberal" rural leaders who maintain links with consumer, environmental, and welfare groups, possibly because the interests of commercial agriculture are increasingly compatible with the interests of these groups.

For example, thousands of poor people who were previously laborers within the agricultural system now relate to it mainly as potential food consumers—likely recipients of school lunch and food stamp programs. Presumably these food programs have considerably enlarged the domestic market for agricultural products. Farmers may also reap benefits from environmental programs that subsidize soil conservation and regulate land use. New regulations that protect human health and safety give large farmers still another competitive advantage over small producers.

One might, therefore, speculate that commercial producers and processors will move toward firmer support of the large USDA programs which were enacted by and for other interests, in which case the USDA could develop the inherent relationships among these programs.

The present administration, however, has opposed a move in this direction. The current secretary of agriculture, Earl Butz, has sought to constrict the roles of the USDA in many areas in order to reduce intervention in the agricultural economy, to reduce citizen dependence upon governmental subsidies, and in the process to reduce the size of the federal administrative establishment. Secretary Butz has frequently voiced his lack of enthusiasm for USDA administration of social welfare functions. He favors transfer of the food stamp program to the Department of Health, Education and Welfare. He also favors a "block grant" in funding the school lunch program—an approach which would, in effect, remove the USDA from major supervision over that program. He has expressed the fear that the growth of such programs within the USDA ". . . will at sometime jeopardize the traditional functions of the Department of Agriculture."[28] Secretary Butz would apparently reorganize the department around the objective of support for commercial agriculture, stressing the agricultural research-technical assistance role provided in the old department.

Secretary Butz has also stressed "management" goals, partly in response to cues from the White House and the Office of Management and Budget, which have been important outside influences upon contemporary departmental affairs. The government-wide management-improvement effort has already reduced the level of per-client personnel in rural housing and other USDA programs. It has also led to an emphasis upon reorganizing agencies along functional lines. But the functional concept is disintegrative as applied to the USDA, whose basis of organization has often been the relationship *between* functions, such as between food production and citizen nutrition, and such as among functions which are all performed in a rural setting. Another, not strictly functional, basis on which USDA roles have accumulated is available research or technical competence, as recognized by the first Hoover Commission's recommendation to transfer all regulation of food products back to the USDA because ". . . the Department is much better equipped for research on these matters."[29]

The zenith of the functional approach was President Nixon's reorganization proposal of 1971, which would have carved the present USDA into four parts, each to be fitted into one of the four proposed new domestic departments.

This effort to terminate the department, though unsuccessful, is one of several possible futures which the department faces.

Institutional-Technological Outputs in LDCs

The outputs of the policy process tend to be especially discriminatory for the welfare of groups in the agricultural sectors of the less developed countries because of cross-national dependency relations and domestic factors. LDCs have little domestic agricultural research capability. As a result, they import most new agricultural technologies from the developed countries. These include machinery, as well as innovations embodied in new biological and chemical inputs such as high-yielding seed and nonorganic fertilizer.[30]

For various reasons, machinery imported from the developed (labor-scarce) countries tends to be substituted for tenants and laborers in production activities in LDCs by landlords and farmers. The displaced laborer has few alternative employment opportunities in many of these labor-surplus economies. Even the "divisible" inputs of seed and fertilizer often have a discriminatory impact on the distribution of benefits between small and large farmers.[31] Unlike machinery, this effect is probably not due to inherent "scale" characteristics of new seed and fertilizer technologies. It is, rather, due to bias in the distribution to farmers of these inputs by public institutions.[32] Widespread institutional bias in favor of large farmers generally reflects the prevalence of so-called "patron-client" relations in the rural localities of many LDCs.[33] Based on generalized social power derived from control over production resources, especially land, in an environment of great scarcity, patrons are able to pose themselves as intermediaries between the national government and their small farmer-clients.[34] Even where they have little power on the national level of policy-making, patrons are in a position to influence the local implementation of public programs (for extension, supervised credit, subsidies, etc.) in such a way that these programs do not disturb the status quo. Indeed, by placing additional resources in the locality, public programs may have the consequence (albeit unintended) of reinforcing the prevailing distribution of wealth and power in the rural localities.

Conclusions

The U.S. agricultural policy process, with its principal outputs—market stabilization and labor-saving technology, has produced changes in the structure of agriculture, and these in turn have increased the control by commercial producers over policy. But recently nonfarm interests have become more influential.

It is appropriate to reexamine the interaction of agricultural process and outputs, because U.S. producers have become larger, fewer, less dependent, and perhaps less influential. The new influences upon agricultural policy arise from impacts outside commercial agriculture, due for example, to impacts upon rural communities, upon consumer food supplies, and upon the natural environment. These interests are in some respects potentially compatible with producer interests, and therein lies a challenge for policymakers. Secretaries of agriculture, for example, are freer than were their predecessors to develop comprehensive approaches to food production and rural development.

In many developing countries, the interaction between policy and technology may be producing new "agricultural revolutions." Governments of developing countries may in some cases feel dependent upon rural patrons to perform a number of functions, among them to extract food from the country for use by urban people, and to invest in technology for raising production. Permitting patrons to exercise a great deal of control over agricultural policy, however, may lead to the extensive displacement of agricultural labor—an outcome that was tolerable at times in the United States, but that is not so tolerable under the conditions of most of the developing countries. Indeed, the challenge for those countries is to find a framework in which they may use their abundant labor resources more productively within agriculture. To face up to this challenge, however, may require political changes to reduce the power of the rural patrons in the agricultural policy process at the national and/or the local levels.

Notes

1. For presentation of these concepts as part of a general "theory of institutional change," see Lance E. Davis and Douglas C. North, *Institutional Change and American Economic Growth* (Cambridge: Cambridge University Press, 1971). Davis and North understand "institutional change" in the broadest possible sense, including public decisions to develop new technologies. See, especially, their chapter "Land Policy and American Agriculture," pp. 83-104. .

2. Robert Evonson, "International Diffusion of Agrarian Technology," *The Journal of Economic History* 34 (March 1974): 55.

3. Harold F. Breimyer, *Individual Freedom and the Economic Organization of Agriculture* (Urbana: University of Illinois, 1965).

4. Fred A. Shannon, *American Farmers' Movements* (Princeton, N.J.: Van Nostrand, 1957), p. 9.

5. *U.S. Census of Agriculture*, 1969, (U.S. Dept. of Commerce-Bureau of the Census), Vol II, pt. 1, chart 2.

6. See, for example, Theodore Schultz, *Production and Welfare in Agriculture* (New York: Macmillan Company, 1949).

7. A well-known statement of the consequences of technological advance, according to which American farmers are caught on a "treadmill," is found in Walter W. Wilcox, Willard W. Cochrane, and Robert W. Herdt, *Economics of American Agriculture* (Englewood Cliffs, N.J.: Prentice-Hall, 1974 edition), pp. 287-290.

8. Carl C. Taylor, *The Farmers' Movement, 1620-1920* (New York: The American Book Company, 1953).

9. Seymour Martin Lipset, *Agrarian Socialism* (New York: Anchor Books edition 1968); Suzanne Berger, *Peasants against Politics* (Cambridge, Mass: Harvard University Press, 1972).

10. Lowell Dyson, "Radical Farm Organizations and Periodicals in America, 1920-1960," *Agricultural History* 45 (April 1971): 111-116.

11. Sidney Baldwin, *Poverty and Politics: The Rise and Decline of the Farm Security Administration* (Chapel Hill: University of North Carolina Press, 1968), pp. 410-411.

12. Grant McConnell, *The Decline of Agrarian Democracy* (Berkeley: Univ. of California Press, 1953), p. 177.

13. Richard S. Kinkendall, *Social Scientists and Farm Politics in the Age of Roosevelt* (Columbia, Missouri: University of Missouri Press, 1966).

14. Reo C. Christenson, *The Brannan Plan* (Ann Arbor: Univ. of Michigan, 1959), p. 106.

15. John M. Brewster, "Socity Goals and Values in Respect to Agriculture," *Goals and Values in Agricultural Policy* (Ames: Iowa State Univ. Press, 1961).

16. Richard Hofstadter, *The Age of Reform* (New York: Alfred A. Knopf, 1968), pp. 23-46.

17. C.E. Bishop, "Economic Aspects of Changes in Farm Labor Force," (p. 48), and Larry Sjaastad, "Occupational Structure and Migration Patterns," (p. 24), both in *Labor Mobility and Population in Agriculture* (Ames, Iowa: Iowa State Univ. Press, 1961).

18. Berger, *Peasants Against Politics*, and Lipset, *Agrarian Socialism*.

19. Charles O. Jones, "Representation in Congress: The Case of the House Agriculture Committee," *The American Political Science Review* (June 1961): 358-372.

20. Gilbert C. Fite, *George N. Peek and the Fight for Farm Parity* (Norman, Oklahoma: University of Oklahoma Press, 1954).

21. Christenson, *Brannan Plan*.

22. John P. Heinz. "The Political Impasse in Farm Support Legislation," *Yale Law Journal* 71 (April 1962): 952-978.

23. Angus Campbell et al., *The American Voter* (New York: John Wiley & Sons, 1960), pp. 404-406.

24. Nick Kotz, *Let Them Eat Promises* (Garden City, New York: Doubleday, 1971), pp. 80-97.

25. "Public Sector Research and Education and the Agribusiness Complex: Unholy Alliance or Socially Beneficial Partnership?" *American Journal of Agricultural Economics* 55 (December 1973): 1001; also Earl Heady, "Allocations of Colleges and Economists," *American Journal of Agricultural Economics* (December 1972): 934-944. The discussions above were prompted by Jim Hightower's book *Hard Tomatoes Hard Times* (Agribusiness Accountability Project, 1972).

26. Philip Selznick, *TVA and the Grass Roots: A Study in the Sociology of Formal Organization* (Berkeley: University of California, 1949), pp. 254, 259, 260, 263.

27. Address by Don Paarlberg, Director of Agricultural Economics, U.S. Department of Agriculture, at the National Public Policy Conference, Clymer, New York. September 11, 1975.

28. U.S. House Agricultural Appropriations Subcommittee, *Hearings on Agriculture and Related Agencies Appropriations for 1976*. (U.S. Government Printing Office, 1975), p. 21.

29. *The Hoover Commission Report*. (New York: McGraw-Hill, 1949), p. 250.

30. Hayami and Ruttan have elaborated on this distinction between "labor-substituting," biological and chemical innovations in terms of their "induced innovation hypothesis." The innovation path in an agricultural sector, whether labor or land-saving, has obvious implications for the distribution of benefits among groups that have different relations to production activities. See Yujiro Hayami and Vernon W. Ruttan, *Agricultural Development: An International Perspective* (Baltimore: The Johns Hopkins Press, 1971).

31. Frankel and Von Vorys, for instance have investigated the political consequences of the seed and fertilizer, "Green Revolution" in India and Pakistan, brought on by this discriminatory impact. See Francine R. Fran-

kel, *India's Green Revolution* (Princeton: Princeton Univ. Press, 1971); Frankel and Karl von Vorys, "The Political Challenge of the Green Revolution: Shifting Patterns of Peasant Participation in India and Pakistan," University of Pennsylvania, Department of Political Science, 1971.

32. For a discussion of the distribution of benefits from technological change within the context of biased institutions, see Carl H. Gotsch, "Technical Change and the Distribution of Income in Rural Areas," *American Journal of Agricultural Economics* (May 1972): 326-341.

33. Clientelism has, of course, become of late a widely used paradigm for analyzing politics in the rural localities of LDCs. Two articles which take account of the patron as intermediary or "broker" between public institutions and peasantry appeared in the *APSR* in March 1972. See Rene Lemarchand, "Political Clientelism and Ethnicity in Tropical Africa: Competing Solidarities in Nation-Building," pp. 53-67; also James C. Scott, "Patron-Client Politics and Political Change in Southeast Asia," pp. 68-90.

34. Tai compares this "non-aggregative" pattern of political participation, where the "landed class . . . continued to interpose itself between the peasantry and the national elite," to the "aggregative" pattern of participation where, following national political change, the elite has had direct access to the peasantry. See Hung-Chao Tai, *Land Reform and Politics: A Comparative Analysis* (Berkeley: University of California Press, 1972), p. 343.

5

U.S. Agriculture in the 1970s: Policy and Politics

Garth Youngberg

Introduction

Since 1970, U.S. farm policy has undergone a number of important changes. The principal effect of recent policy innovations has been the gradual freeing of American agriculture, at least temporarily, from many of the constraints associated with its most important traditional supply management programs. This analysis first outlines the major policy changes introduced in the 1970 and 1973 farm laws, indicates their significance and attempts to show why more permanent reversals in farm policy continue to elude farm policymakers.[1] Second, the changing character of the farm policy system is explored in an effort to show not only what produced recent policy changes, but also what course future policy is likely to take in light of the altered farm policy system and general policy environment.

The Agricultural Act of 1970: Signs of Change

The most significant policy change in the Agricultural Act of 1970 was the elimination of traditional commodity-by-commodity supply management. Unlike earlier programs, the 1970 law provided that once a producer had set aside the minimum acreage required in order to qualify for program benefits, producers were completely free to plant whatever they chose on all of their remaining cropland. This was in sharp contrast to previous legislation wherein producers were required to limit plantings to individual crop bases, thereby regulating the total number of acres under production on a crop-by-crop basis. For example, prior to 1970, if a farmer had a feed grain base of 80 acres on a 160 acre farm and he diverted 20 percent or 16 acres of his base (this was a typical amount due to specific program provisions), he was free to plant only the remainder of his base, or 64 acres, in corn. He was not free to plant the entire remainder of his farm (144 acres) in corn. The same constraints applied for the other major crops. Under this traditional form of supply management, a specific known limit was set on total acres on a commodity by commodity basis. Clearly, the deregulation of individual farmers, i.e., letting them plant whatever they wished on the entirety of their farms once minimum set-asides were made, marked significant departure from traditional supply management policy.

The impact of this change was modified to some extent by the so-called "preservation-of-history" provision. Under the 1970 law, farmers failing to plant 90 percent of their wheat or cotton allotments or 45 percent of their feed grain bases had those bases reduced by approximately one-fifth. Failure to plant one of these crops for three consecutive years resulted in the total loss of that crop base. Liberal departmental substitution rules (e.g., what could be substituted for feed grains and vice versa) did somewhat negate the impact of this measure. Still, farmers were constrained to stay relatively close to a farming pattern roughly proportionate to their traditional practices. They were not, of course, directly discouraged from overall crop increases.[a]

The second noteworthy policy innovation in the 1970 farm bill was the $55,000 payment limitation provision, the first such limitation in farm program history. Previously, individual producers had been allowed to collect whatever level of payment they qualified for under the law. In some cases this amounted to several hundred thousand dollars, with a handful actually getting over one million dollars. This highly controversial aspect of farm policy had been assailed for years by a broad spectrum of the American public, including a growing number of U.S. senators and representatives.

Somewhat paradoxically, the inclusion of a payment limitation itself produced considerable controversy. The 1970 Act, for example, limited payments to $55,000 per commodity program, not $55,000 per individual recipient. Furthermore, critics charged that producers would be able to sell, rent, or lease portions of their farms, thus making each "owner" or "renter" eligible for payments. Still others questioned the fairness of a USDA ruling which limited big farmer acreage set-asides to an amount equivalent to the maximum payment of $55,000. Some suggested that this ruling would allow large operators gradually to acquire larger crop bases since they would be allowed to increase actual plantings relatively more than small farmers. (Crop bases are calculated from actual farming or cropping patterns.) Such potential loopholes and inequities notwithstanding, the mere inclusion of a payment limitation in the 1970 Act was symbolically significant and a harbinger of future policy developments restricting maximum payments.

Price support payments should not be confused with price support loans. Farm program participants are eligible for nonrecourse price support loans from the Commodity Credit Corporation (CCC). These loans are administered by the Agricultural Stabilization and Conservation Service (ASCS). Under the loan program the individual farmer simply indicates to th ASCS that he would like to "seal" a portion of his crop. The CCC then

---

[a] The 1973 preservation-of-history provision is somewhat more compelling in that feed grains are also subject to the 90 percent of allotment minimum planting requirement.

lends the producer a sum of money equivalent to the number of bushels in question times the current loan rate. ASCS, in turn, stores (seals) the crop for the CCC until such time that the market price goes above the support price. At that point the producer would probably elect to sell his crop on the open market, paying the CCC back the money it had lent to him. If market prices fail to rise above the loan rate, the CCC simply takes permanent possession of the crop at the end of the loan period. Many farmers use this loan mechanism as a means of low interest, short-term financing for their farming operations.

One final aspect of the 1970 Act should be noted. Whereas previous legislation, especially since 1965, had included special concessions for small farmers, i.e., higher payment rates on small base operations, the 1970 law omitted all such provisions for producers of feed grains and wheat. Although small cotton farmers continued to receive minimal concessions, overall the 1970 Act made the large commercial farmer the principal beneficiary to an even greater degree than had legislation of the preceding decade or so.

The Agriculture and Consumer Protection Act of 1973: New Concepts And Familiar Features

Target Prices

The introduction of target prices in lieu of traditional price supports represents the principal innovation of the 1973 four year farm bill. Under current legislation eligible farmers (all producers if no set-asides are required) are guaranteed a target price of $2.05 for wheat, $1.38 for corn and 38¢ for cotton. The bill provides that these targets will be adjusted for the 1976 and 1977 crop years according to a cost-price index. If average market prices over a specified period of time for each production year do not equal the targets, producers will receive deficiency payments equivalent to the difference between the target price and (1) the market price, or (2) the loan rate, whichever is smallest. Ultimately, this provision limits maximum payments to the margin of difference between the basic loan level and the target price.

The target price concept differs significantly from previous price support policy in that payments are geared entirely to market prices. If market prices remain above the targets, as in 1974, farmers get no payments. Under former programs farmers were guaranteed a minimum flat rate level of support regardless of market fluctuations. By way of illustration, under the 1970 Act producers were guaranteed a flat rate support price (e.g., $1.35

per bu. for corn) on one-half of their base with maximum payments varying according to percentage of voluntary set-asides. Since a partial payment was made in mid-summer, producers knew what their minimum payments would be when they agreed to participate in the program. They were assured, that is, of at least a minimum payment for agreeing to set aside a portion of their base. The target price mechanism makes no such guarantee. Under present law, setting aside land merely qualifies the producer for target price guarantees. If market prices stay above targets, no deficiency payments are warranted and the producer receives nothing for his diverted acres.

From a policy perspective, it would appear that target prices will work well as long as no set-asides are required. Because none were called for in 1974 or 1975 and because market prices stayed well above the targets, the new scheme appears to be a truly innovative policy change. Should the supply price situation change, as it quite obviously could, the weaknesses of the target price concept as a supply management device will become abundantly clear. Farmers will simply be reluctant to set aside land in any year when market prices are at all likely to range fairly close to the targets. The absence of adequate production adjustment incentives could yet prove to be a serious flaw in the target price mechanism. The major advantage of the target price formula is its administrative simplicity. Since payments depend solely on market prices, administrators and participants are freed from earlier, somewhat complicated, variable payment rates based upon such factors as percentage of voluntary set-aside.

Should circumstance ever require it, the Secretary could, under the 1973 Act, reintroduce a much stronger and more traditional supply management policy by calling for additional voluntary set-asides above the minimum ones required to qualify producers for the target price guarantees. That is, if significant acreage reductions are ever deemed necessary, producers could receive a so-called resource adjustment payment for any set-asides beyond those which may be required under the target price program itself. These resource adjustment payments would be a flat rate guaranteed payment on the set-aside acres themselves, quite similar to the price support payments described earlier. Although policymakers hope that it will never be necessary to implement this awkward provision, its presence in current legislation betrays a certain lack of confidence about the viability of target prices as a permanent and exclusive farm policy innovation.

Other Provisions

The inclusion of a $20,000 payment limitation in the 1973 law is noteworthy.

Unlike its predecessor, the new maximum payment applies to all commodity programs combined, not to each one separately. Although this is a much more stringent limitation than the one inaugurated in the 1970 Act, it is limited to deficiency payments under the target price mechanism. It does not apply to any resource adjustment payments which might conceivably be made under the voluntary additional set-aside program outlined above. Its exclusion from that program would certainly be a strong incentive for large producers to participate should large-scale land diversion become necessary.

For the first time in farm program history, disaster payments were included in the 1973 law. If drought, flood, or other natural condition prevents producers from (1) planting any part of the farm acreage allotment or, (2) harvesting less than two-thirds of the crop base, compensatory payments will be made. Payments are limited to allotment and would equal one-third of the target price on any such unplanted or unharvested acre.

Finally, the 1973 law contains an unprecedented disaster reserve provision formally instructing the Secretary to establish a reserve inventory "not to exceed 75 million bushels of wheat, feed grains, and soybeans for the purpose of alleviating distress caused by a natural disaster."[2] Such stocks are to be acquired through the price support loan program. Inventories under this provision are earmarked exclusively for localized disaster conditions and in no sense constitute a strategic grain reserve. Seventy-five million bushels represents but a fraction of annual U.S. domestic needs. In 1973, for example, U.S. domestic wheat consumption alone was slightly in excess of 757 million bushels.[3]

From Surpluses to Shortage: Policy Continuity in an Uncertain World

As the foregoing illustrates, the impression that U.S. agriculture policy has undergone fundamental change in this decade is unwarranted. Price support loans, acreage set-aside authority and resource adjustment payments are all retained in current legislation. Farmers are constrained through preservation-of-history provisions to stay relatively close to their traditional farming patterns. Even target prices, the most innovative of recent policy changes, would look pecularly similar to former price support policies should they ever become operational.

The changes and continuities reflected in current farm policy result, in a general way, from the same causal mix. Both are needed, that is, because of the intimidating uncertainties of the short- and long-term agricultural supply and demand situation. Given the vagaries of agricultural production, markets, and so on, intermittent cycles of surpluses and shortages seem almost inevitable. A sound agricultural policy must be capable of responding to both sets of conditions.[4] Except for the difficult matter of grain reserves, current U.S. policy reflects this perplexing reality.

External conditions in the 1970s have changed far more than has basic policy. Continuing and unprecedented worldwide demand for U.S. agricultural production has, in the short term at least, freed the American farmer from the controls which, only a few years ago, seemed destined to plague him at least into the 1980s. At the beginning of this decade, for example, some of this nation's most distinguished agricultural economists failed to perceive the radically altered world food supply and demand situation which has so rapidly developed.[5] Nevertheless, today U.S. agriculture is faced with the prospect of periodic shortage and token grain reserves. Presently, the problem for agricultural policymakers is "not finding markets for U.S. crops abroad, but avoiding the use of export controls," a move that could cost the United States "friends and customers elsewhere in the world."[6] In 1973, the United States exported "about three-fourths of all farm sales of wheat, nearly one-half of all farm sales of soybeans, and more than one-third of all farm sales of corn."[7] Fiscal year 1974 agricultural export sales were $21.3 billion—an incredible two-thirds increase in just one year.[8] In 1970, Nick Kotz observed that "more and more one hears in Washington that 'we should be paying people to grow rather than not to grow food'."[9] Today U.S. agriculture policy is in effect doing just that. How long this happy state of affairs will continue remains to be seen.

U.S. Agriculture Policy-Making in the 1970s

From Subsystem to Macropolitics

That policy subsystems tend to dominate policy-making within their respective spheres of influence, interest, and competence has long been part of the conventional wisdom in political science.[10] Furthermore, because the agriculture committees in Congress, the United States Department of Agriculture, and farmer clientele groups all tend to be organized along commodity lines, American agriculture has frequently been cited as a premier example of the existence and operation of subsystem politics in the policy process.[11] The most recent and explicit elaboration of this well-known theme comes from the pen of Theodore Lowi, a prominent American political scientist.[12] Writing in 1969, Lowi concluded, for example, that the notion that agricultural policy should be determined by agriculturalists "is a basic political principle established before the turn of the century and maintained since then without serious reexamination."[13] Agriculture, the analysis continues, "has emerged as a largely self-governing federal estate within the Federal structure of the United States."[14]

The agriculture subsystem has differed from its counterparts in other policy areas by the direct political-administrative linkage which exists between agricultural clientele groups and the remainder of the subsystem. The use of locally elected farmers (potential program recipients) in the administration of farm policy has apparently strengthened and stabilized the agriculture subsystem, thus helping to explain its extraordinary influence upon agriculture policy-making. Indeed, according to Lowi, the decision to use ordinary farmers in the administration of farm policy has resulted in "local self-governing systems" throughout American agriculture.[15] A symbiotic relationship between the local farmer administrations (often linked to specific national farm interest groups), the commodity based agencies of the USDA, and the relevant agriculture subcommittees of the House and Senate has sustained this influential, triangular policy subsystem.

At least with respect to the major commodities considered in this analysis, it now seems clear that what may have been a valid description of the agriculture policy process in the 1960s is no longer adequate.[b] Farm policy has become a macro-political issue in this decade. It has attracted widespread interest among the general public, the media, a broad array of organized interest groups, the Congress, and the Administration. By definition, macro-political issues are salient and visible to a wide spectrum of the body politic. They activate a broad range of both public and private factors. Typically, for example, macro-political issues will involve "party and congressional leaders (who may overlap), the president and the executive departments. The communications media and a variety of group spokesmen are also deeply involved. The range of participants is thus broad."[16] That Congress chose to label its most recent farm bill the Agriculture and *Consumer Protection* Act (emphasis added), is one clear indication that the issue of farm policy has taken on macropolitical traits.

American Farm Policy as a Macro-Political Issue: The
Policy Environment

Evidence of an altered policy environment for U.S. agriculture in this decade is abundant. Moreover the effect of that alteration upon U.S. agriculture policy appears to have been substantial. Senator Herman Talmadge, chairman of the U.S. Senate Committee on Agriculture and Fores-

---

[b] Lowi's analysis dealt with ten policy subsystems found within or closely related to the USDA. The degree to which subsystems continue to dominate policy-making in these other areas is not considered in this review.

try, referred to the macro-political environment of U.S. agriculture as his committee began formal hearings on the extension of farm legislation in February of 1973. As he said,

Our responsibility for drafting new farm legislation this year comes at what is perhaps the poorest possible psychological and political moment.

The U.S. House of Representatives has just been redistricted in such a way that the vast majority of its membership is from large cities and their suburbs.

Food prices are higher than they have been in some time, and many consumers are angry.

The major metropolitan daily newspapers have begun what appears to be a massive campaign on their editorial pages to end the farm program.

The President of the United States indicates that he wants to get government off the farm.

Farm income is higher than it has ever been.

In other words, the pressures on us here today to do nothing—to let existing legislation expire and eliminate permanent legislation on the books—is extremely great. Frankly, given today's climate, this course would seem to be politically expedient, and it would certainly save this committee a great deal of time and energy.[17]

Nearly a month later, Rep. W.R. Poage, then chairman of the House Agriculture Committee, indicated a similar awareness of the rising dissatisfaction with past farm policies at the time his committee began considering extension of the 1970 Farm Act.

As we begin this hearing, I think it is appropriate to make a few comments about a related subject that is very much on the minds of all Americans these days. That is the matter of food costs, and the occasional remarks we hear to the effect that crop price supports authorized in the 1970 Farm Act are no longer necessary or justified.[18]

Although on these two occasions both chairmen also made characteristically strong statements in support of past policies as well as indicating their intention to support such policies in the future, their references to the macro-political character of the agricultural policy environment were harbingers of the changing emphases in agriculture policy which later emerged in the 1973 farm bill and subsequent administrative actions.

Macro-political factors auguring for changes in U.S. agriculture policy grew in number and intensity throughout the spring and summer of 1973. Food prices continued to rise. Domestic and foreign demand for U.S. farm products remained high. The tightness of the supply situation worsened as once plentiful U.S. grain reserves disappeared and bad weather threatened 1973 crop production.[19] High inflation persisted as did pressure from labor and other sources upon the Administration to impose price controls on raw farm products, the one major sector of the economy which remained free from government economic stabilization policy. Administration desires to cut federal spending also entered the picture as did the growing influence within the Administration of the economy minded Office of Management and Budget. An unfavorable balance of payments relationship, which only greater agricultural exports seemed capable of reversing, added credibility to the Nixon Administration's philosophical predilections for returning the American farmer to the market place. Finally, the 1972 presidential election was over and there was no longer a compelling need for the Nixon Administration to court the farm vote.

As a consequence of these and other macro-political developments, on February 15, 1973 President Nixon, in his message to Congress on natural resources and the environment, proposed that farm subsidy payments be gradually eliminated over what he termed "a reasonable transition period. . . ."[20] Two weeks later *Time* magazine editorialized that it was, indeed, "Time to Plant a New Farm Policy."[21] Talbot, a leading and perceptive observer of American farm politics was probably correct in concluding in 1969 that ". . . metropolitan America is just not that much interested in farm policy."[22] By 1973, however, circumstances were different and so was the character of farm policy-making.

Policy-Making in a Macro-Political Arena

Policy-making at the macro level produces different kinds of settlements than decisions reached in the relative obscurity of subsystem politics. This occurs primarily because of the greater salience and visibility of the issues and the broader range of interests which are brought to bear upon them.[23] Often broad public interests at the macro level are represented by the president of the United States. According to Anderson, "a distinctive characteristic of macropolitics is Presidential involvement."[24] For this reason, our discussion of farm policy-making in the 1970s begins with an analysis of President Nixon's impact upon the agricultural policy process.

President Nixon was not, of course, the first president to be actively involved in the area of farm policy-making. Indeed, observers have consistently stressed the importance not only of presidents but also of the president's men, especially the secretary of agriculture, in formulating farm policy.[25] The policy views and actions of former President Nixon did, however, lend a distinctively macropolitical quality to the farm policy debates of the early 1970s. Its macro-political character arose primarily over the ideological void which existed between the former president and the main elements of the traditional farm policy subsystem. (Based upon President Ford's veto of the Emergency Agriculture Act of 1975, these differences seem to be continuing under the present Administration.) Because of these marked ideological and policy differences, presidential farm policy involvement in the 1970s has had a direct bearing upon recent policy changes, helped to convert farm policy into a macro-political issue and contributed to the weakening of the traditional farm policy subsystem.

Presidential and top level USDA resistance to the Agricultural Stabilization and Conservation Service (the agency responsible for the administration of so-called farm programs) was of great concern to proponents of traditional supply-management approaches as early as 1969.[26] At that time, presidential opposition to ASCS conservation programs was, in particular, being interpreted by many within the lower administrative ranks of ASCS as a first step in Administration and top level ASCS agency efforts to diminish the use, size and political effectiveness of that agency. Local ASCS committee consolidations implemented in 1972 and 1973 added credibility to those early fears.

Presidential appointments to top level administrative posts give presidents at least a modicum of control over policy subsystems. Within ASCS these political appointees number in the hundreds and extend far down the administrative hierarchy.[27] The Nixon Administration's widespread use of ideologically compatible ASCS farm program administrators extending from the secretary of agriculture all the way down to ASCS district directors (officials responsible for farm program coordination over several counties within each state), probably represents the Administration's single most important act of presidential involvement in recent farm policy-making. The disquieting and destabilizing effect of such widespread appointments upon the triangular farm policy subsystem was, indeed, profound. When a free market for American agriculture became the rallying cry not only of the president, but also of the key administrative elements of ASCS, the farm policy subsystem had been severed at one of its most critical points, the linkage between the agency and its grass roots administrative, political base.

Recent fissures between top level ASCS administrative personnel and key elements of that agency's traditional and natural political base have occurred at the same time that macro developments continue to erode the autonomy and dominance of the agriculture policy subsystem within the U.S. Congress. The agriculture committees of the House and Senate must be increasingly sensitive to macro-political and economic developments if their committee recommendations are to be enacted into law. While it may be true that basic farm policy is still written within the confines of these committees, it no longer follows that "little emerges, unless it suits the whim and fancy of the sectional and commodity interests which control the committees."[28]

As early as 1970, Nick Kotz reported that Congress was scrutinizing the agriculture committees more closely than it had in the past. At that time these committees were apparently moving into the congressional spotlight because of the growing awareness of their impact upon USDA food aid programs for the poor. According to Kotz, this issue and others had produced "a Congress and general public which is probably more aware of the agriculture committees than ever before . . . there is a growing awareness of the makeup of these committees, particularly among urban liberals. . . ."[29]

The Senate and House agriculture committee hearings held throughout the winter and spring of 1973 in connection with extending the 1970 farm bill provide ample evidence that these committees were, indeed, becoming increasingly aware of the changing character and temper of the Congress, as well as the general public, with respect to farm policy. Despite the clear, personal preferences of most committee members for extending the 1970 Act with equal or greater income protection for farmers, macro-political developments seemed destined, as revealed in their own testimony, to alter future farm policy approaches. As Senator Robert Dole (R-Kansas) put it, "And I do not think we should kid ourselves about the great difficulty we may have in getting any bill passed in the House of Representatives."[30]

Secretary of Agriculture Earl Butz, in testimony before the House agriculture committee, dedicated a similar sensitivity to the general political climate. Admitting that macro developments affect policy formation in the USDA, he further wondered;

> . . . what kind of farm program can you pass with the situation we face now, with the attitude of the public with the alleged high prices of food, which all of us around here know is not true relatively speaking, but that does not alter the fact that they think it is; with the pressures that come on this body right here, and frankly, we have approached this partly from that point of view, that you cannot get by with a continuation of what we have been doing.[31]

The most immediate political threat to traditional agriculture policy arose, of course, from the increasingly unsympathetic urban-suburban oriented House of Representatives. Passage of agricultural legislation in the House requires an ever larger number of nonrural votes. According to Barton, for example, "Rural districts comprised 83 per cent of an absolute majority in the House in 1966; the percentage dropped to 71 by 1969, and to 60 by 1973."[32] Table 5-1 shows the steady erosion, over the past several years, of rural membership in the House of Representatives.

Declining rural membership in the House does not, of course, automatically translate into a loss of rural strength. Indeed, before concluding that macro-political changes in the House of Representatives have diminished the autonomy and influence of the farm policy subsystem in farm policy-making, it must be shown that at least some final policy decisions reflect the wishes of the larger body despite the preferences of subsystem representa-

Table 5-1
Characteristics of House Districts, 1966-1973*

Characteristic	1966	1968	1973	Change, 1966-73
Urban	106	110	102	−4
Suburban	92	104	131	+39
Rural	181	155	130	−51
Mixed	56	66	72	+16

Source: *Congressional Quarterly Weekly Report*, April 6, 1974, p. 878.

*The categories are based upon the following criteria: 50% or more of population in standard metropolitan statistical area (SMSA) central city ("urban"), outside central city but within SMSA ("suburban"), outside SMSA ("rural"), less than 50% of population in any of three above categories ("mixed").

tives. This is not easy to determine. For example, committee compromises made in anticipation of otherwise negative floor reactions are extremely difficult to document. Nonetheless, some indication of the influence of macro-political factors upon the ultimate shape of farm policy may be ascertained by examining floor action.[33] In this regard, passage of the 1973 farm bill provides ample evidence of subsystem capitulation to macropolitical influences in the House.

Floor action on subsidy payment limitations probably provides the best single example of the eroding strength of the farm policy subsystem within the House. In an effort to prevent the adoption of a $20,000 payment limitation, including a prohibition upon allotment transfers, (this amendment by Paul Findlay (R-Ill.) was ultimately adopted),[c] members of the farm bloc themselves put forth a less stringent amendment whereby payments would be restricted to $20,00 but would allow for the sale or lease of acreage allotments. Rep. Robert Bergland (D-Minn.), a leading member of the House agriculture committee and former director of ASCS, introduced the milder amendment in the hope that its adoption would forestall the passage of the more restrictive measure. This strategy developed despite the agriculture committee's earlier approval of a $37,500 payment ceiling. Members of the committee insisted tha more stringent payment limitations would adversely affect farmer incentives to increase production. The Bergland amendment was supported by many members of the agriculture committee despite their preference for the $37,500 limitation. Rep. George Mahon (D-Tex.), chairman of the House Appropriations Committee and a well-known opponent of payment limitations, summed up the frustrations of the weakened farm policy subsystem with these words: "I continue to

[c] House and Senate Conferees later agreed to the Senate version on payment limitations of $20,000 per person with no restrictions on the lease or sale of cotton allotments.

oppose all farm payment limitations, but if we must have some kind of limitation of payments, let us for heaven's sake adopt the Bergland amendment over the Conte and Findley amendments, as they are completely unreasonable and confiscatory."[34]

Although the Bergland amendment did pass (319-89), subsequently, the House also adopted the more stringent Findley measure by a vote of 246 to 163. While a number of factors were involved in the outcome,[35] the overriding explanation seems to have been the general attitude of the House. "That mood might be described as 'hard-line reformist', in the sense that Republicans and Northern Democrats who generally might be called 'reliable traders' yielded to the climate of reform that pervaded the House on the Cotten payments issue."[36] It should also be noted that the Senate Committee on Agriculture and Forestry suffered a similar defeat on the Senate floor when its recommendation to retain the $55,000 per crop limitation was defeated in favor of a $20,000 maximum payment.

Examination of other committee setbacks on the floor of the House and Senate must await more lengthy analyses. Here, it will suffice to say that a number of other committee recommendations were either rejected or modified on the floor. Moreover, several amendments were successfully added on the floor which were opposed by members of the farm policy subsystem. Some of the more important ones, such as the House vote to deny continued funding of the $10 million a year subsidy for Cotton Inc., a cotton research and promotion organization, were ultimately restored in conference. Still, the large number of floor actions considered detrimental to the farm bloc, plus the character of coalition building forced upon farm representatives, particularly in the House, in order to get any farm bill at all passed, adds up to a seriously weakened and compromised congressional farm policy subsystem. The ideological conflict between labor and cotton represents still another problem for successful farm policy coalition building in the future.[37]

What Future for the Farm Policy Subsystem?

We turn finally to an examination of the political base of the triangular farm policy subsystem. After all, in the final analysis, the extraordinary stability and influence attributed to agriculture policy subsystems is predicated on the unique administrative-political relationship which exists between the various USDA agencies and their particular clientele. In the case of the major commodity programs discussed in this analysis, the relevant agency is the Agricultural Stabilization and Conservation Service (ASCS), which is administratively and politically linked to clientele groups through the ASCS Farmer Committee System. The use of some 100,000 locally elected farmers in the administration of farm programs has allegedly insulated this particular subsystem from macro-political influences.[38] The mutual interests, needs and perspective of ASCS farmer-administrators, congressional agriculture committee members, and ASCS agency personnal have historically bound these three elements together in a tightly knit, symbiotic, autonomous policy subsystem. The fact that farmer-administrators have received program benefits as well as per diems for their service on the local committees has added an important and controversial political dimension to this relationship. The normal impulses for organizational survival have contributed to the enduring character of the symbiosis. The tendency, at least during the early phases of supply-management programs, for the agriculture committees of Congress and top level agency staff to use the local farmer committees as grassroots, participative policy input mechanisms added to the parochial nature of the subsystem.

A number of recent developments have substantially undermined the validity of this traditional characterization. For example, the grass roots political base of the ASCS policy subsystem is badly divided over farm program approaches and frustrated in its efforts to influence policy formation at the congressional level. The formation in 1965 of the National Association of Farmer-Elected Committeemen (NAFEC) provides clear evidence of the growing frustration of pro farm-program elements within the Farmer Committee System regarding their diminishing ability to influence farm policy through normal subsystem channels. Had farm policy-making been operating according to the subsystem model, there would have been little need for farm-program proponents to form what can only be described as a typical pressure group.[39] The need for program advocates to find a more direct mode of access to the congressional agriculture committees indicates a failure of normal subsystem processes as well as the growing threat of macro-political influences upon subsystem autonomy. The fact that NAFEC was instigated by increasingly insecure central agency administrators indicates the serious nature of these outside threats, at least as perceived by those administrative elements most dedicated to the continuation of strong farm programs. Moreover, as mentioned earlier, Nixon Administration appointees to ASCS top level administrative positions created profound internal stresses for the subsystem. NAFEC's emphasis upon simply maintaining the Farmer Committee System as a viable administrative form points up the increasingly precarious role of the committee system itself in farm policy-making.

Despite the creation of a formal and active pressure group, macro-political factors continue to frustrate those elements of the farm policy subsystem's political base which have been most dedicated to traditional farm program approaches. That is, NAFEC does not represent simply an alternative form of subsystem dominance. For example, NAFEC favored a straight extension of the 1970 farm act. The following exchange in the winter of 1973 between the chairman of the Senate Committee on Agriculture and Forestry and Frederick Durr, president of the NAFEC, succinctly indicates the organization's position on the future course of farm policy.

The Chairman. Do you support the extension of the existing law?

Mr. Durr. Yes, sir, we do.

The Chairman. Without modification or change in any respect?

Mr. Durr. No sir; we would suggest that there be less discrimination [sic] left to the Secretary in matters pertaining to agriculture. In other words, we would rather presume that the Congress would specifically spell out more details that they have in mind to be implemented.[40]

Although macro-economic developments throughout the spring and summer of 1973 enabled the NAFEC to endorse the general approach adopted in the 1973 farm bill (it is difficult to insist upon set-asides and guaranteed payments with high market prices and seriously depleted grain reserves), it seems clear that the organizaed elements of the farm policy political base did not get what they originally wanted in the 1973 farm bill.

Nor has affiliation with the National Farm Coalition, a loosely knit group of thirty general and commodity based farm organizations, most of which traditionally have been associated ideologically and politically with the Farmer Committee System, arrested NAFEC's declining influence in farm policy-making. For example, the Coalition itself was defeated on nearly every major issue between House and Senate versions of the 1973 farm bill.[41] This, coupled with earlier defeats, resulted in begrudging acceptance of the final bill.

I am sure that some of you are apprehensive, as I am, that this bill takes on an entirely new Federal farm policy. In effect, it is designed to increase production, rather than controlling it as we have done in the past . . . It is, however, we believe a desirable bill and one which if properly administered will offer at least some price protection to farmers in the future.[42]

As the foregoing analysis illustrates, the present constellation of macro-political and economic factors has, at least temporarily, displaced the traditional farm policy subsystem in farm policy-making. That system is simply no longer able, as perhaps it once was, to "resist any type of representation except its own."[43] At precisely what point such displacement renders continued use of the subsystem concept itself inappropriate is debatable. It does seem indisputably correct, however, to conclude that if macro influences become "a regular part of the decisions, it makes little sense to distinguish between the two levels."[44] Careful monitoring of agriculture policy-making will be necessary in the future in order to accurately characterize that process in light of the altered policy environment.

Notes

1. This review will be confined almost entirely to policy changes related to wheat, cotton and feed grains (i.e., corn, grain sorghums, barley, rye and oats), the major U.S. field crops. For a comprehensive historical analysis of farm policy see: Murray R. Benedict, *Farm Policies of the United States 1790-1950*, (New York: Octagon Books, Inc., 1966), or Murray R. Benedict and Oscar C. Stine, *The Agricultural Commodity Programs: Two Decades of Experience* (New York: Twentieth Century Fund, 1956). This latter volume focuses on farm policies only since the New Deal. For a more succinct account of farm policy from the New Deal to the Great Society consult Wayne D. Rasmussen and Gladys L. Baker, "Programs for Agriculture, 1933-1965," in Vernon W. Ruttan, Arley D. Waldo and James P. Houck (eds.), *Agricultural Policy in an Affluent Society* (New York: W.W. Norton and Co., Inc., 1969).

2. Public Law 93-86, "Agriculture and Consumer Protection Act of 1973," 93rd Congress, S. 1888, August 10, 1973.

3. "Wheat Supply and Disappearance," *1974 Handbook of Agricultural Charts*, USDA Agriculture Handbook No. 477, p. 104.

4. Committee for Economic Development, *A New U.S. Farm Policy for Changing World Food Needs* (Georgian Press, October 1974), p. 14.

5. National Farm Institute, *The 70's: Challenge and Opportunity* (Ames, Iowa: Iowa State University Press, 1970).

6. Committee for Economic Development, *New U.S. Farm Policy*, p. 9.

7. Ibid., p. 16.

8. Herman E. Talmadge, "Foreword," *1975 U.S. Agricultural Outlook*, papers presented at the National Agricultural Outlook Conference sponsored by the USDA, December, 1974 (Washington: U.S. Government Printing Office, 1974), p. 111.

9. National Farm Institute, *The 70's*, Nick Kotz, "Changing Politics of Farm Programs," p. 25.

10. James E. Anderson, *Public Policy-Making* (New York: Praeger Publishers, 1975), pp. 50-51.

11. See, for example, Dale E. Hathaway, *Government and Agriculture* (New York: Macmillan Co., 1963), especially Chapter 7.

12. Theodore J. Lowi, *The End of Liberalism* (New York: W.W. Norton, 1969), pp. 102-115.

13. Ibid., p. 103.

14. Ibid.

15. Ibid., p. 110.

16. Anderson, *Public Policy-Making*, p. 52.

17. U.S. Senate, Committee on Agriculture and Forestry, *Extension of Farm and Related Programs*, Hearings on S. 517, 93rd Cong. 1st sess. Part I, February 27, 1973, p. 1.

18. U.S. House of Representatives, Committee on Agriculture, *General Farm Program*, Hearings before Committee, 93rd Cong., 1st sess., March 20, 1973, p. 2.

19. In testimony before the Senate Agriculture Committee on March 29, 1973, Secretary of Agriculture Butz indicated that U.S. government reserve stocks had reached new lows. "Based on our Kansas City Office working numbers the uncommitted grain stocks of the CCC were valued at a little less than $180 million on March 27—the lowest figure since the end of World War II." U.S. Senate, Committee on Agriculture and Forestry, *Extension of Farm and Related Programs*, p. 658.

20. *Weekly Compilation of Presidential Documents*, Vol. 9, No. 7 (Washington: Government Printing Office, 1973), p. 151.

21. William R. Doerner, "Time to Plant a New Farm Policy," *Time* (February 26, 1973), p. 22.

22. Ross B. Talbot, "Political Factors Affecting Public Policy," paper presented at Agricultural Policy Review Conference, North Carolina State University, December 2, 1969, p. 7.

23. E.E. Schattschneider, *The Semi-Sovereign People* (Chicago: Holt, Rinehart, and Winston, 1960), see especially Chapters 1 and 4.

24. Anderson, *Public Policy-Making*, p. 52.

25. Ross B. Talbot and Don F. Hadwiger, *The Policy Process in American Agriculture* (San Francisco: Chandler Publishing Co., 1968), Chapter 7.

26. Ivan Garth Youngberg, "Federal Administration and Participatory Democracy: The ASCS Farmer Committee System," Ph.D. dissertation, University of Illinois, Urbana, 1971. See especially Chapters 3 and 7.

27. Ibid. For a review of the character and extent of political appointments within ASCS, see Chapter 4.

28. Talbot, "Political Factors," p. 11.

29. National Farm Institute, *The 70's*; Nick Kotz, "Changing Politics," p. 25.

30. U.S. Senate, Committee on Agriculture and Forestry, *Extension of Farm and Related Programs*, p. 35.

31. U.S. House of Representatives, Committee on Agriculture, *General Farm Program*, p. 33.

32. Weldon V. Barton, "Coalition Building in the U.S. House of Representatives: Agricultural Legislation in 1973," paper presented at the 1974

Annual Meeting of the American Political Science Association, Palmer House, Chicago, August 29-September 2, 1974, p. 3.

33. Ross B. Hopkins, "Reevaluating the Policy Subsystem Concept with Speculation on the Impact of Congressional Changes on Policy Sub-systems," paper presented at the 1975 Annual Meeting of the Southern Political Science Association, Nashville, Tennessee, Nov. 6-8, 1975, p. 10.

34. "The Farm Bill: A Delicate Compromise Collapses," *Congressional Quarterly Weekly Report* 31, 28 (July 14, 1973): 1919.

35. Karton, "Coalition Building," p. 12.

36. Ibid.

37. Ibid., pp. 2-7.

38. Lowi, *End of Liberalism*, p. 112.

39. Youngberg, "Federal Administration," Chapter 7.

40. U.S. Senate, Committee on Agriculture and Forestry, *Extension of Farm and Related Programs*, pp. 98-99.

41. Copy of telegram sent to all conferees on Farm Bill by John W. Scott, chairman of Washington Steering Committee, National Farm Coalition, July 25, 1973.

42. Letter sent to members of the National Farm Coalition by F.V. Heinkel, chairman of the National Farm Coalition on August 8, 1973.

43. Theorore J. Lowi, *End of Liberalism*, p. 112.

44. Ross B. Hopkins, "Reevaluating the Policy Subsystem Concept," p. 3.

**Part III
Consumer Protection**

6 Consumerism: A Coalition in Flux

Mark V. Nadel

Although one might still regard Ralph Nader as an angry young man, in fact both he and the consumer protection cause he champions are getting older. Consumer protection, having reemerged as a national issue in 1966 in the form of automobile safety legislation, is now entering its second decade. This chapter will highlight some of the most salient trends of consumer protection as a maturing political issue. Also, I would suggest that the maturing of the consumer issue is illustrative of trends in regulatory politics generally.

Implicit in the seminal works on regulatory politics by Huntington, Bernstein, and Edelman[1] is the view that regulatory policy inevitably shifts from its original reform goals as regulatory agencies are overcome by excessive clientelism toward regulated interests, and that the consumer constituency of agencies quickly melts away. While the historic trend of administrative regulation confirms the main thrust of this pessimistic analysis, more recent experience tends to show that the political factors are more complex and random than previously noted. First of all, the re-surgence of vitality and aggressiveness in the Federal Trade Commission shows that there is nothing inevitable or unalterable about the "life cycle" of regulatory agencies.[2]

While much of the discussion of regulatory politics focuses on the agencies, there are also changes in the reform coalition itself—in this case the consumer groups. Contrary to the change one should expect from the early literature on the regulation, the consumer coalition has not simply melted away. If anything, consumer groups have gotten more deeply rooted, more vigorous, more numerous, and more diverse than they were at the height of congressional concern with consumer protection in the late 1960s. But, collectively, they are not necessarily blessed with greater political clout. In fact if there is to be an epitaph for the modern period of consumerism it might well be, "We have met the enemy and he is us."

When consumerism emerged as an issue in the 1960s, consumer activists were fighting for fairly clearly defined goals and there was little dissension in the ranks. As the organizations and issues got older, however, some cracks in the coalition began to appear. There have first of all been heated disagreements within the big consumer organizations. Unhappiness

71

with the style of leadership and positions on some issues led to an unsuccessful attempt by some Consumer Federation of America leaders to oust its executive director, and she eventually did step down. A major source of friction has been the position of labor unions—traditionally a major source of financial support for the Consumers Federation. When issues involving tariffs have surfaced, the CFA has been notably reticent about pursuing the consumer interest in free trade—which often conflicts with the position of organized labor.

Even in that traditional bastion of consumerism, Consumers Union, there has been considerable divisiveness and bickering over a variety of organizational and policy questions. For example, there has been considerable dissension over which kinds of products to rate in *Consumer Reports*. It has been charged that rating items such as outboard motors and full-sized sedans makes the magazine appropriate only for upper middle class audiences and deprives lower income consumers of a rating service they need more than upper income consumers. Furthermore some of the products rated, such as small boat depth sounders, are trivial or useful to only a very small number of consumers.[3]

To some extent, controversies within Consumers Union and other consumer groups reflect differences about priorities. But increasingly there are more fundamental questions about just what policies are in the consumer interest and about which groups actually do represent the consumer interest. This can be seen in the case of no-fault automobile insurance. Since 1969, no-fault insurance has been a high-priority issue for consumer activists in Congress and in 1972 the Hart-Magnuson bill, which in effect mandated national no-fault insurance, was reported out of the Senate Commerce Committee.

An article in the *New Republic* reported that Ralph Nader was not lobbying for the bill and in fact was actually opposed to it. The article also noted that other consumer advocates considered no-fault to be major priority consumer legislation. It went on to charge that Nader's position was influenced by an offer by the American Trial Lawyers Association, which opposes no-fault, to donate $20,000 to the Center for Auto Safety—one of the Nader spin-off organizations.[4] There was, in fact, a contribution made to the Center but it was quickly rejected and returned, and Nader heatedly denied that there was a link between the ATLA offer and his own position on no-fault. More importantly, in terms of the ambiguity of the consumer interest, he stated his own position which attacked the pending legislation as a mere palliative. Nader asserted: "With such widespread revulsion (against the present insurance system) at a rising peak, the opportunity for reform should be broader and deeper than the Hart no-fault bill. . . . My judgment is that Congress has one chance in this decade to make a clean new policy revolution."[5] This was more than just a question of priorities. In contrast to the main thrust of the efforts of Senators Hart, Magnuson and other congressional sponsors who have been aiming at a specific and narrow insurance issue, Nader thus believed that the consumer interest could only be served by seizing the moment to attack a broader range of consumer problems inherent in the present structure of the insurance industry.

Nader's analysis of course parallels the perspective of Gabriel Kolko in regard to the cooptation of consumer interests by industry groups[6]— especially in light of the fact that major insurance companies have come around to backing no-fault. If Nader is correct, we can speculate that the insurance companies were wise enough to realize that no-fault is a cheap price (or no price) to pay for preventing the kinds of reforms and tough regulations that Nader has in mind.

The fortunes of the consumer coalition have also shifted according to the varying interests of varying components. In fact, in political terms it is evident that the distinction between producer and consumer is never a static one. While from a public choice perspective there is a pursuasive case for the inevitable victory of organized issue-specific producer interests over unorganized consumer interests,[7] consumers have been able to win policy battles for two reasons. First, there have emerged "professional" consumers in the form of public interest groups and congressional activists who are functionally equivalent to producer interest groups. Secondly, the distinction between producer and consumer is never static but is instead a description of *roles* in a particular controversy rather than inherent interests. For example, in their role of representing the consumer interests of their members, labor unions have vigorously committed their resources to such consumer legislation as auto safety, product safety, and meat inspection. However, the unions have opposed consumer interests in low tariffs and instead promoted their interests as producers. Similarly, the sugar quota system was ended in 1974 when the bill to extend the quota system was opposed by various processed food manufacturers who were pursuing their interest as industrial consumers in alliance with groups of retail consumers. As consumer issues go beyond the early "good guy" vs. "bad guy" scenarios inherent in such early legislation as auto safety and meat inspection, we will increasingly see more complex mixes of consumer vs. producer interests.

There is also a shifting in the mix of interests of the public that is represented by consumer activists. In an earlier work, I argued that the bulk of the consumer legislation passed in the late 1960s provided collective benefits to consumers rather that differential benefits.[8] That is, most of the laws dealt with health and safety issues and they entailed price rises (for seat belts, better flammability resistance, etc.) that were readily absorbed by middle class consumers. Legislation that imposed real costs on industry and which would save consumers money was systematically defeated.

The same basic tendency has continued, but with a major difference. Previously, it had been only low income consumers who suffered any economic costs resulting from the add-on costs of consumer health and safety legislation. Now, however, the bite of that add-on cost is being felt by an increasing number of consumers. In a period of rapid inflation and recession the ranks of people who could be considered ''low-income'' for political purposes has swelled considerably. The costs of collective benefit legislation are thus increasingly important for middle class consumers who are in a much better political position to make their discontent known. Furthermore, at the farther reaches of consumer protection policies, the add-on costs have increased dramatically. Thus, to consider requiring an auto air bag restraint system, with cost estimates ranging from $100-$200, is probably beyond the bounds of current political feasibility. In short, collective benefit legislation which had previously entailed the least opposition is now also straining the bounds of political feasibility.

Another change to be noted is the shift in roles of consumers from beneficiaries of regulatory legislation to targets of that legislation. The conventional view of regulatory politics is bipolar; consumer interests are opposed to producer interests. If consumers win, producers are regulated. Recent trends, however, make such a view increasingly untenable. First, as we have just seen, the regulations may impose costs that consumers are unwilling to tolerate. Secondly, and more fundamentally, it may be the consumers as well as producers whose behavior is regulated. This is seen clearly in the case of the automobile seatbelt ignition interlock system. The Department of Transportation had required the interlock systems on all 1974 model passenger automoblies. The interesting thing about the systems was that unlike previous auto safety regulation, they directly regulated the behavior of the drivers—the car would not start until the driver fastened his seat belt and shoulder strap. Consumers reacted to this innovation with considerable hostility and resistance—it is estimated that over half of 1974 car owners managed to disconnect the system. In an unusually prompt response to public opinion, the House of Representatives passed an amendment to the Motor Vehicle and School Bus Safety Amendments of 1974 which repealed the interlock requirements. The Senate followed suit and the repeal of the DOT regulation was effected in October 1974. The large congressional majorities in favor of repeal are notable. The vote was 339-49 in the House and 64-21 in the Senate. Although Northern Democrats had previously been the bedrock of support for consumer protection, even among them repeal was voted overwhelmingly. In short, consumers, represented by Congress, were reacting in much the same fashion as any economic sector that is regulated for this first time—they chafed under regulation, resisted it, and sought to reverse it. When consumers were put in a new role as targets of regulation they simply did not like it.

Nonetheless, there are issues on which a broad range of consumer interests are pitted against a broad range of producer interests—typically represented by the United States Chamber of Commerce. The primary issue in this category is the recurrent proposal for a federal Consumer Protection Agency which would act as a consumer advocate before other federal regulatory agencies. The prospect of a centrally institutionalized consumer advocate with legal standing in nearly all regulatory proceedings has profoundly disturbed business groups and brought about near unanimity of business opposition. This proposal has been the most intensely opposed of any consumer issue in the last ten years and has twice occasioned filibusters which killed the proposal in two Congresses—the only consumer bills to fall victim to this ultimate legislative weapon. This kind of outcome is not new or unexpected. As I have argued elsewhere,[9] opposition to consumer legislation has increased as a function of the degree to which that legislation challenged prevailing patterns of economic power. It is not surprising, therefore, that the only new consumer protection agency in the past decade is the Consumer Product Safety Commission, which confers collective benefits with costs readily passed on to consumers. It is by no means an unimportant agency, but it does not seriously challenge the legal and economic superiority of business interests. The proposed federal Consumer Protection Agency, on the other hand, is recognized by both its proponents and its opponents as having the potential for a more fundamental realignment of power relationships.

In summary, the outer limits of consumer protection are still bounded by the inability of consumer interests to obtain fundamental and systemic reform. Within those bounds, issues have become more complex and the form of the consumer coalition has shifted according to the shifting roles of its components who are variously consumers and producers, beneficiaries and targets of regulation.

Notes

1. Samuel Huntington, "The Marasmus of the ICC: The Commission, The Railroads, and the Public Interest," *Yale Law Journal* (1952): 467-509; Marver Bernstein, *Regulating Business by Independent Commission* (Princeton: Princeton University Press, 1955); Murray Edelman, "Symbols and Political Quiescence," *American Political Science Review* 54 (September 1960): 695-704.

2. Andrea Schoenfeld, "FTC's New Boldness Tests Limits of its Authority," *National Journal* 3 (January 30, 1971): 207-219.

3. Morton Mintz, "Consumers Union: Institution in Trouble," *Washington Post*, April 22, 1973, p. A1.

4. Leah Young, "A Chink in Nader's Armor?" *New Republic*, September 2, 1972, p. 11.

5. *New Republic*, September 9, 1972, pp. 13-14.

6. Gabriel Kolko, *The Triumph of Conservatism: A Reinterpretation of American History, 1900-1916* (New York: Free Press, 1963).

7. See, for example, Anthony Downs, *An Economic Theory of Democracy* (New York: Harper & Row, 1961), pp. 238-256.

8. Mark V. Nadel, *The Politics of Consumer Protection* (Indianapolis: Bobbs-Merrill, 1971) pp. 220-227.

9. Ibid., pp. 227-232.

7

Scientific Findings and the Formulation of Public Policy in the Sale of Cigarettes

Charles B. Hagan

I

During the second quarter of this century an enormous increase in the sale of cigarettes got under way. Near the end of the third decade in the United States, advertisements began to include women as a potential market, and the suggestion that cigarettes could be substituted for sweets had a brief interlude. The interlude was stopped in the United States by the Federal Trade Commission's initiation of an unfair practices inquiry. The advertising slogan was then shortened to "reaching for a cigarette instead." The expansion in the sale of cigarettes has been profitable for a variety of segments in the society: the growers, both large and small, the processors, the marketers, the advertisers, the retailers, and last but not necessarily the least has been the interest of government in revenue.

Governments have had a number of links to the tobacco industry. The tobacco crop provided cash income to land owners, and/or to those who leased land and contributed their labor. The manufactured products generated employment and income in the stages that succeeded the growing season and harvest. The smoking products had especially desirable qualities for those engaged in production and distribution, as the customer who overcame the early unpleasant phases of learning to smoke quickly came to enjoy the activity and to become an habitual user. The practice of smoking developed especially strong habits, and as a result the ultimate consumer was tied to the industry. The demand for the product was inelastic, to use the economists' term, and the marketing sector became engaged in keeping its share of linked customers from being attracted to products of competitors. Advertising was the essential skill.

As population increased, and as the proportion of it that smoked cigarettes increased, the industry could ride the wave with ease and with profit. It is not meant to say that changes did not take place in the industry, for there was considerable decline in the use of chewing tobacco and snuff; but cigars and smoking tobacco continued to be the important segments of activity. There were also developments in the technology of the manufacturing processes that required greater capital investments.

Some of the research on this study was done on a grant from the Center for International Comparative Studies of the University of Illinois, Urbana-Champaign.

As might be expected with an increasing market, tobacco production expanded into new areas. The commodity is now produced in many parts of the world, and in each country there are accompanying linkages between the producers, the processors, and the governments. The tobacco plant has a number of varieties; that, combined with the differences in soil and climate, makes the marketable commodity a somewhat different one in the various countries. As may be expected, national regulations in response to the special problems of each country have differed with the expectation of maximizing advantages for each country's concerns. Policies will differ, for the maximization of advantages will depend on the conditions in which each nation finds itself. In a few countries, in which tobacco is not grown, the primary concern may be to maximize tax returns, and in other countries there may be conflicting interests that will need reconciliation. In short there are a number of policy problems that each country will need to resolve even on the basis of economic advantage alone.

The beneficent contribution of cigarettes to national welfare was shaken in some small degree when medical research papers in the 1930s began to find quantitative connections between some illnesses and cigarette smoking. The research papers were few, but they kept coming, and with uniform results. None of the papers developed a theory that causally linked something in tobacco and/or cigarette smoking to the diseases, so there was a theoretical possibility that the explanation could be found elsewhere. By the 1950s papers in the medical and scientific journals began to generate attention in the public and in governmental agencies concerned with health. Two general reports received wide attention: one was published by the British Royal College of Surgeons entitled *Smoking and Health: A Summary of a Report Prepared by the Royal College* (1962), and the other a U.S. study entitled *A Report of the Advisory Committee to the Surgeon General of the Public Health Service on Smoking and Health* (1964). The latter has been followed by annual summaries of additional findings made by research scientists.[1]

The governmental reports have agreed in their assessments of the findings of the research studies. The smoking of cigarettes is linked strongly to lung cancer, to the development of cancers of larynx and oral cavity, to the existence ("the most important cause") of chronic obstructive bronchopulmonary disease, to emphysema, and to chronic bronchitis. Recently cigarette smoking has been found to retard fetal growth in pregnant women. Many other illnesses have been linked in a statistically significant manner to the smoking of cigarettes and even to the inhalation of the smoke of cigarettes[2] smoked by others in enclosed spaces. This finding is frequently designated as "passive smoking."

The reports have had an impact wider than the country of their origin, and all nations concerned with the problem of health and smoking have used the reports in their discussions of policy. The reports, moreover, summarize findings from studies made in many parts of the world.

The findings have not been completely accepted in all countries; even when accepted by many groups, within a country, there have been opponents who reject the conclusions. Their major theme is the failure of research to come up with a clear theoretical linkage between smoking and illnesses, and they make a point of challenging details of the research findings. Nevertheless, the scientific findings have had an impact that cigarette makers have had to cope with, and the most widely used coping device has been the filter. Various observations can be and have been made about the ability of the filter to reduce or remove the elements of the cigarette that generate ill effects. There is certainly no general scientific acceptance of the filter as successful for coping with the health problems that have been linked to the cigarette but there has been a worldwide development in the joining of filters to cigarettes. Most of the cigarettes sold in the Western nations now have filters, and there is a considerable body of literature devoted to their composition and their ability to reduce the dangers of the cigarette. Although many unfiltered cigarettes are still sold, the filtered cigarette has penetrated into the markets of all nations with only one or two exceptions (e.g., Turkey).

The search for alternatives to tobacco has always existed, and the recent health findings have stimulated greater efforts. In fact, in Great Britain the Imperial Tobacco and Imperial Chemical Industries have a research project intended to discover a substitute for tobacco. Other companies in Britain are engaged in similar enterprises. In the United States Celenese Fibers has conducted research and has experimented with mixing its product with tobacco in cigarettes. It is understood that other enterprises are engaged in similar efforts.[3] Bulgaria, a major tobacco-producing country, and an exporter as well, has experimented by crossing tobacco plants with tomatoes and with the thornapple. Both crosses produced a nicotine-free leaf. Apparently nothing has been done with the tomato cross, but the cross with the thornapple produces a leaf with atropine. Bulgartabac, the government monopoly, has produced a cigarette called Atrotabac, which it is suggested is effective when used against asthma and similar ailments.[4]

II

Major policy problems have not been met by these minor improvisations, and the health problems resulting from smoking cigarettes have increased with the expanding use of the cigarette. The illnesses are persistent and expensive and apparently they shorten lives. The costs are of considerable import to those who suffer, and the economy as a whole loses through the reduced productivity traceable to the loss of working time.

Smoking patterns are similar in the industrial nations. An increasing number of adults have developed the habit in the last half century, and the habit of smoking is descending downward in the age groupings, reaching into the secondary schools. It is usually asserted that smoking by parents contributes to the development of the habit among their children.[5] The medical findings associate the extent and depth of the illnesses to the length of time that the individual has smoked. The future of young smokers, on the basis of present day findings, includes extensive illnesses and shorter life spans.

The cessation of smoking is an arduous task, for there are physiological and social habits that must be overcome. The former are often easier than the latter, but there has not emerged in these years any clear and simple route to cessation. Some health agencies believe that success is only to be found in persuading the children not to start. This route requires the public agencies (schools as well as private groupings) to counter the influence of the parents, but it may be partially frustrated by secondary schools which provide smoking rooms which encourage the usual peer group behaviors.

Some countries prohibit the sale of cigarettes to minors. Many of the states in the United States prohibit such sales, but the wide use of the vending machine reduces the effects of the prohibition even though the machines carry a sign making it illegal for minors to purchase cigarettes from the machine. The vending machine companies may agree to locate the machines in the areas that minors are not likely to visit. Even so, there is no prohibition on parents making cigarettes available to their offspring.

No state now prohibits the sale of cigarettes, although a few did so at the beginning of this century. Presumably the interstate movement would frustrate a state policy prohibiting importation. However, most states impose substantial taxes on cigarettes, and so do some local governments. In 1972-73 the states collected $3,010 million and local governments collected an additional $146 million. The state taxes vary from the low of two cents per package in North Carolina (the last state to impose such a tax) to a high of 21 cents per package in Connecticut. (National taxes of $2,229 million were also imposed.) While the taxing power has often been used to regulate or prohibit the marketing of a commodity, it may be that the government's interest in the revenue constitutes an obstacle to prohibition! The average tax rate in the United States, i.e., state, local, and federal, has totaled about 20 cents a pack, yet that is less than the tax in many foreign countries.

No nation has sought to prohibit smoking. Obviously the cigarette is a substantial source of governmental income. Britain, one of the few nations that does not grow tobacco, relies heavily on the import duty that it imposes on tobacco. The duty produces a large item in the national government's revenue, and it is almost certain that those concerned with raising revenue would find it difficult to discover an alternative source with ease. In fact governmental policy has been to impose a tax equal to the import duty if tobacco substitutes were found to make a palatable cigarette.

Among the many nations that operates a governmental monopoly in tobacco products is France. SEITA markets cigarettes and matches and is an important revenue source for the government. The health findings have stimulated SEITA to conduct its own research into the effects of tobacco. The management of SEITA which is concerned primarily with the operations of its marketing side, will determine the use that will be made of these research findings. An indication of the policy direction of the monopoly may be gleaned from the following:

By being the first cigarette ever to exploit a low nicotine level in France (0.8 compared with 1.8 for "*Gauloise*," SEITA's most popular black brand) and backed by publicity declaring unblushingly that [it is] 'three times less dangerous than the others', the brand got immense newspaper and magazine publicity taking up the health challenge; even national TV coverage was provided, making this the biggest (free) publicity campaign for tobacco ever seen in the country.[6]

The three countries provide examples of different institutional arrangements and economic conditions. The United States claims to be a private enterprise economy and is a large exporter of tobacco. Britain is a private enterprise economy (in tobacco products) that imports all of its tobacco. France produces a substantial portion of its tobacco but imports more than half of the tobacco that it uses, and it markets the products through a governmental monopoly. All three are highly industrialized and accustomed to the use of science and its outputs. Two of these have produced damaging reports about the use of tobacco in the form of the cigarette. France has produced no report, but certainly its scientific establishment is aware of the findings that supported the U.S. and the British reports. The policies of these three nations on the marketing of cigarettes are quite similar, but some minor modifications will be noted below.

Yugoslavia produces a large crop of tobacco and exports a substantial portion of its production. It is not as highly industrialized as the above three nations, and it proclaims itself as a Socialist country. It has a complicated regional system for the marketing of tobacco and cigarettes. The health findings have found little support in this nation; an illustrative statement may be the following:

There are only a very few lung cancer cases known in Yugoslavia. Those usual cancer cases are those that affect the stomach and the intestines. Even in the tobacco-producing sections of Yugoslavia, such as Bosnia, Hercegovina, Macedonia, etc. where people are heavy smokers, the occurence of lung cancer seems to be negligible . . ."[7]

The following statement is later in date and may indicate that changes are under way, ". . . Despite the objections of the Tobacco Institute in Prilep the Secretary of Information has supported a move to ban cigarette advertising and to have health warnings printed on pack . . ."[8]

It is not intended by these remarks on Yugoslavia to assert that Socialist countries have taken the health findings less seriously than capitalist countries. Probably a more useful clue is to be found in the stage of industrial development. Many of the African nations that have become producers of tobacco leaf in the years since the First World War have paid little or no attention to the health findings. The same observation may be made about the middle eastern nations that grow and market tobacco on the world markets. On the other hand, the USSR is experiencing increased cigarette smoking, and it has taken many steps to spread health information widely. It prohibits cigarette advertising in all media, but there is no official anti-smoking policy.[9] In Czechoslovakia it is reported that the anti-cigarette information only increased the demand for cigarettes with filter tips. The increased smoking found in other countries has also occurred there. At times some west European cigarettes have been allowed to advertise on television, with the justification that the payments would be made in hard currency. In Bulgaria, which produces a substantial amount of tobacco, the government controls the industry from production through marketing of tobacco products. The government, however, takes a very restrained approach with respect to retail sales:

In fact, in Bulgaria cigarettes are bought, they are not sold. There is very little advertising of any kind, and the only publicity that is ever seen for cigarettes is the appearance in the press or an editorial news story when a new brand is put on sale, and, perhaps, a small tie-in window sticker for retail outlets that tell smokers that they can buy there.[10]

Hungary, another member of the Communist group of nations, has the usual governmental monopoly for the marketing of cigarettes. The filter cigarette has become extremely popular there as elsewhere. The practices surrounding the marketing of a new brand is described:

For the introduction of a new cigarette, the approval of the bodies entrusted in Hungary with quality control, and of the health authorities is also necessary. Having their approval, the general public may be informed of the existence of the new brand by posters, radio, TV, and newspaper advertising, by other means of publicity and of course, by the tobacconists.[11]

One of the striking features of cigarette marketing in recent years has been the large increase in new brands. The practice is found in all of the countries, and it is usually associated with the effort to maintain the quantity marketed. The interchange of brand names between countries is a highly developed part of the marketing process. While advertising is an important facet of such marketing processes, it is not indispensable.

If foreign experience helps, they (United States manufacturers) need not be dismayed. What is now Britain's best-selling cigarette has risen from nowhere to more than 20% of the market without benefit of TV advertising. Nor need the lack of that medium contribute to lack of market growth. That certainly has not been the experience in France, Italy, Switzerland or Britain. Lack of individual brand advertising on TV in Japan has not held back Hi-lite, now the world's largest selling cigarette.[12]

III

Most governments have responded to the health findings with a considerable degree of uniformity. Smokers comprise varying proportions of the population, and majority and minority rights may become an element in the compromises that have emerged. The proportions of the smokers in the various nations is not known, but in the United States it is estimated that thre are 52 million smokers, obviously a minority of the total population. The smokers comprise 42 percent of the men and 31 percent of the women. Most of them have tried to quit and have failed.[13]

One of the regulations with health implications was invented in the United States. This is the requirement that packages of cigarettes carry on them warnings of the dangers to health. The message in the earlier legislation was less assured than is the message that now appears, namely: "Warning: The Surgeon General Has Determined That Cigarette Smoking Is Dangerous to Your Health." Many other nations have followed the same approach, but by no means have all been willing to impose this requirement on the cigarette manufacturers. Of the countries discussed above only Great Britain has required a warning message on its packets.[14]

In the United States, the Federal Trade Commission (FTC) developed a consent order with the six major cigarette manufacturers that requires the same health statement in all advertisements as appears on cigarette packages.[15] Existing national policy also prohibits the advertising of cigarettes and little cigars (the cigarette is wrapped with a tobacco leaf rather than paper) on radio and television stations. Similar policies are effective in Great Britain, the USSR and many other countries. Consideration is being given to the ban in other nations as well.

Some countries have gone further and banned the advertising of cigarettes in all media, i.e., newspapers, magazines and billboards. A problem obviously arises in the circulation of periodicals across nations. In some instances such magazines have been allowed to circulate; others not.[16] Perhaps the most esoteric method of passing along the message is Kuwait's postal canceling machine which imprints the message "Smoking spoils your health" in two languages.[17]

The World Health Organization has urged its members to engage in campaigns against smoking. It specifically recommends restrictions on advertising, warnings on packages, and drives to deter the young from taking up the habit. Its sister organization, the Food and Agriculture Organization, expects the consumption of cigarettes to continue to increase, but concludes that:

Nevertheless, further proof of the adverse relationship between cigarette smoking and health and the increasing attention which is paid to this problem may finally result in a trend toward stagnation or even decrease in tobacco consumption in this whole group of countries as has already been evident in the United States and Canada. However, this is as yet uncertain and at the world level any decline could still be more than counterbalanced by rising consumption in developing countries.[18]

Most estimates of the effect of the health findings do not expect any substantial changes in the consumption of cigarettes. Many observers consider the tax and price factor as the most important restraint. Nonetheless, it may be that the failure to present smoking in advertisements and on television in association with the "good life" will over the long pull reduce the attractiveness of the practice to the young. It is the young who are maintaining the demand for cigarettes in most markets.

IV

The emergence of the concept of "passive smoking" in recent years has presented a more complex health situation. A passive smoker is a nonsmoker who breathes air in which a substantial amount of tobacco smoke has collected. In passive smoking the cigarette, the cigar and the pipe are involved, and the smoke that issues into the surrounding air may be drawn into the lungs of the nonsmoker. There have been studies that measure the comparative quantities of smoke ingested by the passive and the active smoker. The findings usually are that while the passive smoker ingests less, he ingests measurable quantities. Recent studies suggest an increased probability of illness among the passive smokers as compared with nonsmokers not subjected to smoke-filled rooms.

While there have been rules and regulations about smoking in closed spaces, it is probably fair to say that relaxed enforcement has been the custom as the number of smokers have increased. In the United States, at least, in recent years there has been an increased concern for the majority that does not smoke, and the health findings have increased their "clout" in the development of regulations to free air of tobacco smoke. Examples of

this have been the revival or issuance of regulations requiring the maintenance of space without smokers by the Interstate Commerce Commission,
Civil Aeronautics Board, Occupational and Safety and Health Administration, and many other national governmental agencies. The states have also
entered vigorously into this field of legislation, and their subordinate units,
the cities, have sometimes enacted ordinances protecting enclosed spaces
from the smoker. The quality of administrative enforcement is yet to be
determined.

Notes

1. A succinct account of these developments may be found in an essay
by Charles B. Hagan, "Cigarettes and Public Policy: The Inauguration of a
New Policy," in Carl Beck (ed.), *Law and Justice: Essays in Honor of
Robert S. Rankin* (Durham, N.C.: Duke University Press, 1970), p. 249.
See also A. Lee Fritschler, *Smoking and Politics: Policy Making and the
Federal Bureaucracy* (Englewood Cliffs, N.J.: Prentice-Hall, 1975) 2nd
edition; and Joan S. Gimlin "Regulation of the Cigarette Industry, *Editorial
Research Reports* 2, 20 (November 1967); Thomas Whiteside, "A Cloud of
Smoke," *New Yorker*, Nov. 30, 1963, p. 67 et seq., and "Smoking Still,"
New Yorker, Nov. 18, 1974, p. 121 et seq.; Susan Wagner, *Tobacco Coun-
try: Tobacco in American History and Politics* (Praeger, 1973). For a
survey of world comments on the Surgeon General's Report, see *World
Tobacco*, No. 14 (March 1964); 19. *World Tobacco*, published in Great
Britain, reports on all facets of the tobacco industry. It is not a trade journal
in the sense that an organization publishes it, but its reports suggest a
favorable attitude toward the tobacco industry. It will be cited frequently.

2. The 1972 Report of the Surgeon General entitled "The Health
Consequences of Smoking." A summary of this report is published in the
Congressional Record, Feb. 23, 1973, p. H 1087, Daily Edition. The annual
reports of the Surgeon General continue to support the findings of the
original reports.

3. *World Tobacco*, No. 42 (September-October 1973); 47.

4. *World Tobacco*, No. 3 (December 1963); 91. See also No. 6 (September, 1964): 37.

5. This suggestion was made to the author by the public health authorities in Great Britain some years ago.

6. *World Tobacco*, No. 39 (Dec. 1972-Jan. 1973): 147.

7. *World Tobacco*, No. 3 (Dec. 1963); 90.

8. *World Tobacco*, No. 38 (Sept.-Oct. 1972): 36.

9. *ASH*, 4, 4 (July-Aug. 1974), and No. 5 (Sept.-Oct. 1974). *ASH* is the

acronym for Action on Smoking and Health, a vigorous lobbying agency to limit the smoking of cigarettes. It is a useful report of activities.

10. *World Tobacco*, No. 8 (March 1965); 31.

11. *World Tobacco*, No. 26 (June 1969); 119.

12. *World Tobacco*, No. 30 (Sept. 1970); 131, 133.

13. Thomas Whiteside, "Smoking Still," *New Yorker*, November 18, 1974, p. 139.

14. Canada, Ireland, Japan, and Peru require such a message. In 1973 such a message was being considered in Australia, Brazil, Costa Rica and the Philippines. *ASH* 3, 1 (Jan.-Feb. 1973).

15. The order became effective March 30, 1972. *ASH* 2, 4 (July-Aug. 1972). This is the basis for the appearance of the statement on billboard advertisements. The size of the statement is related to the size of the advertisement. The major national legislation on cigarettes, which preempts any state legislation is to be found in PL 89-92 (1965), PL 91-222 (1970), and PL 93-109.

16. *ASH* 3, 1 (Jan.-Feb. 1973). The summary in *ASH* is based on a report by the National Clearinghouse for Smoking and Health, 1972. The Clearinghouse was established in the Department of Health, Education and Welfare to collect information. In 1973 its expenditures were cut by the Office of Management and Budget. No cuts were made in expenditures for the activities of tobacco growers and manufacturers. *ASH* 3, 3 (May-June 1973).

17. *ASH* 2, 6 (Nov.-Dec. 1972). Australia puts the message in nineteen languages for federal government advertisements and the magazines that circulate among the migrant groups in that country. *World Tobacco*, No. 41 (June-July 1973): 43.

18. *World Tobacco*, No. 36 (March-April 1972): 86. It may be noted that Thomas Whiteside found that while the number of cigarettes consumed in the United States had increased, the quantity of tobacco used in making them had declined. See Whiteside, "Smoking Still." There could be many explanations of such a development, among them a more efficient use of the total tobacco plant.

**Part IV
Business Regulation**

8

Regulating the Natural Gas Producing Industry: Two Decades of Experience

Daniel J. Fiorino

The *Phillips* Case and the Origins of Producer Regulation

In June of 1954, for the first time in history, the Supreme Court ordered a federal regulatory agency to broaden the scope of its jurisdiction.[1] The Court ordered the Federal Power Commission to regulate sales of natural gas made by the Phillips Petroleum Company to interstate pipeline companies. Phillips was the largest of several thousands of "independent" producers of natural gas operating in the early 1950s. These independent producers accounted for some nine-tenths of the natural gas sold on the interstate market. The remainder was produced by companies directly affiliated with the interstate pipelines, the so-called "integrated" companies. Although the Commission had been setting rates and regulating the sales of gas produced by the integrated companies for several years, it had always declined responsibility for sales made by independent producers.

The Phillips case was the culmination of several years of uncertainty over the status of the independent producers in the federal regulatory scheme. In the Natural Gas Act of 1938, Congress delegated to the Federal Power Commission authority over three aspects of the natural gas industry.[2] The Commission had jurisdiction over the transportation of natural gas in interstate commerce, the sale of natural gas in interstate commerce for resale to the ultimate consumer, and natural gas companies engaged in such transportation or sale. Among its other responsibilities, the Commission was to ensure that all sales falling within its jurisdiction were made at "just and reasonable" prices.

The question of whether or not Phillips Petroleum was subject to federal jurisdiction would have been clear-cut under these provisions had it not been for another provision of the Natural Gas Act which declared the "production and gathering" of natural gas exempt from federal authority. Phillips was at the same time engaged in the sale of natural gas to the interstate pipelines (who of course would sell the gas in another state) and in the production and gathering of natural gas in the field. The limits of the Commission's responsibilities turned on which jurisdictional provision of the Act one deemed controlling. The Commission had determined in 1951, with one Commissioner dissenting and one writing a concurring opinion, that the second provision was controlling and that Phillips was not subject to federal jurisdiction. The Court of Appeals for the District of Columbia Circuit and later the Supreme Court concluded that the first provision was controlling. This meant that the Commission had jurisdiction to regulate the sales that Phillips (and the thousands of other independent producers) made to the interstate pipelines to ensure that those sales were made at just and reasonable prices. A majority of the Court reached this conclusion over what can only be described as a prophetic dissent from Justice Douglas, who warned against involving the Court in an area "of which we know little and with which we are not competent to deal."[3]

It would be an understatement to say that the Commission did not welcome the *Phillips* ruling. The Commission's reluctance at accepting the Court's mandate was based in part on the administrative burdens the ruling imposed on the agency. The Commission began accepting certificate and rate filings from the independent producers in July of 1954. By June 30, 1955, it had received 6,047 applications for certificates authorizing producers' sales and 10,978 rate filings from independent producers. This was a considerable expansion from the approximately 1,000 annual pipeline certificate applications and pipeline rate filings which had formed the gist of the Commission's workload in the past.[4] Yet the Commission's unwillingness to regulate the independent producers was based on more than just the concern over the growth in the workload. An expansion of federal regulatory authority over private business simply was not compatible with the ideological outlook of a predominantly Republican Commission. As events through the remainder of the 1950s would demonstrate, it was, in the words of one staff official who had been with the agency at the time of the *Phillips* decision, "a Commission that did not want to regulate."

Despite the Court's ruling in *Phillips*, the question of the Federal Power Commission's jurisdiction over the independent producers was still not settled. In 1955, Congress passed the Harris-Fulbright bill, which exempted producers' sales from FPC regulation and, in effect, reversed the Supreme Court's *Phillips* decision.[5] It appeared as though the battle once lost in the courts had now been won in Congress. Similar legislation had passed both houses of Congress in 1949, only to be vetoed by President Truman. A presidential veto was unlikely in 1955, however. President Eisenhower was sympathetic with the aims of the Harris-Fulbright legislation and announced that he intended to sign it. It was only when an attempt by an oil company lobbyist to influence the vote of Senator Case of North Dakota came to light that the president decided to veto the legislation. For the second time in a decade, a legislative attempt to remove the independent producers from federal jurisdiction had failed.

With the president's veto came the realization that legislative relief was not forthcoming, at least for the time being, and the Commission began to deal with the problem of producer regulation. It first tried to set rates for the independents through the "rate base cost-of-service" method, which was what the Commission had always used in regulating the interstate pipelines. This method consisted of determining a company's rate base and cost of service, establishing a fair rate of return on the rate base, and setting rates at a level permitting the company to cover the costs of service and yet earn the established rate of return. As the Commission soon found, however, this form of regulation was not suited to the production and field sales of natural gas. Cost-of-service regulation requires an examination of cost factors on a company-by-company basis. Individual company investigations had been possible with the several hundreds of pipeline rate filings the Commission had been receiving annually over the past several years. But the several thousands of producer rate filings that began to pour into the Commission each year after the *Phillips* decision was more than the agency could handle on a company-by-company basis.

The incompatibilities of the cost-of-service method with producer regulation extended beyond the question of efficiency. Cost-of-service regulation traditionally had been applied to railroads, electric utilities, and pipelines. These are industries in which costs can be determined with some accuracy. Investment bears some predictable relationship with increases in returns, and one company's production costs are comparable with those of others. Natural gas production, however, is an industry characterized by high risk. Investment in discovery and exploration activities frequently yields no return. Costs among companies vary considerably, according to the producing region, the quality of the gas, and such factors as the underground pressure of the gas itself. Moreover, natural gas frequently is produced in conjunction with oil. Determining the cost of producing the gas requires the separation of those costs from those involved in producing the oil. For all of these reasons, along with the administrative problem of processing the flood of producer filings the Commission was receiving, cost-of-service regulation was unsuitable. Yet, the Commission failed to come up with an acceptable alternative. Five years after the *Phillips* ruling, the Commission still had not carried out the Court's mandate.

The Commission was again taken to task by the Supreme Court in 1959. This, the "CATCO" case, involved a Commission practice of authorizing sales by independent producers and reserving for a later proceeding the determination of whether or not the initial prices authorized by the Commission were just and reasonable.[6] The details of the case are complex, but the Commission in effect was permitting producers to sell their gas at unregulated prices for a period of several years. The Court found this unacceptable. It ruled that when the prices proposed in an application to make a sale were excessive, the Commission was to "condition" the certificate by prescribing the prices at which the sale would be made. These prices were to serve as the interim prices until the Commission could make a determination of the "just and reasonable" prices through adjudication. With the CATCO ruling, the Court made it clear that the Commission's jurisdiction over the independents was not discretionary. The Commission had a statutory responsibility to set just and reasonable rates for producers' sales, and this included setting temporary price ceilings when the Commission initially approved a sale.

By 1960, the Federal Power Commission was in an embarrassing position. Its ability to meet regulatory responsibilities in natural gas had reached the point that James Landis, in his report to President-elect Kennedy on regulatory agencies, referred to the FPC as "the outstanding example in the federal government of the breakdown of the administrative process."[7] The agency's deficiencies, Landis wrote, grew out of an unwillingness to assume its responsibilities under the Natural Gas Act and a refusal "in substance to obey the mandates of the Supreme Court of the United States and other federal courts."[8]

Coming to Terms with the Problem: Area and Interim Pricing

In September of 1960, the Federal Power Commission announced that it was abandoning the individual company, cost-of-service method of setting rates for producers' sales.[9] In place of the individual company method, the Commission was adopting a form of wholesale cost-based rate-setting known as area pricing. Natural gas producers were divided into twenty-three regions and five producing areas. The Commission announced that it would begin investigations on the cost of producing gas in each of the five producing areas as a step toward fixing just and reasonable rates for each area. Until the area rate proceedings were completed, however, the Commission would evaluate rates for proposed sales on the basis of a temporary set of price ceilings for each area. These "interim" or "in-line" price ceilings were based primarily on the average price of producers' sales prevailing in each producing area through the late 1950s. The in-line prices met the Supreme Court's requirements in the CATCO case by providing a standard for evaluating initial requests for authorization to make sales.

The 1960 policy statement provided little in the way of detail on the way in which the more permanent area prices would be set. Further elaboration of the area pricing policy came in the Commission's 1965 decision setting rates for the Permian Basin area of New Mexico and West Texas.[10] The central feature of the rate formula for the Permian Basin area was a system of two-tiered pricing. One set of prices applied to "old" gas, which included gas produced from wells which had begun production and sales to interstate commerce prior to 1961 and all gas produced in conjunction with oil (termed "associated" gas). Gas from wells which began production after January of 1961, and which was not associated with oil production, was priced on the basis of a "new" gas schedule. The rates for new gas, which were higher than those for old gas, were designed to encourage producers to sell more gas on the interstate market. The reasoning was that once the gas was committed to the interstate market, or if it was produced in conjunction with oil, there was no need to offer a higher price. The price of the old gas was thus tied to the historical costs of producing gas in the Permian Basin, while that of new gas would take into account the current national cost of finding and producing natural gas. If the Commission found that the new price was not sufficient for inducing the necessary levels of production, then it had the option of establishing a "new, new" price to provide greater incentive.

The Commission was relying on two different formulas in determining what was a "just and reasonable" price for producers' sales. Prices for "old" gas were set on the basis of the average historical costs of producing the gas in each area. It was a form of cost-based pricing, but it was anchored in historical, and not current, costs. In determining the price ceilings for "new" gas, however, the Commission said that it was considering the current national costs of finding and producing the gas. The problem with the "new" gas rate was that the determination of current costs was such a long process that by the time the Commission arrived at price ceilings for a producing region those price ceilings were already outmoded.[11] Compounding the problem was the Commission's reliance on "in-line" prices for controlling rates until the area rate proceedings were completed. They were designed to be only temporary price ceilings, but the in-line prices governed sales in most producing regions through the 1960s. Although the area rate proceeding for the Permian Basis was completed in 1965, proceedings for the other producing areas were not completed until the late 1960s or early 1970s.

The disagreement which had characterized relationships between the Supreme Court and the Federal Power Commission through the 1950s was replaced in the 1960s by a pattern of agreement between the Court and the Commission. The Democratic commissions of the 1960s apparently were more in tune with the Court's thinking on the matter of producer regulation than the earlier Republican commissions had been. In 1963, the Supreme Court upheld the Commission's departure from individual company, cost-of-service regulation in *Wisconsin* v. *Federal Power Commission*.[12] Five years later, in the *Permian Basin Area Rate Cases*, the Court demonstrated that it approved of area pricing in practice as well as in principle and upheld the Commission's 1965 Permian Basin decision in its entirety.[13]

The Natural Gas Shortage and the Commission's Response

By 1969, the nationwide structure of area rates envisioned in the Commission's 1960 policy statement was nearly complete. The Commission established the basic formula for the determination of area rates in the 1965

Permian Basin decision. The Supreme Court upheld the legal validity of the area rate policy in 1968. Proceedings for the Southern Louisiana areas were completed in 1968, and proceedings for the other producing areas were either near completion or well under way.

Yet a problem was developing in the natural gas producing industry. Since 1946, when the American Gas Association had begun collecting production and reserve statistics, the amount of newly discovered gas supplies had always exceeded the amount of gas produced in any one given year. In 1968, however, production was greater than were additions to reserves, indicating a net decline in available gas resources.[14] By 1970, interstate pipelines began experiencing difficulties in meeting their contract commitments because not enough gas was being sold on the interstate market. The shortage was not one of natural gas resources, but one of gas production. Conservative estimates made by the industry indicated that the nation had at least a thirty-year supply of gas. More liberal estimates by the U.S. Geological Survey in 1974 forecast sufficient potential gas reserve to last over one hundred years at current rates of production.

There was no doubt that by 1970 adequate supplies of gas were not forthcoming; nor was there any doubt that adequate reserves did exist, if they were sought and tapped. The uncertainty, and the controversy, revolved around why the pool of available gas reserves was shrinking and why discovery and production of natural gas was not keeping pace with demand. To critics of producer regulation, the source of the problem lay in the low prices the FPC had imposed on producers through the 1960s, which had not only discouraged exploration and production but had also channeled supplies into the intrastate market, where prices were several times what they were on the interstate market. Paul MacAvoy and Stephen Breyer, for example, argued that the natural gas shortage was "a direct result of FPC regulation of producers' prices" and that "gas price regulation at the wellhead should be substantially abandoned."[15] Another critic, Edmund Kitch, charged that the Commission had frozen the field price of natural gas at 1959-60 price levels.[16] Artificially low prices, these critics argued, had dampened incentives to produce natural gas in quantities sufficient to meet the rising demand for the fuel. Only if the prices at which producers sold their gas were permitted to rise to unregulated market levels would adequate supplies be available to the interstate pipelinees.

To others, however, the cause of the shortage lay elsewhere. Lee C. White, chairman of the Commission from 1966 to 1969, attributes the shortage not to artificially low prices but to a marked increase in the demand for natural gas, flowing primarily from the growing concern with the environment, and to the industry's expectations of price increases and possibly deregulation raised by the election of a Republican administration in 1968.[17] Similarly, Charles Wheatley, general manager of the American Public Gas Association, traces the current shortage in supplies to judicial validation of the area rate policy in the Permian Basin and Southern Louisiana areas in the late 1960s. It was after these decisions, Wheatley testified before the Senate Commerce Committee, "which the producers had lost on the merits, that the 'gas shortage' became apparent."[18] Both White, who is chairman of the Consumer Energy Task Force of the Consumer Federation of America, and Wheatley, as general manager of the APGA, have been advocates of continued regulation of independent producers. Their position is that the prospect of deregulation and increased prices has kept producers from producing more gas and selling it on the interstate market. The first step toward increased production would be to eliminate the uncertainty about the future of federal regulation.

Since the early 1970s, a majority of the Federal Power Commission has favored the first set of explanations for the shortage. In September of 1969, one month after he became chairman of the FPC, John Nassikas announced his intention to increase the field price of natural gas to provide incentive for exploration by producers. Prophetically, the *New York Times* reported at the time that Chairman Nassikas "intends to review, and probably alter, the whole pricing policy . . ."[19] By 1973, four of the five commissioners were openly espousing some form of deregulation of independent producers through legislative revision of the Natural Gas Act. In the 1974 Annual Report of the Federal Power Commission, four of the five commissioners were still on the record in favor of producer deregulation, with the fifth, Don S. Smith, favoring only the deregulation of small producers.

Despite the open avowal of at least a partial deregulation of independent producer sales by a majority of the Commission over the past several years, the Commission has never attempted a frontal assault on the very concept of regulation at the wellhead. Rather, the Commission has pursued the twin goals of permitting an upward revision of prices and injecting greater certainty and stability into the contractual relationships between the producers and their customers in a series of incremental steps. Gradually, over the past six years, "cracks in the wall" of the cost-based area pricing structure have appeared. Why has the Commission attempted incremental rather than wholesale revision of its policies toward independent producers? The next section briefly considers policy changes the Commission had introduced since 1969 and offers and explanation for the Commission's reliance on marginal change.

**The Commission, the Courts, and Producer Regulation
Since 1969**

In July of 1970, the Commission issued a notice of proposed rulemaking entitled "Exemption of Small Producers From Regulation."[20] The rule provided that small producers, defined as those whose sales were less than

ten million m.c.f. annually, were to be relieved of nearly all filing requirements under the Natural Gas Act, and were to be permitted to contract with
the interstate pipelines and large producers to whom they sold their gas at
prices in excess of the maximum allowable area rates. The proposed rule
would not constitute deregulation of small producers, the Commission
argued, because they would be regulated indirectly through regulation of
the pipelines and small producers. The customers of the small producers—
the interstate pipelines and large producers—would be permitted to reflect
the higher rates charged by small producers by filing "tracking increases"
in their own rates when the prices at which they purchased the gas from the
small producers exceeded area rate ceilings.

The Commission justified the small producer exemption on grounds
that it would relieve small producers of the burdens and costs of meeting
regulatory filing requirements, ensure greater stability in the contractual
arrangements between small producers and their customers, and permit
small producers to sell their gas at something nearer the prevailing market
price of natural gas in a particular area, thereby increasing the incentives
for small producers to commit gas to the interstate market. Because the
producers included in this category accounted for only 10.5 percent of the
gas sold on the interstate market, the Commission concluded that any
increase in rates obtained by the small producers would have a minimal
effect on the consumer. Yet the large number of producers falling within
this category meant a reduction in the administrative burdens the agency
faced in processing producer filings. The exemption rule would thus
achieve several objectives—increasing the gas supply, relieving small producers of unnecessary costs, and easing the agency's workload—without
unduly harming the consumer.

Another policy change initiated by the Commission was an "optional
procedure" for certifying sales of new gas. The objective of this procedure,
according to the Commission, was "to provide an alternative method to
stimulate and accelerate domestic exploration and development of the
nation's natural gas preserves."[21] The procedure was designed to permit
producers and their customers who met certain conditions to obtain certificates of "public conveniences and necessity" authorizing sales at price
levels above area ceilings. These conditions included the requirement that
both the producer and its customers agree to the use of the optional
procedure, and that the acreage covered by the sale has not previously been
dedicated to the interstate market.

Like the small producer exemption, the optional procedure created a
category of producers and producers' sales for which the normal area price
ceilings were not controlling. In creating both categories of exemptions, the
Commission was attempting to encourage producers to make more gas
available on the interstate market yet maintain in its basic form the area rate
program.

Both the small producer exemption and the optional procedure were challenged in court. Neither emerged intact. The Court of Appeals for the District of Columbia, and later the Supreme Court, overturned the small producer policy because the Commission had failed to ensure that the prices of sales by small producers would be just and reasonable.[22] The Commission had said it would permit customers of the small producers to file "tracking increases" when the prices they paid to the small producers exceeded the area rates. These increases were subject to refund (and thus would not be passed on to consumers) only to the extent that they were "unreasonably high" relative to two standards: (a) the highest contract prices for sales by large producers in the same producing area, or (b) the prevailing market price for intrastate sales in the same producing area. The Commision was saying, and the Supreme Court identified this as the "essential flaw" in the agency's exemption rule, that price increases were subject to refund only if they appeared exorbitant when evaluated against the standards of the marketplace. The Court concluded that the statutory standard of just and reasonable precluded the Commission from relying on comparisons with market prices in establishing rate ceilings. If just and reasonable meant anything, it surely did not mean the standards of the market.

The Court of Appeals' rejection of one of the first applications of the optional procedure in 1974 provided a further judicial elaboration of the just and reasonable standard.[23] The Commission had issued certificates to three producers authorizing them to make sales to the Tennessee Gas Pipeline Company at a price 70 percent higher than the applicable area rate ceiling. The Court's primary objection was to the weight the Commission had given to noncost factors in determining what was a just and reasonable rate for the sale. Noncost factors include negotiated contract rates, rates for intrastate (which are not federally regulated) sales, the cost of substituting alternative fuels for natural gas, and the cost of importing gas. Although the courts have permitted the Commission to weigh such noncost factors in determining rates for producers' sales, Chief Judge Bazelon noted, "it is doubtful that such non-cost factors can sustain a decision by the FPC which is unsupported by sound cost data."[24]

The judicial definition of "just and reasonable" rates was becoming clear. Embodied in that definition was a fundamental disagreement in policy between the courts and the Commission. The main objective of both the small producer and optional procedure policies had been to permit limited departures from the cost-based pricing formula of the area pricing policy. The Commission saw such departures as the key to stimulating producers to produce more gas and sell more of it on the interstate market. Yet the courts objected to both policy innovations precisely because they deviated from the principle of cost-based regulation. The courts viewed such policies as inconsistent with *Phillips, CATCO,* and the line of cases woven into the fabric of the Natural Gas Act since then. Other policy changes pursued by the Commission since 1969 have encountered similar objections from the courts.[25]

What is significant about the Commission's policies toward the independent producers in recent years is that the Commission has not attempted a frontal assault on cost-based pricing in determining rates for producers' sales. Although four of the five commissioners favor a wholesale revision of policies toward independent producers by Congress, the Commission has never proposed such a wholesale change through its own actions. Certainly a major explanation for this is the certainty that no court of appeals would have permitted the agency to make that kind of policy change. By the early 1970s, the agency was presented with an accretion of judicial interpretations of the Natural Gas Act which foreclosed certain options in producer regulation. For nearly twenty years, the courts had been telling the Commission that its responsibilities included the regulation of independent producers' sales, that regulation meant ensuring just and reasonable rates to consumers, that just and reasonable meant some reference to costs, and that just and reasonable did not mean the unfettered application of prevailing market prices. It is not difficult to follow the line of cases establishing these principles: *Phillips Petroleum* (1954); *City of Detroit* v. *FPC*, in which the Court of Appeals refused to permit the Commission to certify sales at prices reached through armslength bargaining; *CATCO* (1959); and in recent years, *Texaco, Consumers Union*, and the *MacDonald* case, where the court overturned a settlement agreement reached between the agency and a producer because it was not based on a full evidentiary record of costs of production and the producer's expected profits.[26]

One major change in the Commission's policies toward the producers was upheld by the courts. Under the area rate policy, prices for producers' sales had always been established on the basis of trial-type, adjudicative hearings. These proceedings were cumbersome, however, and in 1969, the Commission announced its intention to abandon rate-setting based on adjudication and determine rates for the Appalachian and Illinois Basin area in a rule-making proceeding.[27] When, in 1971, the Commission announced that it was undertaking a similar rule-making proceeding to set rates for the Rocky Mountain area, it was challenged in court. The Court of Appeals found no inconsistency between the Commission's transition to rule-making and the requirements of the Natural Gas Act or the Administrative Procedure Act, and upheld the rate proceedings.[28] In June of 1974, the Commission carried its success in the transition to rate-setting by rule-making one step further. The Commission announced that it was replacing the area rate concept with a national uniform rate for all "new" gas (post-December 31, 1972 sales).[29] In the future, producers' rates for all areas would be determined in one national rule-making proceeding.

Judicial decision-making has been characterized as "incremental"—proceeding in small steps, making change at the margin, and allowing for remedial adjustment.[30] As the history of relationships between the Commission and the courts reveal, however, incrementalism may be a consequence as well as a characteristic of judicial decision-making. The Commission's attempts to implement what it conceived as the appropriate response to the natural gas shortage were not incremental enough to satisfy the courts. Even the major innovation which was upheld by the courts, setting producers' rates through a national rule-making proceeding rather than adjudication, was accomplished in two careful steps.

Congress and the Future of Natural Gas Regulation

If any fundamental change in federal regulatory policies toward the natural gas producing industry is to be made, it must come from Congress not the Commission. The Commission has innovated and experimented as far as the courts are likely to permit under the terms of the Natural Gas Act.

There has been renewed congressional interest in recent years in modifying the Natural Gas Act. Although a multitude of proposals have been put forth, two kinds of proposals illustrate the legislative options receiving the most serious consideration. One set of proposals provides for the deregulation of new gas supplies and of old gas supplies as existing contracts between producers and their customers expire. This ultimately would place producer regulation where it had been prior to the *Phillips* decision in 1954, although without the statutory ambiguity that had clouded the status of the independents. This approach is based on the assumption that the natural gas producing industry is reasonably competitive, and that the removal of federal price controls would have a limited effect on the consumer.

The second type of proposal would maintain federal price controls but in a substantially modified form. All but the approximately twenty or thirty largest producers would be exempt from federal price controls. This would remove nearly four thousand small producers from the Commission's jurisdiction. The Commission's authority over the largest producers would include not only sales on the interstate market but sales made within a state as well. Because prices for natural gas sold within the producing states are several times what they are on the federally-regulated interstate market, much of the available gas is not leaving the state where it is produced. The extension of federal price controls to the intrastate market would reduce the price differential and increase supplies on the interstate market. The Commission also would be permitted to include several noncost factors in calculating price ceilings for the large producers remaining within its jurisdiction.

As the shortage in natural gas supplies continues, deregulation increasingly may appear as a convenient way out of the dilemma. Yet, although the industry may be reasonably competitive, there is no assurance that it is sufficiently competitive to permit deregulation. Estimates of the probable increase in the price of new gas that would accompany the deregulation of new gas supplies vary considerably. Moreover, the gradual removal of price controls on old gas as existing contracts expire could trigger rounds of price increases as pipelines scramble to restore their supplies. Higher prices may be necessary, both to stimulate increased production and to encourage gas conservation, but not to the extent that they could increase after deregulation.

Undoubtedly, federal price controls through the 1960s did contribute in some measure to the shortage. The reliance on "in-line" prices based on historical costs imposed low price ceilings on producers' sales. The lengthy adjudicative proceedings meant that once area price levels were determined they very likely were outmoded. Yet, we have learned much about the pitfalls in the regulation of the natural gas producing industry in the last two decades. Imperfections in the early stages of the area pricing policy should not be used now as an argument against any kind of regulation of producers. The Commission's abandonment of areawide adjudicative proceedings in favor of a national rulemaking proceeding was a major step in making federal regulation of the gas producing industry workable. Legislation which would permit the explicit incorporation of certain noncost factors in the calculation of price ceilings would overcome many of the limitations of the rigid, cost-based pricing formula. An extension of these more flexible price ceilings to intrastate sales would increase the willingness of producers to commit more gas to the interstate market.

The least acceptable policy alternative would be the maintenance of the current regulatory situation. If the deregulation forces are correct in their analysis of the causes of the shortage, the continuation of federal regulation through a cost-based pricing formula will not alleviate the shortage. If the advocates of continued regulation are correct, a continuation of the uncertainty about the future of federal regulation will only encourage producers to limit production in anticipation of higher prices. A choice must be made in favor of one or the other set of legislative options.

Observations on Two Decades of Regulatory Experience

The decision to include the independent producers within the Commission's jurisdiction was one of the most significant decisions in the history of federal regulation of the economy. Yet that decision was made not by Congress, nor by the Commission to which Congress had delegated authority over the natural gas industry, but by the Supreme Court. This is not to say that the Court should not have decided the way it did in the *Phillips*. The Court arrived at a reasonable conclusion based on two conflicting provisions of the statute. There is evidence that the producing industry was less competitive in the early 1950s than it is now, providing some policy justification for the Court's ruling.[31] The Court was called upon to resolve a dispute over the meaning of the Natural Gas Act. In the course of resolving that dispute, the Court made a major policy decision which set the pattern for federal regulation of the natural gas industry for at least the next two decades.

The inadequacies of federal regulatory commissions are frequently attributed to the quality of the commissioners, or to notions of the capture of the agencies by the industries they regulate. The quality of the Federal Power Commissioners since 1960 has been reasonably high. It would be difficult to ascribe the problems in natural gas regulation to any kind of capture hypothesis. The problem is that when Congress speaks in the area of economic regulation its words are not clear and, worse yet, are followed by long periods of legislative silence. Since it passed the Natural Gas Act in 1938, Congress has made only one change of any significance in the statute. That amendment, passed in 1942, removed certain constraints from the Commission in certifying the extension of pipeline facilities. Congress has shown a similar reluctance to make changes in the statutes outlining the authority of other major regulatory agencies.

These long periods of legislative silence mean that an agency is left to regulate a changing industry with a statute that soon becomes outmoded. The courts are called upon to clarify statutes when disputes over their meaning arise, as they inevitably do. Yet the courts cannot be counted upon to adapt outmoded legislation to changing circumstances. Judicial reasoning is designed to have the opposite effect—to introduce stability, to look retrospectively rather than prospectively. A court may innovate, as the Supreme Court did in *Phillips*, but that is when it rules on an issue for the first time. After that, lacking further guidance from the legislature, courts are more likely to consolidate than to innovate. This is the important lesson of the relationship between the courts and the Commission since 1969.

The natural gas industry has undergone fundamental change since the Natural Gas Act was passed in 1938. Yet the Act is essentially the same document it was nearly four decades ago. Regulatory statutes provide the framework within which agencies and the courts must struggle to attain certain policy objectives. If that framework is anachronistic, or if the policy objectives established by it are inconsistent or unclear, the task of the agency and of the courts has been made that much more difficult. Two decades of federal regulatory experience with natural gas producers illustrate the need for occasional legislative revision of regulatory statutes in response to changing circumstances.

Notes

1. *Phillips Petroleum* v. *Wisconsin*, 347 U.S. 672 (1954).

2. 15 U.S.C. §§ 717-717 w.

3. 347 U.S. 672, 690.

4. U.S., Federal Power Commission, Annual Report, 1955, p. 1.

5. S. 1853, 84th cong., 1st sess. (1955).

6. *Atlantic Refining Company* v. *Public Service Commission of New York*, 360 U.S. 378 (1959).

7. *Report on Regulatory Agencies to the President-Elect*, printed for use of the Senate Committee on the Judiciary, 86th cong., 2d sess. (1960), p. 54.

8. Ibid., p. 55.

9. Statement of General Policy No. 61-1, 24 F.P.C. 818 (1960), *as amended*, 18 C.F.R. § 2.56 (1967).

10. Area Rate Proceeding 61-1 (Permian Basin), 34 F.P.C. 159 (1965).

11. For a discussion of this weakness in the area pricing system, see Edmund W. Kitch, "Regulation of the Field Market for Natural Gas by the Federal Power Commission," in Paul W. MacAvoy (ed.), *The Crisis of the Regulatory Commissions* (New York: W.W. Norton, 1970), pp. 169-186.

12. 373 U.S. 294 (1963).

13. 390 U.S. 747 (1968).

14. The extent of the decline in reserves is documented in the Federal Power Commission's Annual Reports, 1969-1971.

15. Stephen Breyer and Paul W. MacAvoy, "The Natural Gas Shortage and the Regulation of Natural Gas Producers," *Harvard Law Review* 86 (April 1973): 943. See also, by Breyer and MacAvoy, *Energy Regulation by the Federal Power Commission* (Washington, D.C.: Brookings Institution, 1974).

16. "Regulation of the Field Market for Natural Gas," *The Crisis of the Regulatory Commissions*, p. 169.

17. Personal interview, Washington, D.C., January 8, 1975. See also James G. Phillips, "Energy Report/Congress Nears Showdown on Proposal to Decontrol Gas Prices," *National Journal Reports* (May 25, 1974), p. 767.

18. Hearings before the Senate Commerce Committee, 92d cong., 2d sess. (1972). Reprinted in *Natural Gas Regulation* (Washington, D.C.: U.S. Government Printing Office, 1973), p. 168. (The American Public Gas Association consists of 225 publicly-owned gas distributors.)

19. Eileen Shanahan, "F.P.C. Chief Urges Price Rise for Gas," *New York Times*, September 21, 1969, p. 67.

20. 35 *Federal Register*, pp. 12220-12221; later issued as Order 428, 45 FPC 454 (1971).

21. Federal Power Commission News Release, "Docket No. R-441: Optional Gas Pricing Procedure," April 6, 1972; "Optional Procedure for Certificating New Producer Sales of Natural Gas," 37 *Federal Register*, pp. 7345-7347 (1972); later issued as Order 455.

22. *Texaco* v. *Federal Power Commission*, 474 F. 2d 416 (C.A.D.C.; 1972); *Federal Power Commission* v. *Texaco*, 417 U.S. 380 (1974).

23. *Consumers Union* v. *Federal Power Commission*, 510 F. 2d 656 (C.A.D.C.; 1974).

24. Ibid., 660.

25. See, for example, *Memphis Light, Gas and Water Division* v. *Federal Power Commission*, 504 F. 2d 225 (C.A.D.C.; 1974).

26. *City of Detroit* v. *Federal Power Commission*, 230 F. 2d 810 (C.A.D.C.; 1955); *MacDonald* v. *Federal Power Commission*, 505 F. 2d 355 (C.A.D.C.; 1974). Breyer and MacAvoy reach a different conclusion when they note: "Nothing in the *Phillips Petroleum* decision *requires* the FPC to set prices; the decision simply gives the Commission jurisdiction to do so." "Natural Gas Shortage," *Harvard Law Review*, p. 986. Over twenty years of judicial interpretations suggest just the opposite.

27. 34 *Federal Register*, p. 17341 (1969); *Appalachian and Illinois Basin Areas*, 44 F.P.C. 1112 (1970).

28. "Opinion and Order Establishing Initial Natural Gas Rates in the Rocky Mountain Area," 36 *Federal Register*, p. 13586; upheld in *Phillips Petroleum Company* v. *Federal Power Commission*, 475 F. 2d 842 (C.A. 10th; 1973).

29. Opinion No. 699 (June 21, 1974).

30. Martin Shapiro, "Stability and Change in Judicial Decision-Making: Incrementalism or Stare Decisis?" *Law in Transition Quarterly*, (1965), p. 134; Martin Shapiro, *The Supreme Court and Administrative Agencies* (New York: Free Press, 1968).

31. Paul MacAvoy found in 1962 that "pricing was generally becoming more competitive during the later 1950s." *Price Formation in Natural Gas Fields: A Study of Competition, Monopsony, and Regulation* (New Haven: Yale University Press, 1962), p. 243.

9

The Supreme Court and National Bank Merger Policy

William Jenkins, Jr.

Since the Great Depression, which resulted in over 15,000 bank failures,[1] two opposing forces have shaped national bank regulatory policy. The depression implanted a deep fear of overbanking and "rampant competition" leading to bank failures, resulting in legislation designed to promote banking stability and security. Conversely, the national antitrust laws, based largely on a fear of concentrated financial power, push for greater competition. Public policy since the 1930s has been an uneasy compromise between these two concerns. The total number of banking offices declined from 31,000 to 17,000 during the years 1921 to 1933.[2] Banking concentration remained relatively stable for the next twenty years, but the 1950s saw a resurgence of bank mergers leading to increased concentration in banking. The trend was highlighted by several Brobdingnagian bank mergers in the late 1950s.[3] By 1960, the four largest banks in sixteen of the nation's largest financial centers controlled 60 percent of the bank assets in those centers.

During the 1950s banks were able to merge with little or no supervision from the three major national bank regulatory agencies: the Comptroller of the Currency, the Federal Reserve Board (FRB), and the Federal Deposit Insurance Corporation (FDIC). Unless the merged banks had fewer assets than the aggregate total of the merging banks separately, a most unlikely possibility, none of the federal bank regulatory agencies had any say in the matter. Section 7 of the Clayton Act, as amended in 1950, was the primary antitrust statute designed to deal with anticompetitive corporate mergers. Though it was clear the statute was applicable to stock acquisitions or consolidations by banks, the Justice Department was on record as doubting that it could be used to challenge anticompetitive asset acquisitions by banks. This doubt arose from the wording of section 7, which seemed to make only asset acquisitions by corporations subject to the jurisdiction of the Federal Trade Commission (FTC) liable to antitrust attack. Banks were clearly not subject to the FTC's jurisdiction.

The 1960 Bank Merger Act

At the urging of the Justice Department and the federal bank regulatory agencies, Congress passed a statute to deal with bank mergers which were not clearly monopolistic, but which nevertheless had anticompetitive effects. The result, the 1960 Bank Merger Act, was a compromise between the preservation of banking security and stability and the promotion of competition. The federal bank regulatory agencies were given jurisdiction over bank mergers which paralleled their jurisdiction over banks generally. The Comptroller of the Currency had to approve bank mergers in which the resulting bank would be a national bank. The FRB supervised mergers between state banks, one of which was a member of the Federal Reserve System. (All national banks are required to be members of the system, and these were subject to the comptroller's jurisdiction.) Finally, the FDIC passed on mergers between state banks which were not members of the Federal Reserve System but were members of the FDIC. Together, these three categories encompassed about 95 percent of the banks in the United States. Only state banks not insured by the FDIC were beyond the scope of the new law.

The 1960 Bank Merger act required the banking agencies to consider six "banking" factors and a competitive factor in evaluating bank merger applications. The banking factors focused on the financial soundness of the institutions involved plus the convenience and needs of the community to be served by the merged bank. The competitive factor was defined simply as the effect of the transaction on competition, including any tendency toward monopoly.[4] The statute also required the Justice Department to submit a report to the appropriate banking agency on the probable competitive impact of the proposed merger.

The law raised as many questions as it answered, and it was inevitable that the courts would be asked to interpret the scope and exact nature of the new statute. Among the issues to be settled were: (1) What was the proper weight to be given to the various factors enumerated in the law in passing upon bank merger applications? Under what circumstances were the banking factors to outweigh the competitive factor? Congress had intimated no views on the matter. (2) Did the statute immunize all bank mergers approved under its provisions from subsequent attack under the antitrust laws? (3) If not, what were the criteria to be used in measuring the anticompetitive impact of bank mergers? What was the quantity and quality of the proof necessary to condemn a bank merger as anticompetitive and illegal? As is often the case in economic matters, Congress had passed a general, vague, and ambiguous statute indicating only that bank mergers should be subject to some type of scrutiny for their prospective benefit and harm, but had left to the courts the task of determining the specific standards to be applied in individual cases.

The Supreme Court and the 1960 Bank Merger Act

The Justice Department wasted little time in bringing a case to court. The Department was unhappy with the standards being applied by the comptroller of the currency, believing that he gave too little weight to competition in his deliberations. The case at issue was the merger of the second and third largest banks in the Philadelphia area. The Justice Department had brought suit under both the Sherman Act and section 7 of the Clayton Act. However, because of its continuing doubts about the applicability of section 7 to asset acquisitions by banks, as in this case, the Department stressed the Sherman Act aspects of the merger in its briefs.

When the case reached the Supreme Court, the majority ignored the Sherman Act allegations and focused instead on the applicability of section 7 to bank mergers. The majority opinion of Justice Brennan in this case, *Philadelphia National Bank*,[5] is an ingenious bit of statutory interpretation. Affirming the district court conclusion that the 1960 Bank Merger Act did not immunize bank mergers from attack under the antitrust laws,[6] the Supreme Court used the opinion in *Philadelphia National Bank* to transform section 7 into a formidable weapon for challenging horizontal mergers (those between directly competing firms) and made the effect on competition the paramount consideration in passing on bank merger applications.

Justice Brennan began his opinion by disposing of any doubts concerning the applicability of section 7 to asset acquisitions by banks. The wording of the statute was intended to mean that the stock and asset provisions, *taken together*, embraced the full range of possible mergers from simple stock to simple asset acquisitions and all combinations thereof.[7] Such an interpretation was necessary to prevent the creation of a new loophole in a statute designed to close a loophole (the original section 7 had not been applicable to asset acquisitions, and the 1950 amendment was designed to correct this oversight), to give effect to congressional desire to cover all mergers via section 7, and, in any event, immunity from the antitrust laws is not lightly implied.[8] Realizing that these views differed from some of the key sponsors of the 1960 Bank Merger Act, the Court merely noted that the "views of a subsequent Congress are a hazardous basis for inferring the intent of an earlier one"[9] (the Congress which had passed the 1950 amendment to section 7). The Court had done nothing more, it said, than make certain what had been previously uncertain, and in so doing did no violence to the Bank Merger Act.[10]

The Court then considered the standards to be used in judging bank mergers under the provisions of section 7. Section 7 requires that two preliminary determinations be made before the anticompetitive aspects of a merger can be considered. The first is the "line of commerce," or product market (e.g., bottles, cans, cars, etc.), and the second is the "section of the country," or geographic market (e.g., Chicago, Illinois, a group of states, or the entire United States). Once the appropriate product and geographic markets have been defined, one can consider the effect of a merger on competition in those markets. The Supreme Court's findings on these two questions have formed the basis for all subsequent bank merger litigation.

The cluster of financial services offered by commercial banks was sufficiently distinct to provide some insulation from competition from other types of financial institutions, such as savings and loan associations.[11] Thus, "commercial banking" was the relevant product market. The Court also concluded that convenience was such an important factor in a customer's choice of a bank that the geographic market for banking was a very localized one. The Court thus rejected the claims of the merging banks that the merger would increase competition for large commercial loans by allowing them to better compete with their large New York rivals.[12] The needs of all the customers of a bank, not just a selected portion, were what was important, said the Court.

Having made the requisite determinations of the product and geographic markets, the Court then moved on to consider the nature and quantity of proof necessary to prove that the merger would indeed "tend to substantially lessen competition" or "tend to create a monopoly," as section 7 requires. Prior to *Philadelphia National Bank* the Supreme Court had written but one opinion interpreting the amended section 7.[13] In that decision it had refused to formulate any simple rules for enforcing the statute. This it did in *Philadelphia National Bank*. Any merger which resulted in a one-third increase in existing concentration and created a firm with a 30 percent share of the relevant market was presumptively anticompetitive and unlawful. This approach to horizontal mergers had been suggested no where in the briefs of counsel, and was first broached by Justice Goldberg in oral argument.[14] The Court declined to say whether or not 30 percent was the minimum market share necessary to invoke the new rule, merely stating that it was sure that 30 percent was a sufficiently large share to make such a rule appropriate, and that this was consonant with economic theory.[15]

The Supreme Court justified its new approach on the need to simplify the burden of proof in complex antitrust litigation, to give effect to the congressional desire, embodied in section 7, to halt the trend toward economic concentration, and to provide some degree of certainty in antitrust enforcement, thus facilitating business planning by implanting a greater degree of predictability in the standards of illegality.[16] The part of the opinion which aroused the greatest controversy was this:

If anticompetitive effects in one market could be justified by pro-competitive ones in another, the logical upshot would be that every firm in an industry could, without violation of §7, embark on a series of mergers that would make it in the end as large as the industry leader . . . We are clear . . . that a merger the effect of which "may be substantially to lessen competition" is not saved because on some ultimate reckoning of social or economic debits and credits, it may be deemed beneficial. A value choice of such magnitude is beyond the ordinary limits of judicial competence, and in any event, has been made for us already by Congress when it enacted the amended §7. Congress determined to preserve our traditional competitive economy. It therefore proscribed anticompetitive mergers, the benign and the malignant alike, fully aware we must assume, that some price might have to be paid.[17]

It was doubtful Congress had meant any such thing. Sponsors of the 1960 Bank Merger Act, bankers, and antitrust lawyers were all surprised by the Court's opinion. Their surprise was echoed in the exhaustive, and persuasive, dissenting opinion of Justice Harlan who argued that Congress had rejected the pleas of the Justice Department to bring asset acquisitions by banks with the ambit of section 7. Considerations other than competition—the sole concern of the majority of the Court—were deemed necessary because of the central importance of banks in determining the value of the dollar, the volume of money and credit in the country, and the stability of the currency system. Furthermore, the Senate Report on the Bank Merger Act specifically noted that the banking agencies were not bound by any findings of anticompetitive impact issued by the attorney general in his advisory reports.[18] Harlan did not seem to exaggerate much when he said that the result of the *Philadelphia National Bank* decision was that the "Bank Merger Act is almost completely nullified."[19]

The *Philadelphia National Bank* decision exhibits distrust of big business, concern for the smaller competitor, fear of oligopoly, and a disdain for the type of complex economic analysis favored by corporate antitrust counsel which would prolong and complicate antitrust litigation. As one observer noted,[20] had the justices found a way to blend section 7 and the 1960 Bank Merger Act, instead of making a clear choice in favor of section 7 and competition, they might have avoided the rage and bitter criticism which followed the *Philadelphia* decision.

In its next term, the Supreme Court, in a less controversial action, invalidated a bank merger in which the resulting bank would have been bigger than all its remaining competitors combined.[21] The Justice Department relied solely upon the Sherman Act in this case, partly because of the size of the merged bank and partly because of uncertainty concerning the applicability of section 7 at the time of the trial. The Court ruled that any merger which eliminated a "major competitive factor in a relevant market" was a violation of section 1 of the Sherman Act. Harlan saw the decision as striking at bigness per se,[22] and one commentator said the decision merely demonstrated that the Court was hostile to any interpretation of banking statutes which would limit the use of the antitrust laws to regulate competition in banking.[23]

The 1966 Bank Merger Act

The result of the controversy was the passage of the 1966 Bank Merger Act, designed to limit the impact of the Supreme Court's *Philadelphia National*

Bank decision. Bank mergers consummated before the date of the *Phila-delphia* decision were specifically exempted from any future antitrust liability under section 7. As a result, two cases pending in the courts were dismissed by the government, one of which it had won in the district court.[24] The larger banks supported a bill which would have given the national bank regulatory agencies "exclusive and plenary" authority over bank mergers and immunized all approved mergers from subsequent anti-trust attack.[25] Small banks, represented by the Independent Bankers Association, wanted a provision inserted that would allow the Justice Department to sue under the antitrust laws within a specified period of time. This was accepted. The three-year delay in the passage of the bill was largely attributable to the intrepid opposition of Congressman Wright Patman, an old foe of banks, and the chairman of the House Banking and Currency Committee. The bill was finally reported out of committee in a meeting called without informing Mr. Patman.

The 1966 Bank Merger Act still required the banking agencies to gather advisory reports from their sister banking agencies and the attorney general. They could, however, forego the reports if required to prevent a failure of one of the banks involved in the merger. Any merger resulting in a monopoly or an attempt to monopolize was not to be approved. A new provision of the law, aimed at the Supreme Court's condemnation of both "benign and malignant" mergers, stated that where the merged bank's success in meeting the "convenience and needs of the community" which it served "clearly" outweighed the anticompetitive effects of the merger, the merger was to be approved.[26] A key question to be resolved, of course, was the type of evidence necessary to establish that the convenience and needs of the community outweighed the anticompetitive aspects of a merger. A corollary question was which party—the government or the banks—had the burden of proving that the merger did or did not come within the new provision.

The new law also delayed the consummation of any approved merger for thirty calendar days in order to give the Justice Department time to file suit. If the Department did not file suit within thirty days, all future antitrust attack, save under the Sherman Act for monopolization, was forbidden.[27] If the Department did file suit, however, the merger was enjoined pending the resolution of the suit in court. A "review de novo" by the courts was provided for any merger approved and subsequently challenged by the Justice Department, with the courts to consider the same issues and factors as the relevant banking agency in initially approving the merger application.[28] Finally, any banking agency had the right to intervene in a court challenge to a merger which it had approved.[29] In the view of two prominent antitrust attorneys and the *Wall Street Journal*, the new law had solved little, and was an open invitation to the Supreme Court to resolve a major and difficult policy question.[30]

The Supreme Court and the 1966 Bank Merger Act

Before the Supreme Court had a chance to interpret the new law, six lower courts had issued opinions. Three of these cases involved mergers pending in the district courts when the statute was passed,[31] and three were cases filed after the passage of the law.[32] It is enough to observe here that there was a consensus among the district court judges that the act had created new and substantive changes in the manner in which bank mergers were to be judged.[33] All agreed that the government had the burden of proof in balancing the anticompetitive impact of a merger against the convenience and needs of the community. Each held that the courts were to sit as reviewing bodies, evaluating the propriety of the banking agency's approval of the merger, and not as a court sitting at a "trial de novo."[34] (The term "review de novo" was unprecedented in federal administrative statutes; the usual expression was "try de novo," and there was some confusion over the exact meaning to be given the new term.[35]) None of the lower courts came close to the Supreme Court's interpretation of the 1966 Bank Merger Act.

The first case to reach the Supreme Court was *Houston National Bank*,[36] which had been initially dismissed by the district court because the government had filed suit under section 7 rather than the new bank merger law.[37] The comptroller, who had approved the merger over the objections of the FRB, FDIC, and the Justice Department, intervened on behalf of the merging banks. The Supreme Court, in its only unanimous bank merger opinion, turned the 1966 Bank Merger Act into a potent enforcement tool for the Justice Department. The Department, in its brief, had launched a frontal assault upon the judgment of the bank regulatory agencies, particularly the comptroller, in evaluating bank merger applications.[38] The Supreme Court accepted the Justice Department's contention that the banks had the burden of proving that the convenience and needs of the community "clearly" outweighed the anticompetitive impact of a merger. The Court ruled that the convenience and needs defense was an *exception* to the normal ambit of the antitrust laws, and it was well-established that those seeking refuge under an exception to a law have the burden of proving it applies to them.[39] This interpretation was a tremendous boon to the Justice Department and actually did no great harm to the banks. Since there is an automatic stay in effect under the terms of the 1966 Bank Merger Act, a quick resolution of the issues benefits the banks as well as the government. Furthermore, if the bank merger application had been properly prepared, the merging banks should have such evidence readily available.[40]

Focusing on the words "de novo" in "review de novo" in the statute, the Court concluded that Congress had intended that the trial court make a fresh evaluation of the case, particularly in light of the fact that hearings were not normally held before approval by the banking regulatory agencies. No special weight should be given the approval of the merger by the relevant banking agency since "it is the court's judgment, not the [agency's], that finally determines whether the merger is legal."[41] Additionally, the automatic stay provided by the statute pending the resolution of litigation was not to be dissolved except in extraordinary circumstances. The status quo should be maintained during litigation lest there be grave problems of divestiture should the stay be dissolved, the merger consummated, and the government eventually prevail on the merits.[42]

The Supreme Court did not address itself to the nature of evidence needed to establish the "convenience and needs" defense. This it did in its next decision, *Third National Bank of Nashville*.[43] The Court overruled the district judge, who had determined a rule-of-reason sort of approach was required by the 1966 Bank Merger Act.[44] The same standard which had been applied in *Philadelphia National Bank* was to be used in judging the competitive effects of a merger under the new statute. The convenience and needs defense could be established only upon the most "clear" showing of its benefits compared to the loss to competition resulting from the merger. It was apparent the Court did not intend for this to be an easy defense to establish. Additionally, the courst were to determine if the banks had made a reasonable effort to solve any financial or management problems they claimed necessitated the merger or at least find that these efforts would not have been successful. The Court must "sufficiently or reliably establish the unavailability of alternate solutions" to merger.[45] This particular merger had been defended largely on the grounds that the acquired bank was "floundering" with little hope for recovery short of merger. The case was remanded for reconsideration in light of the Supreme Court's opinion.

The result of *Houston Bank* and *Nashville Bank* was to leave the 1966 Bank Merger Act largely a hollow shell. The banks which received a specific exemption from further prosecution (i.e., all those which had merged prior to the *Philadelphia Bank* decision); the Justice Department, which benefited immensely from automatic statutory stay; and antitrust lawyers were the primary beneficiaries of the new statute. Since few banks could keep a merger in a stage of suspension for very long, one of the results of the statutory stay was the abandonment of many approved mergers once the Justice Department filed suit. (See table 9-1). The "convenience and needs" defense had been rendered rather harmless by the Supreme Court, and was of no particular benefit in defending horizontal bank mergers.

Phillipsburg National Bank,[46] the Supreme Court's final decision regarding horizontal bank mergers, is also a summation of the standards to be applied to bank mergers under the 1966 Bank Merger Act. The decision eliminated any remaining hope that the 1966 Bank Merger Act had altered significantly the standards for judging competition in banking. The Court reaffirmed that all alternative solutions short of merger should be explored by the courts as a solution to any problems one of the merging banks may have, and established that it was the market share held by the merging banks, rather than their absolute size, which was the test of illegality.

The district judge had used two separate geographic markets for judging the competitive impact of the merger and the convenience and needs of the community. In so doing, he gave the merging banks the best of both worlds, for he gauged the convenience and needs of the community in the smaller market, and the competitive impact in a broader area, which minimized the market shares of the merging banks.[47] The Supreme Court reversed, noting that this subverted clear congressional purposes to judge both the competitive impact and convenience and needs of the community in the same geographic market. Under the approach taken by the district court, anticompetitive effects in one part of the relevant market could be justified by community benefits in another part. This standard was rejected by the Court in *Philadelphia Bank* and rejected here as well.[48] Also echoing its *Philadelphia Bank* opinion, the Court reminded the district court that the convenience and needs of the community includes all the customers of a bank, large and small, and not just those customers seeking larger loans or specialized services.

The Court pointed out that to fail to apply the antitrust laws to mergers between leading banks in small communities would be to deny small businesses the protection afforded by those laws. Indeed,

[I]f anything it is even more true in the small town than in the large city that if the businessman is denied credit because his banking alternatives have been eliminated by mergers, the whole edifice of our entrepreneurial system is threatened; if the costs of banking services and credit are allowed to become excessive by the absence of competitive pressures, virtually all costs, in our credit economy, will be effected.[49]

Compared to the hail of criticism which greeted the *Philadelphia Bank* decision, there was surprisingly little criticism of the Court's decisions interpreting the 1966 Bank Merger Act. The Court had essentially gutted the 1966 Bank Merger Act and maintained the predominant emphasis on competition which was the focus of the *Philadelphia Bank* decision. Perhaps, everyone had merely braced themselves for the worse, and the Court's decisions were consistent with previous decisions. In any case, *Phillipsburg Bank* represented the end of the halcyon days of bank merger enforcement, for the Justice Department has not since won a single bank merger case in the Supreme Court.

Potential Competition and Bank Mergers

The concept of potential competition in merger litigation is one both well-developed and endorsed by the Supreme Court in a series of nonbanking decisions.[50] The Court has yet to formulate the sort of simple rules of thumb for potential competition cases, that it established for horizontal mergers. As the term implies, potential competition is that which is possible or probable; given certain conditions, it can become actual and direct. The theory of potential competition holds that a company on the edge of a particular market, ready, eager, and financially able to enter that market will, should prices and profits rise to a level justifying such entry. As such, a potential competitor, when perceived as such by those firms already in the market, acts as a restraining force on those firms by causing them to maintain prices and profits at a level below that which would cause the potential competitor to become an actual one. This benefits both competition and the consumer.

Antitrust policy has built on this theory to attack mergers of a conglomerate nature, that is mergers between noncompeting firms in related geographic or product markets. The Justice Department has tried to transfer the theory to market extension mergers between banks. A market extension merger is one in which a firm acquires another firm in the same industry—dairy products, men's clothing, or whatever—but in a different geographic market from the one in which the acquiring firm is a direct competitor. The Justice Department has been singularly unsuccessful in this effort, having lost every single case it has litigated to date—nine losses in the district courts, and three of those losses upheld in full opinions by the Supreme Court.[51] The Justice Department cases have been concerned with basic structural changes now taking place in banking, in no small part because of the Supreme Court's decisions strictly limiting the ability of banks to undertake horizontal mergers. The change has been a phenomenal growth of the banking holding company, a company which may hold controlling interest in, or own outright, a number of banks in a particular state, or several states. What the Justice Department has been trying to encourage is bank expansion through either de novo entry or toehold acquisition. In every case filed to date, it has challenged either the merger of large banking organizations in contingent areas of a state,[52] or the acquisition by a large banking organization of a small, but leading, bank in another part of the state, with the concomitant possibility of entrenching the market position of that bank and reducing any hopes of deconcentrating the market.[53] In other words, the Justice Department has sought to encourage challenges to the status quo rather than having acquiring banks become the inheritors of it.[54]

The Justice Department has filed suit in potential competition cases when three conditions have been met: (1) the acquiring organization is one of only a few large, capable, and eager potential entrants legally capable of entering the market in which the acquisition takes place; (2) the acquired bands is a leading bank in a market which is already highly concentrated;

and (3) the acquiror has some other means of entry—either a de novo entry or the acquisition of a smaller bank, whose market share it would try to increase.[55]

There are, however, basic problems with attempting to apply potential competition principles to banking. One is the highly regulated nature of the banking industry. Entry into banking is subject to the approval of both federal and state banking authorities. There are restrictions on branching by banks, with some states allowing branching statewide (e.g., California); some allowing branching only in counties contiguous to the bank's home office (e.g., Pennsylvania); and so-called "unit banking" states, which allow a bank to have one, and only one, office (e.g., Texas). In addition, many states have what are termed "home office protection" statutes which forbid branching into counties in which a bank has its home office by banks which are not headquartered in the same county (e.g., Connecticut). It is because bank expansion is restricted by a plethora of state and federal regulations that both the district courts and the Supreme Court have been somewhat skeptical of the Justice Department's claims.[56]

The decisions of the district courts have been remarkably similar. All have given considerable weight to the testimony of various bank regulatory officials, particularly the comptroller of the currency, who have testified that the markets were "well-banked" or even "overbanked" thus foreclosing the possibility of de novo entry, since such an application would not be approved.[57] (One might be inclined to view such testimony with some caution, since the regulatory agency has a vested interest in defending its approval of the merger under attack.) The credibility of defense witnesses, as contrasted with government witnesses, has been crucial in almost every case.[58] Many district judges have also placed considerable reliance on the testimony of the officers of the acquiring bank that they would not enter the market except through the acquisition in question.[59] The Justice Department has now amassed a considerable body of evidence to prove that this is not always the case, and that is one method of entry is blocked, another, perhaps more competitive one, will be tried.[60]

The Supreme Court, in three decisions involving market extension acquisitions by large statewide bank holding companies, has ruled that while potential competition in banking is a viable concept, it has limitations owing to the peculiar nature of the banking industry. The Justice Department has found itself a victim of its past success, since the Court has insisted that banking is a localized market. The Court has thus not been receptive to the Justice Department's concern over the acquisition of leading banks in various local communities by statewide bank holding companies which would create a series of oligopolistic banking markets linked statewide through their common ownership by the three or four largest holding companies in the state. Thus, in each local market, the holding companies would face one another through their locally owned and/or controlled banks, and patterns of mutual accommodation, rather than vigorous competition, would be the result. The Court has rejected this contention in the cases to date, as "possibility" rather than "probability."[61]

Any application of the potential competition doctrine to banks must take into account the regulatory limitations on entry into the market, and the effect these limitations will have on the perception of the bank seeking entry as a potential competitor by those banks already in the market. Where the "potential competitor" is not viewed as such because of these limitations, it can have no pro-competitive effects from its position on the edge of the market, and therefore there is no loss of potential competition through merger.[62]

In contrast to the Court's decisions on horizontal mergers, the Court's decisions regarding potential competition and banking have made the government's burden of proof a heavy one. The standard which the Warren Court would have applied (all the potential competition decisions have been made by the Burger Court) can be seen in Justice White's dissenting opinion in *Marine Bancorporation*. Since the local banking market was highly concentrated, and there were alternative means of entry which were less anticompetitive than the instant merger, White would have held that the government had established a rebuttable prime facia case which entitled it to judgment.[63]

An Overview of the Supreme Court and Bank Merger

Throughout the 1960s, the Supreme Court was a vigorous supporter of the strict application of the antitrust laws to bank mergers. As table 9-1 shows, the Court consistently ruled in favor of the government in bank merger cases, overturning nine of thirteen district court losses which were appealed by the government. Actually, the record is even more distinct. Through 1970, the Supreme Court had reversed every single government loss which it had chosen to appeal. Since 1972, the Supreme Court has divided evenly in one case,[64] summarily affirmed one government loss,[65] vacated one loss,[66] and affirmed two losses in full opinion.[67] The Supreme Court can no longer be counted upon to bail out the government when it looses in the district courts. The government chose, for one reason or another, not to appeal any of its early losses in potential competition bank merger suits, and when it did finally decide to take a case to the Supreme Court, it was too late.[a]

---

[a] In interviews with Justice Department personnel and corporate antitrust attorneys, there was a consensus that the Department could have won an earlier appeal, but chose not to appeal its early losses because the Department wanted to present the Supreme Court with a "really strong case" on potential competition.

Table 9-1

Supreme Court Decisions in Bank Merger Cases by Results in District Court: 1962-1975

	District Court Decision	
Supreme Court Decision	For Government	For the Banks
Summary Affirmance		1
Summary Reversal		3
Affirmed in Full Opinion		2
Reversed in Full Opinion		6
No Appeal Taken	2	6
Affirmed by 4-4 Vote		1
Total	2	19

Neither can the district courts be counted upon suddenly to become enforcement minded either, both for reasons already cited—their reliance upon the testimony of officials who have a vested interest in seeing the merger consummated, and their demonstrated hostility toward government claims in some cases[68]—and because the requirements of both the 1966 Bank Merger Act and section 7 of the Clayton Act require district court judges to do something which is somewhat alien to them: make a prediction about what may happen in the future on the basis of economic evidence which is generally contradictory and uncertain. Trial judges normally determine, through rules of evidence and testimony of witnesses, what has *in fact* happened in the past, not what *may* happen in the future. Additionally, the Justice Department is usually trying to expand the applicability of the law to mergers in its litigation, and trial judges are reluctant to blaze new legal ground.

Through 1972, the Supreme Court supported the efforts of the Justice Department to apply a single, competitive factor to bank mergers, rejecting all efforts to include special extenuating factors. In so doing, the Court greatly eased the burden of proof borne by the Justice Department in challenging bank mergers, and simultaneously complicated the defense of merger suits. The Court's decisions on potential competition in banking, particularly that of *Marine Bancorporation*, represent a significant setback for Justice Department efforts to apply to banks the principle of potential competition, developed in nonbank merger cases with few modifications.

Table 9-2 shows that the Justice Department has never challenged an appreciable portion of the total number of bank mergers, or banking assets acquired, in any one year. The 1966 Bank Merger Act did have the effect of increasing the number of bank mergers challenged, however, as table 9-3 demonstrates. Since the Justice Department must file suit within thirty days of the merger's approval or lose its right to challenge the merger, there is a "put-up-or-shut-up" character to the law. One result of the automatic

Table 9-2

Bank Mergers Approved by Federal Banking Agencies, and Number of Justice Department Suits Filed, 1961-1973

Year	Number of Bank Mergers Approved	Number of Bank Mergers Challenged
1961	135	4
1962	191	1
1963	153	2
1964	135	1
1965	151	1
1966	143	4
1967	139	3
1968	170	10
1969	181	8
1970	167	5
1971	132	9
1972	165	6
1973	179	5
TOTAL	2,041	59

statutory stay of the law, plus the Supreme Court's restrictive interpretation of the "convenience and needs" defense in the statute, was a rather dramatic increase in the number of bank mergers abandoned when the Justice Department filed suit (table 9-3). Indeed, since the Supreme Court's *Philadelphia Bank* decision, only three horizontal bank acquisitions challenged by the Justice Department have been consummated.

The most obvious result of these developments is that banks have largely abandoned attempts to undertake horizontal mergers with direct competitors, have formed bank holding companies in rapidly increasing numbers, and have channeled their urge to merge into market extension mergers. It was in response to this development that the Justice Department began trying to establish the use of potential competition to challenge bank mergers by holding companies. Thus far that effort has been singularly unsuccessful.

This lack of success, and the recent setback in *Marine Bancorporation*, have combined to decrease the number of bank mergers challenged by the Justice Department's Antitrust Division. Prior to 1973, the Justice Department was agressively challenging bank mergers in selected markets which it felt were rapidly becoming oligopolistic, or in danger of becoming monopolies.[b] However, since then, the number of cases filed has dropped

[b] The Antitrust Division had filed three cases against Virginia bank holding companies, three cases in 1971 and 1973 challenging bank mergers in the Atlanta, Georgia, metropolitan area, four against bank holding companies in Colorado between 1971 and 1973, and three attacking bank mergers in the state of Washington.

Table 9-3

District Court Decisions and Bank Merger Cases, 1961-1975, by Year, Type of Merger, and Results in Litigated and Non-Litigated Cases

Year	Type		Litigated		Consent		Order		
	H	CG[1]	Win[2]	Loss	Divestiture	Other Relief[3]	Merger Abandoned	Case Dropped	Case Pending
1961-65	9	1	1	5	1	-	1	2[a]	
1966-69	18	8	-	6	1	3	15	-	1
1970-75	10	14	1	8	1[b]	1	8	2	3
Totals	37	23	2	19	3	4	24	4	4

[1]H is horizontal; CG is conglomerate (market extension).

[2]Connotes a government win or loss.

[3]Non-divestiture relief is most commonly a ban on future mergers for a period of 5 to 10 years.

[a]Both of these cases came within the exemption clause of the 1966 Bank Merger Act.

[b]Bank had to divest itself of controlling interest in savings and loan association, but allowed to keep minority interest provided it did not attempt to convert it to controlling interest for 10 years.

precipitously. Every case since 1973, has involved a challenge to a horizontal merger, though several cases have attacked horizontal acquisitions in particular communities by bank holding company subsidiaries. From 1968 to 1972, the Justice Department filed no fewer than five cases annually. While it also filed five in 1973, three of these were separate actions challenging three acquisitions by subsidiaries of the same banking holding company. The only case filed in 1974 was a refiling of the same suit, which was dismissed by the district court, as prematurely filed. In the first ten months of 1975, the Department has not filed a single bank merger suit.

The Supreme Court's role in halting horizontal bank mergers is an important one, and there is little doubt among those in the field that the result could have been expected in the absence of the Court's decisions. Similarly, the growth of bank holding companies is unlikely to have been so rapid as it has been had banks been freer to expand via horizontal merger. The shift by the Burger Court toward a more skeptical attitude toward Justice Department claims of illegality insures the continued growth of bank holding companies through market extension acquisitions, at least for the near future. It seems likely that concentration in banking in leading financial centers in the nation would be greater than it is in the absence of the Supreme Court's decisions.[69] While the Supreme Court may no longer longer strike down economic legislation by Congress, its role as statutory interpretor continues to give it a voice in economic policy through its ability to restrict or encourage the ability of administrative agencies, like the Justice Department, to enforce the laws. The role of the Supreme Court in bank merger policy suggests that while the Court may not be the primary policymaker, it is hardly an insignificant bystander.

Notes

1. Earl Kintner, *Primer on the Law of Mergers* (New York: Macmillan Co., 1973), p. 412. The introductory portion of the chapter draws heavily on Kintner and three additional articles on the 1960 Bank Merger Act: Tynan Smith and Nathaniel Greenspun, "Structural Limitations on Bank Competition," *Law and Contemporary Problems* 32 (1967): 40-57; William T. Lifland, "The Supreme Court, Congress, and Bank Mergers," *Law and Contemporary Problems* 32 (1967): 15-39; and Paul M. Horvitz and Bernard Shull, "The Bank Merger Act of 1960: A Decade After," *Antitrust Bulletin* 16 (1971): 859-871.

2. Kintner, *Primer on the Law of Mergers*, p. 412.

3. Ibid., p. 416. Some notable large bank mergers of the late 1950s include: Chase National Bank (Assets: $5.7 billion) acquired the bank of Manhatten ($1.6 billion) and the Bronx County Trust Co. ($76 million) to form the Chase Manhatten Bank; Bankers Trust ($2.3 billion) merged with Public National ($500 million) to form National Bankers Trust; National City Bank ($6 billion) bought First National ($715 million) to form First City National Bank; and on the West Coast, Crocker National Bank ($1.5 billion) acquired Anglo National Bank ($1 billion) to form Crocker-Anglo National Bank.

4. Kintner, *Primer on the Law of Mergers*, p. 417. For an exhaustive analysis of how these various factors were applied by the three banking agencies and the Justice Department see: G. Hall and C. Phillips, *Bank Mergers and the Regulatory Agencies—Application of the Bank Merger Act of 1960* (Federal Reserve Board, Washington, 1964).

5. *U.S.* v. *Philadelphia National Bank*, 374 U.S. 321 (1963).

6. *U.S.* v. *Philadelphia National Bank*, 201 F. Supp. 348 (E.D. Pa. 1962).

7. *Philadelphia National Bank*, 374 U.S. at 342.

8. Ibid., pp. 342-49.

9. Ibid., pp. 348-49.

10. Ibid., p. 349.

11. Ibid., pp. 356-57.

12. Ibid., pp. 357-62.

13. The case was *Brown Shoe* v. *U.S.*, 370 U.S. 294 (1962).

14. Transcript of oral argument in *U.S.* v. *Philadelphia National Bank*, p. 30.

15. *Philadelphia National Bank*, 374 U.S. at 362-64.

16. Ibid.

17. Ibid., pp. 370-71.

18. Ibid., p. 383.

19. Ibid., p. 384.

20. Lifland, "The Supreme Court and Bank Mergers," p. 26.

21. *U.S.* v. *First National Bank of Lexington*, 376 U.S. 665 (1964).

22. Ibid., p. 680.

23. Quoted in Kintner, *Primer on the Law of Mergers*, p. 485, without reference.

24. The cases were suits against Continental Illinois National Bank and Manufacturers Hanover Trust. The government had won a district judgment against the second: *U.S.* v. *Manufacturers Hanover Trust*, 240 F. Supp. 867 (S.D.N.Y. 1965).

25. Kintner, *Primer on the Law of Mergers*, p. 426. For a good description of the legislative history of the 1966 Bank Merger Act see: David Searls and Harry Reasoner, "The Bank Merger Act of 1966—Its Strange and Fruitless Odyssey," *Business Lawyer* 25 (1969): 133-156.

26. The relevant portion of the statute reads:

the agency shall not approve—

(A) any proposed merger or transaction which would result in a monopoly, or which would be in furtherance of any combination or conspiracy to monopolize or attempt to monopolize the business of banking in any part of the United States, or

(B) any other proposed merger transaction whose effect in any section of the country may be substantially to lessen competition, or to tend to create a monopoly, or which in any other manner would be in restraint of trade, unless it finds that the anticompetitive effects of the proposed transactions are clearly outweighed in the public interest by the probable effect of the transaction in meeting the convenience and needs of the community to be served.

12 United States Code §1828 (c)(5)(A) and (c)(5)(B)

27. 12 U.S.C. §1828 (c)(7)(C)

28. 12 U.S.C. §1828 (c)(7)(B) and (c)(7)(A)

29. 12 U.S.C. §1828 (c)(7)(D)

30. *Wall Street Journal*, February 8, 1966, p. 1; and Sears and Reasoner, "The Bank Merger Act of 1966," p. 133.

31. *U.S.* v. *Third National Bank of Nashville*, 260 F. Supp. 869 (N.D. Tenn. 1966); *U.S.* v. *Crocker-Anglo National Bank*, 263 F. Supp. 125 (N.D. Calif. 1966); and *U.S.* v. *Mercantile Trust Co. National Assoc.*, 263 F. Supp. 340 (E.D. Mo. 1966).

32. *U.S.* v. *First National Bank of Hawaii*, 257 F. Supp. 591 (D. Hawaii 1966); *U.S.* v. *Provident National Bank*, 262 F. Supp. 397 (E.D. Pa. 1966);

and *U.S.* v. *First City National Bank of Houston*, 1967 Trade Cases Par. 71970.

33. Sears and Reasoner, "The Bank Merger Act of 1966," pp. 144-48, reviews the district court decisions which preceded the Supreme Court's interpretation of the new law.

34. Ibid.

35. Kintner, *Primer on the Law of Mergers*, p. 428.

36. *U.S.* v. *First City National Bank of Houston*, 386 U.S. 361 (1967).

37. *U.S.* v. *First City National Bank of Houston*, 1967 Trade Cases Par. 71970.

38. The Justice Department was rather perturbed with the bank regulatory agencies, and this was reflected in the brief of the Solicitor General which noted that as many as 30 percent of the mergers approved by the banking agencies may have resulted in concentration as serious as that condemned in Philadelphia National Bank, and that the proper antitrust standards had been evolved not by the banking agencies but by the courts. The banking agencies, in contrast to the courts, did not seem to view increases in concentration as particularly significant from a competitive standpoint. Brief for the *United States* v. *First City National Bank of Houston*, pp. 26-28, 49-50.

39. *First National Bank of Houston*, 386 U.S. at 366.

40. See Lifland, "The Supreme Court and Bank Mergers," p. 39; and Kintner, *Primer on the Law of Mergers*, p. 439.

41. *First City National Bank of Houston*, 386 U.S. at 369.

42. Ibid., p. 370.

43. *U.S.* v. *Third National Bank of Nashville*, 390 U.S. 171 (1968).

44. *U.S.* v. *Third National Bank of Nashville*, 260 F. Supp. 869 (M.D. Tenn. 1966).

45. *Third National Bank of Nashville*, 390 U.S. at 189.

46. *U.S.* v. *Phillipsburg National Bank*, 399 U.S. 350 (1970).

47. *U.S.* v. *Phillipsburg National Bank*, 306 F. Supp. 645 (D.N.J. 1969).

48. *Phillipsburg National Bank*, 399 U.S. at 371.

49. Ibid., p. 358.

50. *U.S.* v. *El Paso Natural Gas*, 376 U.S. 651; *U.S.* v. *Penn-Olin Chemical Co.*, 378 U.S. 158 (1964); *U.S.* v. *Continental Can*, 378 U.S. 441 (1964); *F.T.C.* v. *Procter & Gamble Co.*, 386 U.S. 568 (1967); *Ford Motor Co.* v. *U.S.*, 405 U.S. 562 (1972); and *U.S.* v. *Falstaff Brewing Co.*, 410 U.S. 526 (1973).

51. The cases were: *U.S.* v. *Crocker-Anglo National Bank*, 277 F. Supp. 133 (N.D. Cal. 1967) (three-judge court); *U.S.* v. *First National Bank of Jackson*, 301 F. Supp. 1161 (S.D. Miss. 1969); *U.S.* v. *First National Bank of Maryland*, 310 F. Supp. 157 (D. Md. 1970); *U.S.* v. *Idaho First National Bank*, 315 F. Supp. 261 (D. Idaho 1970); *U.S.* v. *First National Bancorporation*, 329 F. Supp. 1003 (D. Colo. 1971); affirmed by equally divided Court, 410 U.S. 577 (1973); *U.S.* v. *United Virginia Bankshares*, 347 F. Supp. 891 (E.D. Va. 1972); *U.S.* v. *Connecticut National Bank*, 362 F. Supp. 240 (D. Conn. 1973), vacated and remanded, 418 U.S. 656 (1974); *U.S.* v. *Marine Bancorporation*, 1973-1 Trade Cases Par. 74496, affirmed 418 U.S. 602 (1974); and *U.S.* v. *Citizens & Southern National Bank*, 372 F. Supp. 616 (N.D. Ga. 1974) affirmed, 43 U.S. Law Week 4779 (17 June 1975).

52. E.g., *Connecticut National Bank*.

53. All other cases in Note 51 except *Connecticut National Bank*.

54. See Donald Baker, "Potential Competition in Banking: After Greeley, What?" *Banking Law Journal* 90 (1973): 365-369.

55. Ibid., p. 367. For a full discussion of the government's policy goals and consideration in potential competition banking cases, see both the Baker article (Baker recently resigned as the director of policy planning of the Antitrust Division of the Justice Department) and Shiela Solomon "Bank Merger Policy and Problems: A Linkage Theory of Oligopoly," *Banking Law Journal* 89 (1972): 116-127.

56. Justice Powell attributes the Justice Department's lack of success in potential competition bank cases to this very lack of consideration for the unique regulatory status of banks. *Marine Bancorporation*, 418 U.S. at 628.

57. See, e.g., *First National Bank of Jackson*, 301 F. Supp. 119-200; *Idaho First National Bank*, 315 F. Supp. at 263; *United Virginia Bankshares*, 1971 Trade Cases Par. 73466 at 92845; *Crocker-Anglo National Bank*, 277 F. Supp. at 154; *First National Bank of Maryland*, 310 F. Supp. at 160; and *Marine Bancorporation*, 1973-1 Trade Cases Par. 74496 at 94245.

58. See, e.g., *Philadelphia National Bank*, 201 F. Supp. at 348, but especially *Marine Bancorporation*, in which the judge specifically ordered defense counsel, in preparing the findings of fact and conclusions of law in the case, to include his reasons for discounting the credibility of key government witnesses. See Jurisdictional Statement for the United States, Marine Bancorporation, Appendix E, p. 55.

59. This is questionable since the officers of the bank can be expected to make self-serving statements to justify their decisions to acquire the

particular bank they want. The Supreme Court has recognized this fact in a nonbanking case, *U.S.* v. *Falstaff Brewing Corp.*, 410 U.S. 526, 537-38 (1973).

60. Donald I. Baker, "Banking Competition in the Age of the Computer," *Banking Law Journal* 90 (1973): 208-212.

61. *Marine Bancorporation*, 418 U.S. at 640-41.

62. Ibid., pp. 639-40.

63. Ibid., p. 646.

64. *U.S.* v. *First National Bancorporation*, 410 U.S. 577 (1973).

65. *U.S.* v. *Trans Texas Bancorporation, Inc.*, 412 U.S. 946 (1973).

66. *U.S.* v. *Connecticut National Bank*, 418 U.S. 656 (1974).

67. *U.S.* v. *Marine Bancorporation* 418 U.S. 602 (1974) and *U.S.* v. *Citizens & Southern National Bank*, 43 U.S. Law Week 4779 (17 June 1975).

68. In *United Virginia Bankshares*, for example, the district judge viewed the government's attempt use potential competition theory with some skepticism:

Reduced to simplicity, this case is another attempt by the Department of Justice to engraft the theory of potential competition on banking. Five previous cases, designed to accomplish this end, have been tried—all without success.

United Virginia Bankshares, 1971 Trade Cases, Par. 73466 at 92845.

69. For some empirical evidence on this point see Horvitz and Shull, "The Bank Merger Act of 1960: A Decade After," Antitrust Bulletin 16 (1971): 859-871.

10

The National Labor Relations Board and the Duty to Bargain in Good Faith: Consistency or Confusion?

Charles Bulmer and John L. Carmichael

Probably no question constituted a greater strain on the American social fabric than the labor organization issue. In the latter part of the nineteenth century and the first half of the twentieth century the right of working people to organize and confront their employers as an organized unit was one of the most seriously contested issues since the resolution of the slavery question. Violence and threats of violence when workers attempted to organize were all too common. The very right of laboring people to organize and engage in collective bargaining with their employers had to be established, and the early history of the attempt was all too often written in fraternal blood.

Labor organizations were originally viewed as illegal conspiracies in restraint of trade and were prosecuted as such.[1] Big business and government were initially in agreement that this new menace to the free enterprise system had to be stamped out. Many clung stubbornly to the notion that employers and employees should be viewed as individuals. It seemed perfectly reasonable that as individuals they should be able to negotiate with one another and reach mutually satisfactory agreements. If, for whatever reason, the employee did not choose to accept the terms of employment offered by a particular employer, he did not have to work.[2] He would not be compelled, and the decision would be his. He should not, however, expect to combine with others of his kind in order to bring pressure to bear upon the employer. Such a thing smacked of conspiracy and would not be tolerated.

Such thinking, of course, already belonged to another age. The notion that employers and employees were equal bargaining units and could work out the terms of employment was wholly unrealistic and was destined to be recognized as such. However, this recognition was a long time coming. Much strife and agony had to be endured before it was realized that the corporate employer and the individual workers were not equal, and that on the worker's side an organized bargaining unit was needed to balance the power of the company.

Of course, workers made the discovery long before it was recognized generally. The labor movement had to fight a long and sometimes lonely struggle before the rest of society was willing to concede its right to organize and negotiate as a unit.

The first major positive recognition of labor's right to organize came in the form of the National Labor Relations Act[3] passed in 1935. This Act was supplemented in 1947 with the passage of the Labor-Management Relations Act[4] which amended the 1935 Act. The basic intent of these pieces of legislation was, first of all, to recognize and establish, once and for all, the right of the worker to organize, and, secondly, to impose duties on the part of both labor and management to bargain collectively.[5] The realization had finally been reached that the best way to eliminate the strife and violence which had characterized the labor movement was, not to challenge labor's right to organize, but to impose an obligation on both labor and management to settle their differences in a peaceful and orderly manner. That is, labor and management would be required to meet and bargain with one another and attempt to reach a mutually acceptable agreement through the peaceful process of negotiation, rather than through armed confrontation, as had been the case in the past. In effect, the Congress decided to impose the standards of an orderly process on both parties. In addition, the legislation attempted to establish certain standards with regard to the negotiating process itself. That is, the legislation provided that in the negotiating process certain actions would be regarded as improper or demonstrative of bad faith and would be designated as unfair labor practices. For example, the National Labor Relations Act (or Wagner Act of 1935) made it an unfair labor practice for an employer to refuse to bargain collectively with the union representing the employees.[6] Subsequently, the Labor-Management Relations (or Taft-Hartley Act of 1947) imposed the duty on employees, through their unions, to bargain in good faith with employers.[7]

It is the National Labor Relations Board, established by the National Labor Relations Act, which must determine what constitutes good faith bargaining, and in making such determinations the Board exercises considerable discretion. The questions for the National Labor Relations Board have become: What constitutes good faith bargaining? What factors should be used in determining whether the broad intent of Congress is being achieved and good faith collective bargaining is taking place? Are the employers and employees, in fact, bargaining in good faith as required by the legislation; or is one or the other reneging on his obligation and defeating the intent of the legislation and the Congress. One might put it negatively, as in fact the Board has done, by asking what factors indicate bad faith bargaining. In the process of answering such questions, the Board uses its discretionary prerogatives to shape policy within the broad commands of the legislation. As the history of the application of the legislation will show, it is one thing to determine that an employer and his employees must bargain in good faith and quite another to determine in individual cases just exactly what constitutes good faith efforts.

The Board has attempted to identify various types of actions on the part of the employer which might constitute a lack of good faith effort. The Board has identified unfair tactics such as: using dilatory tactics, unilaterally changing conditions, bypassing employee representatives, imposing prior conditions, surface bargaining, and refusing to make concessions. Some of these tactics are relatively easy to identify. Bypassing the employee representative or unilaterally changing conditions are rather obvious violations which do not require very much subjective judgment by the Board. These are usually referred to as "per se" violations, that is, conduct which obviously violates the provisions of the legislation and is flagrant in nature.[a]

The second category of violations is more difficult to define because it does not involve obvious flagrant violations, but is concerned with more subtle acts which often require the Board to make subjective judgments with regard to the employer's state of mind and intentions. The Board has experienced great difficulty in attempting to establish doctrinal precedents to serve as guides in these more subjective areas of possible violation. The result has been that the Board's policies and decisions seem to vacillate from one case to another without ever establishing clear rules for future conduct and judgment.

Two notable aspects of bargaining with respect to which rule-making difficulties have been experienced by the Board are employer surface bargaining and the expectation of concessions on the part of the employer. Surface bargaining is defined as entering into the negotiations with an intent not to reach an agreement. The important element in determining surface bargaining is a *prior disposition* not to reach an agreement. The employer is trying to defeat or subvert the negotiating process.

Failure to make concessions is a more difficult posture to assess. The essential distinction is that, while there is no *prior* disposition not to reach an agreement, the unyielding and inflexible nature of the employer's bargaining position may demonstrate bad faith. Concessions imply that there must be willingness to accommodate the other party in the interest of reaching an agreement. The criteria used to demonstrate when surface bargaining or failure to make additional reasonable concessions has taken place are very similar.

The discussion which follows will be limited to an examination of these two aspects of the employer duty to bargain in good faith and the way in

---

[a] The Board is on firmer ground when it can find flagrant violations of the duty to bargain in good faith. Sometimes these infractions are termed per se violations. These violations are defined to be conduct which by itself violates the Act on its face. Examples are: (1) refusal to negotiate at reasonable times and (2) refusal to reduce a final agreement to writing.

which the Board has dealt with them in some recent cases. Efforts to perceive the occurrence of surface bargaining by employers and the need for employer concessions have been critical to the determination of acceptable collective bargaining and have provided fruitful spheres of policy-making by the Board. Focus on the refinement of obligations imposed on employers is not intended to suggest that the duty of employees to bargain in good faith has not given rise to questions posed by surface bargaining and lack of concessions by unions, but most of the cases have involved employers and major policy-making by the Board has concerned actions by employers.

Surface Bargaining

The problem of determining when surface bargaining has occurred is one of the most difficult problems facing the Board. It is difficult to define what surface bargaining is, and any definition can only be in the most general terms. One definition is that surface bargaining occurs when an employer refuses to accept a union proposal, makes a proposal of his own, and fails to make attempts to reconcile differences. Surface bargaining is sometimes described as "sham" bargaining. The difficulty for the Board lies in applying the definition in specific cases in order to determine whether a serious, good faith attempt has been made to bargain.

Furthermore, the Board must make a distinction between "hard bargaining" and "surface bargaining." When is an employer taking a hard line in seeking to secure acceptance of his proposals and when is he merely discussing matters with no real intention of reaching an agreement? Some general guidelines are available to determine if the employer is making a good faith attempt to reach agreement and is not making a sham of the negotiating process. First there must be a genuine desire on his part to enter into meaningful negotiations; he must not evidence a take-it-or-leave-it attitude. Secondly, some negotiating or exchange of views must occur, and he must give reasons to support the position taken. Otherwise the parties have not really met and conferred. Thirdly, he has the right to maintain previously made proposals even if they do not appear "reasonable" to the union; however, the Board insists that he maintain some flexibility and be willing to compromise lest the proceedings become meaningless.[8]

In specific cases the Board will often consider a variety of factors in attempting to determine surface bargaining. For example, if the employer has insisted on inflexible terms and used stalling tactics, he very likely has engaged in surface bargaining. On the other hand, if he presents a counter-proposal to the union in the bargaining negotiations that is almost certainly to be rejected, this fact alone probably does not constitute surface bargaining. In fact there is no absolute obligation by the employer to make counterproposals, but the Board may construe a refusal as a factor tending to show a prior disposition not to reach an agreement.[9] There is a duty to make some reasonable proposal to reconcile differences with the union; otherwise surface bargaining will probably exist.[10]

A failure by an employer to reconcile differences with the union was found by the Board in *National Automobile and Casualty Insurance Company*.[11] The Board determined that the company had illegally failed to bargain as shown by an obstinate refusal to offer any wage increases or to discuss any other benefits. Presumably if the employer had been willing to make some compromise, the Board would have found that he had met the requirement of good faith bargaining. However, the determination is difficult in any event, because there is no absolute requirement to make concessions or counterproposals. If the position taken by the employer is adamant, but "reasonable," should not the Board find bargaining in good faith? Otherwise, the employer will be placed in a highly unsatisfactory position vis-à-vis the union.

In a case with similar facts, the *Hartford Fire Insurance Company* case,[12] the Board again found an unwillingness to reconcile differences. Here, the Board considered the failure to make counterproposals a factor in determining bad faith bargaining.[b] In this case no agreement had been reached by the end of the fourteenth bargaining session and the company rejected a proposal previously agreed upon. The Board found that surface bargaining existed. It should be noted, however, that length of the negotiating period is not, by itself, evidence of bad faith bargaining, nor should it be. If the employer has taken a "reasonable" position with respect to the union's position, then a lengthy period of negotiations alone would not evidence surface bargaining.

If a failure to reconcile differences can indicate surface bargaining, does "hard bargaining" also demonstrate surface bargaining? The answer is that it does not. Throughout its decisions the Board has consistently ruled that "hard bargaining" is not surface bargaining. Although one can make this categorical statement, a serious problem exists in trying to determine when "hard bargaining" rather than "surface bargaining" has occurred. Certainly the employer cannot satisfy the obligation to bargain merely by going through the motions without actually seeking to adjust the differences. If he is firmly convinced that his position is fair with respect to the union, then is it not asking too much to insist that he compromise? Assuredly he cannot present the union with proposals which evidence a take-it-or-leave-it attitude. He cannot simply present the union with a "package" proposal, and then insist that the union accept it.

Even though an employer previously may have committed certain

---

[b] Although it is not mandatory that the employer make counterproposals, the Board may consider the failure, when combined with other elements, as showing bad faith. See footnote a, supra.

unfair labor practices, he is not guilty of surface bargaining when it can be shown that he did not engage in dilatory tactics, and that he did not impede efforts to reach agreement. This was the decision in *American Rubber and Plastics Corporation*.[13] Here, the Board relied heavily on the outcome of negotiations in determining that good faith rather than surface bargaining occurred. The company was found to have made a serious effort in the bargaining process, and the Board stressed that "results" were forthcoming in the negotiations.

An obvious case of surface bargaining was found in *Murietta Hot Springs*[14] where the company stalled and "lulled" the union with concessions. At the same time the employer's agent denied that he had authority to negotiate and the company increased the employees' wages without offering to do so in its negotiations with the union.

Also, the Board looked to a combination of tactics in *Valley Oil Company, Incorporated*[15] to find surface bargaining. It found a breach of the obligation to bargain in good faith by the employer's general conduct combined with a specific withdrawal from agreements previously reached and a failure to give its agents authority to carry on meaningful negotiations. What are "meaningful negotiations" is highly subjective and the criterion is less satisfactory.

Assuredly, the problem of finding legitimate hard bargaining as opposed to surface bargaining is most difficult, and the Board is imposing upon itself a task in which subjective judgment must necessarily play a large part. Without question this procedure is less than ideal, and the Board should seek to base its determination of bad faith bargaining on other factors.

Lest the cases cited should suggest that the employer has an almost impossible burden in showing hard bargaining, the following case should be mentioned. In *Typeservice Corporation and Indianapolis Typographical Union No. 1*[16] hard bargaining was found on the part of both management and the union. In this decision the Board ruled that an employer was under no obligation to accept certain terms in a contract merely because they were present in an earlier contract; it found that the union was just as adamant in its position as the employer. What the Board seemed to be saying is that it will allow rather wide latitude to the employer in his bargaining efforts so long as his position is reasonable and he is not clearly seeking to undermine the bargaining process by placing the union in an untenable position. The Board recognizes that the union may also be engaged in hard bargaining and to prevent the employer from taking the same stance would be unfair.

Frequently, in deciding whether surface bargaining has occurred, the Board will consider the totality of the employer's conduct during the bargaining sessions. Examination of some recent cases suggests that the Board is constantly looking at totality of conduct to find if good faith bargaining has occurred. In fact this determination appears implicit in the very concept of surface bargaining. For example, in *Columbia Tribune Publishing Company*[17] the Board decided that the totality of the company's behavior showed surface bargaining. The company proposed to lower wage rates, impose a longer workweek, and require a prohibition against strikes without accepting any provisions for handling grievances. The company justified its position, arguing that it was converting to a more efficient process which would require fewer and less skilled employees. The Board concluded that "no self-respecting union" would accept such proposals and rules that there had been a mere pretense at bargaining on the employer's part. In the company's favor it should be noted that it felt that the more efficient production process demanded less skilled labor; however, to keep the same employees and to pay them less per hour was questionable reasoning on its part. This would appear to be the critical factor that tipped the scales and caused the Board to construe the actions as a mere pretense at bargaining.

Another case in which the Board found surface bargaining rather than hard bargaining was *Continental Insurance Company*.[18] Again, in this case it was the totality of action that proved surface bargaining. Many factors were considered by the Board: prolongation of negotiations on the part of the employer, dealing directly with the employees rather than with the union representatives, failing to give the union notice of disciplinary action against an employee, making wage increases and transfers of employees without consulting the union, and taking "unreasonable" positions in negotiations with the union. Implicit in all of these activities was an attempt on the part of the employer to bypass the union and thereby to undermine the union.[c] The Board would appear justified in its determination; otherwise, the union would cease to serve a useful purpose and the attempt of the labor legislation to protect employees would be thwarted.

In *Evergreen Convalescent Home, Incorporated*[19] the Board again found surface bargaining where, among other things, the employer's representative lacked diligence in finding reasonable times to meet, took unreasonable positions, and withdrew from previously reached agreements. The employer objected to the inclusion in the contract of a grievance procedure, and it refused to accept a check-off provision for union dues on the ground that it was opposed to compulsory union membership. There also was a finding that the employer reduced benefits previously offered to the union and accepted by it. The Board had a rather clear-cut case of surface bargaining when all factors are considered together; however, the authors

---

[c] Board Chairman Miller, dissenting in part, concluded that there was not sufficient evidence in the case to indicate surface bargaining. He even questioned whether the Board should undertake this type of review—trying to ascertain what the motivations of the negotiators were.

doubt that the rejection of the check-off provision by the employer, alone, would have much probative value.

Finding that the positions of union and employer were not balanced, the Board determined, the *Czas Publishing Company, Incorporated*[20] that surface bargaining had occurred. When all of the evidence was considered, the Board found that the employer had placed the union in a clearly disadvantageous position. The Board observed that the employer had participated in only two negotiating sessions, had made no counterproposals and attempted to induce the employees to withdraw from the union by offering increased benefits without tendering this proposal to the union. By attempting to turn employees against the union, the employer was subverting the very purpose of the labor legislation—to preserve the right of employees to collective bargaining. This was a clear-cut case of surface bargaining.

In the bargaining process the Board may consider behavior on the part of both union and employer in determining whether the employer was engaged in surface bargaining. For example, in *Unoco Apparel, Incorporated and International Ladies' Garment Workers' Union*[21] the Board ruled that the employer had engaged in hard bargaining and not surface bargaining. Of all of the recent cases handled by the Board, this case has presented the greatest difficulty for the Board in making a "fine" distinction between hard bargaining and surface bargaining. The Board concluded that although there was some evidence of surface bargaining, the totality of the employer's conduct showed that it had engaged in hard bargaining. Arguing that the employer's proposals and agreements on some items indicated a willingness to conclude a contract with the union, the Board found that both union and employer had adopted an attitude of hard bargaining and inflexibility on such major items as wages and benefits.[d] The Board seems to be looking for comparable activity on the part of both union and employer in the negotiating sessions to make the difficult distinction between surface and hard bargaining. If each side is taking the same stance, it appears that the Board will accept the idea of hard bargaining. This position is surely a sound one.

Finally, it should be noted that the Board generally looks for flexibility in bargaining position on the part of the employer to determine whether surface bargaining has occurred. If this criterion is met, the Board will find absence of surface bargaining. Such requirement was met in *Los Angeles Herald-Examiner*.[22] Although there were only five negotiating sessions, the Board found a serious attempt on the part of the employer to reach

---

[d] Board member Penello, dissenting in part, disagreed with his colleagues that hard bargaining existed on the part of the employer. He found that the employer's negotiator in effect lacked authority to negotiate and that his intrasigence on almost all issues demonstrated that he was only going through the motions of bargaining without any intention of reaching agreement. He beleived the employer had engaged in surface bargaining.

agreement, since the area of dispute between union and employer was small. It might be added that the labor legislation[23] does not compel the parties to reach agreement, and even though extensive negotiations do not produce a contract, there is no conclusive inference that the employer is engaged in surface bargaining.

Concessions

In the previous cases the essential element in determining surface bargaining was an apparent prior disposition not to reach an agreement. We shall now turn to a discussion of concessions. This is a very difficult and controversial area which the Board must deal with in the course of deciding cases. Does the legislation require the employer, in the course of the negotiations, to make concessions to the union? The courts have generally held that there is no such requirement and have overturned Board decisions which seemed to require concessions.[24] But the legislation does require the employer to negotiate "in good faith" with the employee representative. The question for the Board in deciding cases in which refusal to bargain collectively has been alleged is: how does one distinguish good faith, but hard bargaining, which is legal under the legislation, from refusal to bargain, which is not legal?

In addition, the Board has had to deal with the question of: how does one require good faith bargaining, without at the same time requiring that concessions be made? The difficulty seems to be in deciding what can be used as evidence of good faith bargaining if concessions cannot be employed as evidence of such bargaining. What other factors might be considered in determining good faith bargaining? Part of the difficulty lies in the fact that there is no precise answer to this question. Generally the Board has tried to adopt the position that movement in the negotiating process should be considered in determining good faith. But what is meant by movement? The Board has held that the employer must demonstrate a willingness to move from a fixed position, not necessarily making concessions to the union, in order to achieve a mutually acceptable agreement. Admittedly this is a rather nebulous concept, and the attempt to apply it has resulted in some rather controversial and, at times, apparently contradictory decisions; but the fact remains that no other more precise standard is available. The Board must grapple with such difficult questions as: has the employer taken a fixed position, and is that position reasonable; has the employer shown a willingness to move from his original position and made counter proposals which could be reasonably accepted by the union in lieu of its original bargaining position; has the employer shown a willingness to consider alternatives offered by the union and has the employer offered reasonable explanations if he rejects those alternatives? The answers to the questions must demonstrate a willingness to negotiate in good faith on the part of the employer, but they do not require him to make any specific concessions. This is not always an easy task and the Board has been severely criticised for involving itself in the details of the bargaining process and requiring concessions not required by the legislation.

Consideration of a few cases in which the Board dealt with the problem of concessions will help to demonstrate the difficulty of making a determination in those cases. A case which reflects the Board's traditional position is the *American Steel Building Company*[25] case in which the Board held that an employer had failed to bargain in good faith because he had not offered any new counterproposals which reflected any substantial change in his original negotiating position. There was not an initial predisposition not to reach an agreement but the Board felt that the employer had failed to make any significant moves in the direction of reaching an agreement.

Another element in this case was the consideration by the Board of the employer's obligation to make counterproposals if the union has evidenced a willingness to do so. The Board pointed out that the union had offered to relent on several important points in the interest of reaching an accommodation with the employer, but the employer remained adamant and refused to make any concessions beyond his original position. Again the evidence did not demonstrate a predisposition not to reach an agreement; however, it appears that the employer's duty to make additional proposals is related to the flexibility of the union's negotiating stance. That is, if the union has shown a willingness to relent on some of its proposals, then the employer should be willing to reciprocate, and failure to do so may be considered evidence of bad faith.

An interesting question which might be raised with regard to this decision is: as a matter of strategy, wouldn't the effect of this kind of decision be to cause employers to withhold their real bargaining position until later on in the negotiations in order that they will not be accused by the Board of intransigence?

Another position which the Board has taken with regard to the duty of the employer to make concessions is that while the employer does not have to make specific concessions, he does, apparently, have to make positive counterproposals. That is, the employer cannot simply reject the union's proposal and not make any concrete proposals of its own. In the *Big Three Industries*[26] case, for example, the Board held that the employer's position consisted solely of rejecting the union's proposals and agreeing only to the suspension of certain employee rights which had already been established in previous negotiations. The Board found that not only did the employer not make any concessions, but his position was so unreasonable that the union could not have been expected to accept it. In other words, in the negotiating process the employer cannot refuse to offer anything and, indeed, propose to withdraw rights which were already established. The employer must be willing to offer something, although not necessarily specific concessions. Again the evidence failed to indicate a prior disposition not to reach an agreement.

In the *Food Service Company*[27] case the Board ruled that an employer had not shown bad faith even though he had adopted a take-it-or-leave-it attitude in the negotiations with the union. In this case, the Board found that both sides had taken fixed positions in the negotiations and that neither had shown any evidence of flexibility. The fact that the employer had refused to make additional concessions was not considered evidence of bad faith. The Board seemed to be taking the position that, if during the negotiating process both the union and the employer became rigid in their positions, then the employer should not be expected to make additional concessions, if he had not displayed a prior attitude against reaching an agreement. The Board seems to be trying, with regard to the need to make concessions, to establish some sort of principle of reciprocity or mutual obligation, although its rulings in this area have not always been consistent.

In the *Wal-Lite Division of United States Gypsum Company*[28] case the Board ruled that a fixed "take-it-leave-it" bargaining position did amount to bad faith bargaining because the employer had offered nothing and was attempting to withdraw existing employee benefits. Such a position is not consistent with good faith bargaining, even though there was no prior disposition not to reach an agreement. Of course the difficulty is apparent. If the employer is not required to make any concessions then how can the fact that he has not made any concessions be used as evidences of bad faith? The dilemma provoked by the inconsistency of this policy has caused serious problems not only for the Board, but also for the employer trying to meet his responsibilities under the legislation, while at the same time trying to maintain his bargaining position.

In the *State Farm Mutual*[29] case the Board concluded that the employer did not bargain in bad faith even though he adamantly refused to yield on certain important issues such as weekly hours and union security. The Board found that the employer had made concessions in other areas and therefore good faith bargaining had been established. Apparently in this case the Board felt that intrasigence on certain substantial matters was proper as long as flexibility was shown on other matters. However, one is still faced with the fact that, while claiming otherwise, the Board is basing its decision on the apparent willingness of the employer to make concessions.

Conclusions

Two unhappy consequences seem to flow from the Board's case-by-case approach to fostering good faith in collective bargaining by probing for employer surface bargaining and the need for employers to make concessions. First, the employer comes to the adjudicative procedure without a clear notion of precisely what actions are required or prohibited on his part and, although the Board presumes not to involve itself in the actual bargaining process, the practical effect of its decision is to make its influence pervasive and even determinative throughout subsequent bargaining sessions. Secondly, employers' ignorance of the behavior expected of them is compounded by the failure of the Board's inconsistent and confusing decisions to provide clear and instructive precedents for future cases. Under the case-by-case approach, as Theodore J. Lowi has observed, "the rule is not known to the bargainer until he knows the outcome, and its later application must be deciphered by lawyers representing potential cases.[30] In some instances, under the existing policy, it is extremely difficult or even impossible for the employer to determine when he is taking a legitimate hard bargaining position in the negotiations and when he is engaging in surface bargaining or refusing to demonstrate flexibility. The specific obligations and responsibilities in these areas need to be spelled out more clearly.

It may be argued that the Board's decisions in the areas of surface bargaining and the making of concessions appear at times either questionable or contradictory essentially because the legislation itself is vague. For example, while the legislation establishes the obligation to negotiate in good faith, it does not at the same time either define the obligation further or spell out in any detail what factors should be used by the Board in making its determination of good faith. Such lack of specificity is often typical of delegated legislation. The Congress simply proclaims broad objectives and standards and then instructs and empowers an administrative agency to pursue the objective by applying the standards. The agency—the National Labor Relations Board in this case—must interpret both objectives and standards. In fashioning policy under these circumstances the Board has deliberately chosen to proceed on a case-by-case basis rather than to follow a rule-making approach. It has, as a result, failed to establish consistent substantive policy. The solution to the problem would appear to have been early and frequent administrative rule-making, producing a body of detailed guidelines. Such rules would have become known and certain factors guiding all parties involved or to be involved in bargaining.

On the other hand, so elusive are the notions of surface bargaining and of the need for concessions that the Board, having acknowledged them as important, may have done the best it can. It may well be that the two notions simply cannot definitively be formulated into general rules applicable to all cases. If so, the issues can be dealt with perhaps, only by a case-by-case approach.

The dilemmas produced by the case-by-case approach nevertheless remain. If the Board cannot successfully resolve them, the ultimate resort is legislative revision in which Congress undertakes more precisely to define the elements required in demonstrating good faith in collective bargaining. It might, for example, specify the making of concessions by both unions and employers to be such a required element. Given the complex nature of the collective bargaining process and the uniqueness of each instance, however, there can be no assurance that more rigid and necessarily arbitrary definitions imposed by Congress would, even if they could be formulated, achieve the objectives of the acts of 1935 and 1947 more satisfactorily than has the Board's case-by-case attempt to realize those objectives.

Notes

1. See *Loewe* v. *Lawlor*, 208 U.S. 274 (1908).

2. See *Lochner* v. *New York*, 198 U.S. 45 (1905).

3. 49 Stat. 449 (1935).

4. 61 Stat. 136 (1947).

5. Relevant portions of the Labor Management Relations Act are: "Sec. 8(a) It shall be an unfair labor practice for an employer—

. . . . . .

(5) to refuse to bargain collectively with the representatives of his employees, subject to the provisions of section 9(a).

. . . . . .

(d) For the purposes of this section, to bargain collectively is the performance of the mutual obligation of the employer and the representative of the employees to meet at reasonable times and confer in good faith with respect to wages, hours, and other terms and conditions of employment, or the negotiation of an agreement, or any question arising thereunder, and the execution of a written contract incorporating any agreement reached if requested by either party, but such obligation does not compel either party to agree to a proposal or require the making of a concession . . .

6. See Sect. 8(a)(5). The Act also imposes other duties and limitations on the employer. See Sect. 8(a) 1-4.

7. See Sect. 8(d).

8. See "Note, Good Faith Bargaining and the G.E. Case—The NLRB Views 'Boulwarism' and other Bargaining Practices," 53 *Georgetown Law Journal* 1115.

9. Sect. 8(d) of the Labor Management Relations Act, as originally proposed, had a statement that an employer was not obligated to make counterproposals in order to meet the requirement of good faith. The final

version did not include such a statement. It was left out because the NLRB objected that such a statement would preclude it from considering a lack of counterproposals as indicating bad faith. See Archibald Cox, ''The Duty to Bargain in Good Faith,'' 71 *Harvard Law Review* 1401, 1421 (1958).

10. See *NLRB* v. *Reed & Prince Manufacturing Co.*, 205 F.2d 131 (1st Cir. 1953).

11. 199 NLRB 1 (1972).

12. 191 NLRB 78 (1971).

13. 200 NLRB 127 (1972).

14. 198 NLRB 118 (1972).

15. 210 NLRB 47 (1974).

16. 203 NLRB 183 (1973).

17. 201 NLRB 70 (1973).

18. 204 NLRB 129 (1973).

19. 209 NLRB 161 (1974).

20. 205 NLRB 158 (1973).

21. 208 NLRB 88 (1974).

22. 197 NLRB 15 (1972).

23. National Labor Relations Act (1935) as amended by the Labor Management Relations Act (1947).

24. See e.g., *White* v. *NLRB*, 225 F.2d 564 (5th Cir., 1958); *NLRB* v. *Reed & Prince Manufacturing Co.*, 205 F.2d 131, 134 (1st Cir., 1953), cert. denied, 346 U.S. 887 (1953); and *NLRB* v. *American National Insurance Co.*, 343 U.S. 395 (1952).

25. 208 NLRB 141 (1974).

26. 201 NLRB 105 (1973).

27. 202 NLRB 107 (1973).

28. 200 NLRB 132 (1973).

29. 195 NLRB 155 (1972).

30. Theodore J. Lowi, *The End of Liberalism* (New York: W.W. Norton, 1969), p. 300.

**Part V
Government-Business
Relationships**

11

Some Recent Policy Trends in the Mixed Economy

Lloyd D. Musolf

The idea of greater state intervention in the economy went, of course, very much against the American grain; it had to be introduced on a provisional basis and frequently through the back door. If America now has a mixed economic system, this has come about not as the result of the pressure of the Left, but because more and more industrialists and bankers asked the federal authorities for subsidies and thus, indirectly, for state intervention.

> Walter Laqueur, "The Next Ten Years: A Review of History Yet to be Written," *Harper's Magazine* 249 (December 1974): 70, 73.

Probably few Americans would find much disagreement with the predictive statement above. Penn Central, Lockheed, Pan American, and other giant firms have recently become better known as mendicants than as symbols of free enterprise, thereby tending to confirm Laqueur's accuracy in depicting the source of greater state intervention. Nor is it surprising that the "land of opportunity" would find it distasteful to have "greater state intervention." Our business civilization usually finds it persuasive to locate the spirit of the pioneers in commercial ventures, no matter how insulated they are against competition.

Government intervention in the economy through subsidizing, regulating, operating, and planning are—in different degrees for each—commonplace in twentieth century America. Why pay any special attention to them at the moment? After all, it could be maintained that if a problem exists it is psychological rather than policy-centered. That is to say, the apparent gap between the operative myth of free enterprise and the existence of a mixed economy can be dismissed as a problem of cognitive dissonance, the very human need to assure consistency in strongly-held beliefs by downplaying information that contradicts them.[1] Cognitive dissonance there may well be, but more is involved, as we shall see.

In a dynamic economy, many areas clamor for attention. How shall a selection be made? The criterion employed here is the evidence of at least preliminary steps in policy-making. It has been well said that policy agenda-setting involves identifying problems in need of a solution, agreeing that a governmental response is required, and evaluating and choosing among competing approaches.[2] Thus, the fascinating topic of multinational corporations has been omitted because, though Congress has shown increasing concern about the power of these giants, the agenda setting process is still at an inchoate level. The three areas selected for attention are not the only ones in which policymakers have taken at least preliminary steps, but they are significant areas. They are also interesting because they incorporate changed elements (one hesitates saying "new," when government intervention in the economy dates from the Massachusetts Bay Colony). Finally, these three areas suggest a further blurring of the line between government and the private economic sphere and the prospect of an even more intricate mixed economy in the future.

Foreign Governments and Domestic Policy

First of all, it is now apparent that foreign governments have more influence than in the recent past on the shaping of public policy that involves defense contractors. In a sense, of course, this policy area came under foreign influence, for example, when this country became the "arsenal of democracy" in both world wars. More direct influence than that is meant here. Consider, for example, some recent dealings between oil-rich foreign governments and defense contractors (with policymakers peering over their shoulders). In 1974, the well-known financial difficulties of the Lockheed Aircraft Corporation prompted an offer from several of these governments to purchase 41 percent of its common stock, an offer which Lockheed prudently rejected.[3] Subsequently, the government of Iran made several approaches. Initially it tried to have the U.S. government share the cost of reopening the Lockheed production line for the giant C-5A military transport plane through the addition of Pentagon purchase orders to its own. This failed because of the Defense Department's fear that reopening production would rekindle a bitter controversy with Congress over massive cost-overruns in earlier production of the C-5A. The Shah's government then shifted to another proposal. It offered to pay for the reopening of the production line on its own and to buy ten of the $55 million planes.

The Grumman Corporation, another hard-pressed defense contractor, was also involved with the government of Iran. With the knowledge of the State and Defense departments, Iran had arranged to make advance payments to Grumman (via the Pentagon) in order to enable it to produce 80 F-14 fighters for sale to Iran.[4] This arrangement was later placed in doubt because of our government's fear that it would create overdependence on a foreign government in the sensitive area of national defense. Faced with a Hobson's choice between advancing public funds and relying on those of a foreign government, Congress, in the person of influential senators, ultimately threw its weight behind a resumption of Iran's advance payment schedule. The senators' reasoning was that resumption would persuade American bankers to reestablish a line of credit to Grumman and so avoid the necessity of U.S. government loans. Foreign government influence is not, however, limited to public policy involving defense contractors. In early 1975, the ubiquitous Iranian government bought 13 percent of the stock of Pan American World Airways.[5] That the sale affected public policy was indicated by the fact that it required consideration and approval by the U.S. government and occurred against a backdrop of Pan American's cries for help (see below).

Extending the Concept of Essentiality

This incident leads into a second (and related) fresh element in the blurring phenomenon: the erosion of the old distinction between the government's treatment of defense-related and "civilian" industries. The essentiality of the former has been much better established in public policy than has been the case for "civilian" industries. Emergency assistance to the latter in times of severe economic depression has of course been extended in the past, as when the Reconstruction Finance Corporation temporarily acquired many businesses in the 1930s. Under the terms of a 1971 statute, however, this notion was enshrined in law without regard to general economic conditions. The statute, which narrowly passed both houses of Congress, permits the government to guarantee up to $250 million in bank loans to any corporation whose failure would "adversely and seriously" affect the national economy or that of any region.[6] The occasion for congressional action was to assure the production of a Lockheed plane (the L-1011 Tri-Star Airbus) designed for sale, not to the Air Force, but to commercial carriers. Treasury Secretary John Connally's assertion that the loan guarantee was necessary for defense purposes was not confirmed by Undersecretary David Packard, who conceded that an economic rather than a defense issue was involved.[7] Has a principle been established? Lockheed's defense-contractor status muddies the picture, but, taking the statutory wording at face value, the answer is, yes. Any firm able to establish its economic essentiality can at least try for assistance via this law. Even when the law is not invoked—and it has not been since the Tri-Star incident—important nondefense companies now receive close official attention when they are in trouble. Last year's collapse of the Franklin National Bank, barely in the top twenty among the nation's banks, attracted the concern of the government because of its fear that the public would think all banks were unsafe. The Comptroller of the Currency therefore requested the Federal Deposit Insurance Corporation to negotiate for Franklin's purchase in order to keep its doors open.[8] (The successful bidder, it may be noted, was a European bank.) Also in 1974, Pan American made a desperate appeal to the Civil Aeronautics Board for what it boldly called a "national interest payment."[9] Though the request was rejected, the airline received the assurance of some government steps to ease its situation.[10]

Organizational Confusion

The final trend to be noted is the increased use of policy instruments that defy neat labeling as public or private. The mushroom growth of a third sector with some of the characteristics of both has been widely noted,[11] but it is doubtful whether there is yet much consciousness among citizens of the extent of their entanglement in this sector. In particular, the proliferation of loan-guarantee programs—often under the auspices of a "government-sponsored private corporation"—have attracted little attention because they have been outside the national budget. This is an undoubted attraction to policymakers, sensitive to the size of the budget deficit. Both the Johnson and Nixon administrations employed extra-budgetary credit to the point where the government's own projections for fiscal 1974 placed the commitments at around $250 billion.[12]

Confusion results not only from uncertainty as to how the loan guarantees will actually be employed but also from the organizational arrangements that often follow in the wake of joint public-private action. A prime example of the latter is the Regional Rail Organization Act of 1973. Lack of space permits not even a brief summary of this voluminous statute, which seeks to financially rescue eight bankrupt railroads in the Northeast and Middle West along with their employees. A measure of the law's complexity is *Congressional Quarterly's* comment that "Observers disagreed on whether it was likely to save the railroads as a private-enterprise operation or constituted a first step toward railroad nationalization."[13] Another illustration of the difficulty in sorting out the governmental from the private is the Act's establishment of "an incorporated nonprofit association to be known as the United States Railway Association" to plan and finance a new rail system out of the present chaos and a "for-profit corporation" to be known as the Consolidated Rail Corporation to run it.[14] So long as half of the latter body's outstanding indebtedness consists of obligations of the Association or of the federal government, seven or eight of the fifteen members of the Corporation's board of directors will be government appointees.[15] A reasonable arrangement under the circumstances, one might say, but joint boards have contributed little to clarifying accountability in the past. For example, government directors sat as a minority on the board of the Union Pacific Railroad from 1862 to 1897—as they do now for the Communications Satellite Corporation—but neither in these nor other cases have they had a significant influence on policy-making.[16] Perhaps they will have if they are temporarily in the majority, but this possibility would create another and greater anomaly: government direction of a "for-profit corporation" in the land of free enterprise.

The Prospects for Public Policy

It can be safely said that the three elements in public policy that have been noted add up to a more intricate mixed economy and that we can expect even more intricacy in the future. This raises the question of whether the United States has reached a policy crossroads. Has the blurring of the public-private distinction reached the point where piecemeal action does not suffice to deal with it?

Certainly there is no consensus that this is so. Those who are aroused about the power of private corporations often propose steps that go beyond incrementalism. Thus, they may urge that the country adopt a national development plan so as to prevent global corporations from continuing to be "the principal planners of the society."[17] Or, when certain corporate giants draw the public's ire, as the international oil companies did recently, there are often calls for nationalization or at least the creation of a rival company owned by the government. Though the United States has moved closer to the point where seminal legislation is seriously considered, public opinion still is some distance, say, from the nationalization and partial nationalization going on in Great Britain. Support for this statement can be found in the public opinion polls. In 1974, Louis Harris found a 50 to 39 percent split against "the federal government taking over big companies that have gone broke, such as Lockheed and the Penn Central Railroad, which are essential businesses."[18] Even the statement that the federal government should put up money "to save big companies that have gone broke but are essential businesses" lost out by 46 to 43 percent. Under these circumstances, it is not surprising to find that, though Congress enacted the principle into law of aiding enterprises essential to the economy, it then proceeded in its usual incremental, ad hoc fashion by authorizing only enough loan guarantee funds to rescue the corporation whose troubles were the occasion for the law. This action suggests that, short of economic catastrophe, the more intricate mixed economy of the future will emerge only gradually and with the usual pluralistic policy-making methods.

If it is likely that piecemeal action will continue, are there any indications of the kinds of policy proposals that will gain high visibility? An unusual feature, such as the involvement of foreign governments or the extension of the concept of essentiality beyond national defense consid-erations, appears to attract notice, as has been observed above. Will a gigantic program do so? There is evidence that size alone is not sufficient to arouse the interest and concern of the public. Take the matter of govern-ment involvement in mortgage transactions, for example. According to the latest figures,[19] mortgage insurance loans made by the Federal Housing Administration total almost $2 billion in direct loans or credits and almost $85 billion in guarantees and insurance. When the mortgage guarantee program of the Veterans Administration is added in, the total obligation of the government is around $116 billion! Yet, these agencies operate these vast programs with a minimum of public attention. It is also worth noting that the total amount of federal direct and guaranteed loans outstanding as of June 30, 1975, was almost $360 billion.

Given these facts, one suspects that an unusual element in a program, rather than its size, is what attracts attention to it. This suspicion is reinforced when one considers the proposal of the Ford Administration, in mid-1975, for a $100 billion Energy Independence Authority. The plan was stimulated by the shock of the 1973 oil crisis and a desire to achieve national self-sufficiency in energy. The Authority was to have a life of ten years, during which it would have at its disposal up to $25 billion in equity capital and authority to underwrite $75 billion worth of commercial loans. Thus, it would not only provide financial aid to private industry but would also—at least for a short time—own operating facilities related to energy produc-tion, transportation, or transmission. The Authority was the brainchild of Vice President Nelson A. Rockefeller, who told a business gathering that the proposal did not mean a government takeover of energy production but "exactly the opposite"—a new system of federal aid that would help the private sector help the nation achieve energy self-sufficiency.[20] Despite such reassurances, the plan faced strong opposition within the administra-tion before it was presented to Congress and a mixed reception afterwards. On the basis of extensive interviews in Washington, a *New York Times* reporter found that the critics included "environmentalists worried about pollution, liberal Democrats opposed to giving handouts to big business, philosophic conservatives concerned about the growing power of the Fed-eral Government, fiscal conservatives worried about the possible threat to the free flow of capital and oil state representatives uneasy about assisting energy competitors."[21] Supporters of the plan generally echoed the Rock-efeller view that "the minute the President declared a national policy that self-sufficiency was our goal, this automatically cut across the basic free market structure and concept."[22] Though the Rockefeller plan appeared, by the end of 1975, to be as dead in the water as the vice president's own political fortunes, the notion of vastly expanding energy production through active government participation remained alive. For example, in February 1975, Senator Henry M. Jackson had in fact introduced a bill that went far beyond the administration plan in terms of government involvement in energy operations.[23] Whatever the ultimate fate of proposals for vast government involvement in energy production, it is apparent from the kinds of issues they generate that the subject will be viewed as attention-demanding and controversial.

Notes

1. Leon Festinger, *A Theory of Cognitive Dissonance* (Stanford, California: Stanford University Press, 1957). See also, Harold H. Kassarjian and Joel B. Cohen, "Cognitive Dissonance and Consumer Behavior: Reactions to the Surgeon General's Report on Smoking and Health," *California Management Review* 8 (Fall 1965): 55-64.

2. Jack L. Walker, "Performance Gaps, Policy Research, and Political Entrepreneurs: Toward a Theory of Agenda Setting," *Policy Studies Journal* 3 (Autumn 1974): 112-113.

3. *New York Times*, December 2, 1974.

4. *Ibid.*, August 20, 1974.

5. *Ibid.*, February 9, 1975.

6. Emergency Loan Guarantee Act of 1971 (Public Law 92-70), Sec. 4. (85 Stat. 178) and Sec. 8. (85 Stat. 181), respectively. See also *New York Times*, August 3, 1971.

7. *New York Times*, Editorial, June 11, 1971.

8. *Time*, October 21, 1974, p. 56; *New York Times*, October 4, 1974.

9. *Time*, September 23, 1974, p. 83.

10. *New York Times*, October 7, 1974.

11. Eli Ginzberg, Dale L. Hiestand, and Beatrice G. Reubens, *The Pluralistic Economy* (New York, McGraw-Hill Book Co., 1965). Bruce L.R. Smith, "The Future of the Not-for-Profit Corporations," *The Public Interest* (Summer 1967): 127-142.

12. Special Analysis. *Budget of the United States, Fiscal Year 1972,* p. 83.

13. *Congressional Quarterly Almanac*, 1973, p. 465.

14. Regional Rail Reorganization Act of 1973 (Public Law 93-236), Sec. 201 (87 Stat. 968) and Sec. 301 (87 Stat. 1004), respectively.

15. *Ibid.*, Sec. 301 (d). The Association is a government corporation of the District of Columbia whose eleven-member board of directors includes

"seven nongovernment members" selected by the president and confirmed by the Senate from a list of nominees submitted by private organizations as well as the National Governors Conference, National League of Cities, and Conference of Mayors. The president of the Association, who is chosen by the board of directors, has the swing vote on the fifteen-member board of directors of Consolidated Rail Corporation. As the "nongovernment members" dominate the Association's board, presumably they would elect one of their number.

16. See Lloyd D. Musolf, *Mixed Enterprise: A Developmental Perspective* (Lexington, Massachusetts: Lexington Books, D.C. Heath and Company, 1972), Chapter 4.

17. Richard Barnet and Ronald Muller, "A Reporter at Large: Global Reach-II," *The New Yorker*, December 9, 1974, p. 149.

18. *Sacramento Bee,* September 9, 1974.

19. Figures in this and the succeeding three sentences are taken from the *Treasury Bulletin* for October 1975, pp. 132-138, published by the United States Treasury, Washington, D.C.

20. *National Journal*, October 25, 1975, p. 1469.

21. *New York Times,* October 9, 1975.

22. *National Journal*, October 25, 1975, p. 1469.

23. *Ibid.*, p. 1471.

12

The Debate on Public Ownership of U.S. Railroads: A Comparative Perspective

James A. Dunn, Jr.

As the U.S. federal government becomes inexorably involved in a massive program of loans and subsidies to the financially hard-pressed railroad industry, the perennial debate over the question of public versus private ownership of the railroads has flared anew. "Nationalization" of the railroads involves many different political, economic, and legal issues and is much too broad a topic to be fully treated here. But one important element in the public debate over nationalization, *viz.*, the relevance of other nations' experience with publicly-owned rail systems to the current American problem, appears increasingly central to the arguments of both sides and deserves to be examined at greater length. Indeed, since most of the references to other nations' rail experience are made for the purpose of bolstering ideological positions on one side or the other, the way in which this potentially valuable comparative policy debate is conducted appears in need of a reformulation that will inhibit polemics and encourage thoughtful scrutiny from a public policy perspective. The purpose of this chapter is to show the direction that such a reformulation might usefully take.

Ideology and the Nationalization Debate

On one side of the argument spokesmen for the rail industry/regulatory complex not only continue to profess their faith in a free enterprise "income-based" solution to current rail problems, they also claim that other countries' experiences with publicly-owned rail systems prove that nationalization is less efficient and hence less desirable than America's privately-owned rail system. Former Secretary of Transportation Claude S. Brinegar undoubtedly represented the views of the vast majority of members of the rail industry/regulatory complex when he told a congressional subcommittee that

Rail nationalization is unnecessary and would solve little, except perhaps hide some of the short-term Northeast area problems under the bed of the Federal budget. Experiences elsewhere indicate that nationalization only means increasing subsidies and declining resource efficiency—something our nation can ill afford. The largely state-owned rail systems of Japan, Britain, Germany, France, and Italy now report losses that in total exceed $2 billion per year.[1]

On the other side are the critics who see too much private enterprise as the root of the problem and call for government ownership and operation of the railroads as the only way to achieve a variety of socially desirable ends. Environmentalist Barry Commoner, for example, excoriates the

. . . apologists for private ownership [who] would have us believe that the unprofitability of the nationalized railroads is a result of their "inefficiency." What the evidence really shows, however, is that U.S. railroads—or at least some of them— run at a profit because they have refused to provide passenger services. . . . The choice is between social and private profit.[2]

The ideological nature of this exchange becomes painfully evident when the reader discovers that both Secretary Brinegar and Professor Commoner were basing their arguments *on the same set of data!* The "facts" they each were referring to were compiled by the Union Pacific Railroad Corporation (which could hardly be accused of bias in favor of nationalization), and were published by the railroad as *A Brief Survey of Railroads of Selected Industrial Countries*. The survey compiles economic and financial data on all American Class I line-haul railroads and a number of publicly-owned rail systems, including the five mentioned by Brinegar: Britain, France, West Germany, Italy, and Japan.

Differences Between U.S. Railroads and Five Publicly-Owned Systems

The salient points of the Union Pacific's Data are summarized in table 12-1. A close examination of the data reveals that, compared to American railroads, the five publicly-owned rail systems exhibit the following characteristics:

1. They have much higher operating deficits and receive much larger public subsidies.
2. They have many more employees.
3. They have many more maintenance-of-way employees per mile of track.
4. They produce a much greater amount of passenger transportation.
5. They get a much greater share of their revenue from passenger transportation.
6. They produce much less freight transportation.
7. They get a much smaller share of their revenue from freight transportation.
8. They have a much shorter average freight haul.

Table 12-1
Comparison of U.S. and Five Publicly-Owned Rail Systems, 1971

	U.S.	U.K.	France	W. Germany	Italy	Japan
Route Length (Miles)	205,000	11,643	22,940	18,227	10,185	12,976
No. of Employees	544,333	268,562	296,411	415,788	199,834	450,338
Av. No. of Maintenance of Way Employees per mile of track	.4	2.6	3.1	4.3	4.5	6.4
Passenger Miles (Millions)	6,939	18,720	25,448	23,359	21,094	118,260
Freight Ton Miles (Millions)	739,743	15,073	45,629	44,016	11,799	41,339
Passenger Revenues As % of Total R. R. Operating Revenue	2,3%	48.2	34.0	22.5	47.8	74.0
Freight Revenues As % of Total R. R. Operating Rev.	93.1	35.8	51.8	59.2	38.3	21.9
Av. Length of Freight Haul (Miles)	532	71	173	122	197	203
Govt. Subsidies and Other Payments (Millions of $)	34	180	1,184	831	470	N.A.

Source: Adapted from *A Brief Survey of Railroads of Selected Industrial Countries*, pp. xi-xii

These data suggest that we are in the presence of two very different types of rail systems, not just in terms of their ownership but in terms of their physical and economic characteristics and functions as well. The difference between the U.S. railroads and those in each of the five foreign countries is much like the difference between a wholesale-industrial enterprise and a retail commercial one. American railroads are wholesale-industrial factories that produce freight transportation in trainload lots for a relatively few large shippers. They benefit from much longer average hauls, automated freight handling systems, and lower maintenance costs on road-beds devoted mainly to freight trains. The European and Japanese railroads, on the other hand, are much more heavily involved in the retail-commercial business of passenger transportation. From conductors to porters, dining car stewards, and maintenance-of-way employees, passenger transport is much more labor-intensive and hence more costly than freight transport.

In their freight operations, the European and Japanese railroads do not have the advantages of the long hauls, the large amounts of bulk cargo (coal, grain, wood products, etc.) or the huge GNP that U.S. railroads have. Other things being equal, then, we would expect these systems to be more costly to operate and probably to lose more money than American railroads, whether or not they were publicly owned.

Differences Within the U.S. Rail System

The northeastern rail crisis did not result solely or even principally from the alleged mismanagement and/or financial chicanery of the officers of the Penn Central and other area railroads.[3] It stemmed mainly from the nature of the rail net in that region. Built earlier than roads further west, Northeast railroads developed into a spider web of local and branch lines serving a relatively dense population over fairly short distances. They transport a high percentage of manufactured goods and they retained a substantial amount of the nation's passenger traffic until the arrival of Amtrack in 1971. Western and southern railroads, on the other hand, tend to be primarily long-haul trunk lines with a minimal amount of branch line service. They rely heavily on the kind of freight traffic that railroads are best equipped to ship at a profit: bulk commodities going long distances. In other words the profitable railroads like the Southern Pacific, Union Pacific, Norfolk and Western and the like are more similar to the archtypical American railroad mentioned above, whereas the northeastern railroads are closer to the European type railway.[4]

These regional differences should be kept in mind during discussions of the question of public ownership. The position of the railroad industry, especially the western and southern companies, is that since the nation's railroads comprise one interdependent system, "nationalization of one segment of this system would lead, ultimately, to government ownership of the whole industry. It is difficult to see how privately-owned and financed carriers could compete on equal terms with railroads financed by taxpayers through the federal treasury."[5] While this argument may seem superficially plausible it is actually an unfounded assertion which ignores the regional differences between U.S. railroads. There is no reason to suppose that any program of public ownership of unprofitable railroads in the Northeast would entail "nationalization" in the sense that all the nation's railroads, regardless of economic prospects and financial condition, would come under government ownership. As for competition between private and publicly-owned carriers, the northeastern roads are such an important part of the total U.S. rail system, in terms of the amount of extra-regional traffic that originates or terminates there, that railroads in other parts of the country would clearly benefit more from a publicly-owned Northeast rail system which continued a high level of service than a private one that was dramatically shrunken.

The industry's contention that public and private systems could not long coexist also ignores the experience of several other nations which saw precisely such a coexistence for a considerable number of years. In France, for example, the government operated a railway made up largely of unprofitable lines that it nevertheless considered necessary for the military defense and economic expansion of the country. This State railway functioned side by side with the five major private companies for a period of fifty years (1878-1938) until the collapse of the private companies during the Great Depression made their nationalization inevitable.[6] Closer to home, the successful operation of the publicly-owned Canadian National and the privately-owned Canadian Pacific railroads shows that even in a North American geographic and economic environment public ownership of one segment does not automatically and inevitably entail nationalization of the entire rail system.[7]

Thus when spokesmen for the rail industry/regulatory complex emphasize the deficits of publicly-owned railroads abroad and imply that this is somehow due to the inherent inefficiencies of public ownership, or when these spokesmen express a kind of domestic "domino theory" by implying that public and private railroads cannot coexist within the same system, they are doing a great disservice to the truth. On the other hand, advocates of the nationalization of all U.S. railroads must realize that at the present time this is not necessary, given the great regional differences between them. Partisans of public ownership should realize that the recent experi-

Table 12-2

Changes in Route Length of Publicly-Owned Railways in Five Industrial Countries, 1960-1971

	1960 Route-Km.	*1971 Route-Km.*	*Absolute Change*	*Percent Change*
Britain	29,562	18,746	−10,786	−36.5
France	38,858	35,624	−3,234	−8.3
W. Germany	30,608	29,267	−1,341	−4.4
Italy	16,339	16,099	−300	−1.8
Japan	20,482	20,883	+401	+2.0

Source: James Sloss, Thomas J. Humphrey, and Forest N. Krutter, *An Analysis and Evaluation of Past Experience in Rationalizing Railroad Networks* (Washington, D.C.: U.S. Department of Transportation, Office of University Research, 1974), p. 156.

ence of the five industrial nations that were used in the comparisons above indicates that public ownership of all or part of a country's rail system is far from being a panacea for its rail problems.

Public Ownership Is a Policy Parameter, Not a Panacea

All railroads in modern democracies, regardless of ownership, have been contending with the same unfavorable trends in the general economic and technological environment. Publicly-owned railroads in Europe and Japan have seen a steady decline in their relative share of total transportation activity. In France, for example, the National Railways hauled 62.1 percent of the nation's total freight kilometers in 1958 but only 39.2 percent in 1972.[8] Britain saw her railway passenger miles fall from 22,150 million in 1961 to 18,895 million in 1970.[9] Not only is rail's share of the transport market declining but in most industrial nations public ownership has not prevented the physical size of the railroads from shrinking also. Table 12-2 reveals that this shrinkage was quite severe in Britain and moderate to slight in the other European nations. Over the same period from 1960 to 1971 the U.S. railway system underwent a moderate decline of 5.9 percent, going from 217, 552 to 204,696 miles of class I line-haul route.[10]

Thus nationalization does not immunize railroads against the problems of modern post-industrial society. When a democratic government attempts to deal with the crucial problem of intermodal competition (railroads versus truck, car, bus, plane, barge, etc.), the question of public versus private ownership is not so much a policy as a policy parameter. Rail ownership does not, in itself, directly affect the modal split. Rather it determines, or at least helps to determine, the types of policies a government can adopt that do directly or indirectly affect the modal split.

Types of Rail Regulatory Policies

What it means to say that a rail system's ownership acts as a parameter of government policy can be better understood in the context of the types of policies that Western democratic governments use to affect the role of the railroads in the national transport system. There are three basic types of such policies:

1. Policies that *encourage economic "efficiency" (profit) in the rail transport enterprise.* This includes the dropping of unprofitable branch lines, reductions in the labor force, new technology, mergers, and reorganizations of the structure of relations between the railways and the government.

2. Policies that *protect the rail transport enterprise from the effects of economic "inefficiency."* This includes such things as government loans, grants, and loan guarantees for capital construction, operating subsidies, tax privileges, cancellation of railway debts owed to the public treasury.

3. Policies that *directly change the balance of competitive advantage between rail transport and competing modes.* These include higher taxes and tolls for trucks and barges, limitations on the number of road haulage licenses issued, increased taxes on petroleum products with railways and other public transport enterprises exempted from the tax, restrictions on size and weight of trucks, etc.

It should be clear that some types of policies are more likely to be stressed in systems where the railroads are privately owned while others will be adopted more readily under public ownership systems. For example the third type of policy, changing the intermodal split, would be more likely to be acceptable to the general public in nations where the rail system is publicly owned. This has indeed been the case in several European countries. In France the policy of *contingentement*, i.e., severely restricting the issuance of licenses for long-haul truck routes that compete with the S.N.C.F. National Railways, is still followed.[11] In West Germany, the Leber Plan (named after Social Democratic Transport Minister Georg Leber) provided a tax on all modes of transport as a means of raising money to subsidize the Deutsche Bundesbahn.[12] One does not need a terribly vivid imagination to envisage the political outcry likely to be unleashed in the United States by truckers, teamsters, and shippers if the federal government were to attempt to shift a significant portion of freight out of trucks and onto the privately-owned railroads in order to increase the profits of the private rail companies.

Constraint of Other Transport Modes Is the Key Rail Policy Issue

One thing, at least, is certain. The federal government is engaged in an escalation of its involvement in the operation of the nation's rail system. It will soon be spending much more than the $2 billion that so horrified Secretary Brinegar in 1973. A recent report by the U.S. Railway Association has called for an outlay of $7.3 billion to restructure and rebuild the railroads in the Northeast.[13] There is very little chance that the Consolidated Rail Corporation, the would-be recipient of these funds, will ever be able to repay a dime of that sum. Congress is also preparing grant programs which would fight unemployment by paying railroads to hire unemployed workers to rebuild the roadbeds.[14] The country will soon have the frustrating and seemingly paradoxical experience of spending more and more public money for less and less rail service. In the long run, however, massive public subsidies are likely to create pressures of their own for public ownership.

Thus one sees that the policy debate over rail transportation can no longer be a question of preserving privately-owned railroads in order to save the public billions of dollars. The public subsidies are going to be given no matter who owns the railroads. Nor can it be only a question of appropriating money for nationalized railroads and providing the country with efficient rail service and many ecological and energy benefits. The nationalized systems abroad have had to struggle to get along, and merely increasing public funding has not resolved their fundamental problems. The questions that should be posed in the course of the policy debate are: how much and what kinds of rail service do we need now and in the foreseeable future? How much constraint will the various nonrail transport interests stand for if constraints are necessary to preserve a viable rail system for the country? How much more constraint would be acceptable if the railroads were publicly owned than if they remained privately owned?

Making hard decisions on these questions is bound to offend at least some vested interests in the transportation industry. And these kinds of constraints are never popular with public opinion which is still responsive to certain kinds of anti-statist, laissez-faire slogans and shibboleths. The Ford Administration recognizes this and has chosen to cloak its modest efforts to shift the balance of competitive advantage more toward the railroads under the guise of abolishing government constraints on the transport industry. While President Ford makes speeches to the U.S. Chamber of Commerce calling for "deregulation," his Secretary of Transportation, William Coleman, indicates he plans to ask barges and trucks to pay heavier taxes.[15] The deregulation theme may have many political benefits to a president guarding his right flank against a conservative challenge to his renomination, but it is not likely to clarify public debate on transportation policy. It all but assures that the ideological theme of free-enterprise versus government control will continue to obscure the real transport policy options.

Conclusion

The United States has the largest rail system in the world, and the only one which has been almost totally privately-owned from its inception to the present day. These two facts are obviously related to the present difficulties it is experiencing. But they do not mean that the problems facing U.S. rail policymakers are unique and that the experience of other nations is irrelevant. There is a clear need for thorough and unbiased studies of foreign transportation policies and problems. Political scientists have an important role to play in providing these studies. The successes and failures, the differences and similarities, the underlying principles and assumptions of a variety of other national transport policies need to be examined by political scientists—who are professionally sensitive to the political and ideological uses that can be made of their work—as well as by the more specialized transportation "experts," be they engineers or economists. The results of this type of comparative study, when presented to policymakers in the executive and legislative branches, to the scholarly community, and to the general public, can not fail to improve the quality and utility of debate in this increasingly important area of public policy.

Notes

1. U.S., Congress, House, Committee on Interstate and Foreign Commerce, Subcommittee on Transportation and Aeronautics, *Northeast Rail Transportation*, 93rd Cong., 1st sess., 1973, serial no. 93-30, p. 218.

2. Barry Commoner, "Nationalizing the Railroads," *Current* (February, 1974): 53, 55.

3. The financial activites of these officers will ultimately be judged in the courts. An assessment of their management practices and problems is offered in Joseph R. Doughen and Peter Binzen, *The Wreck of the Penn Central* (Boston: Little, Brown and Co., 1971).

4. The regional differences in the U.S. rail system and the ways public policy should respond to them are discussed in the testimony presented by L.E. Dennis, executive director, Brotherhood of Railway, Airline, and Steamship Clerks, Freight Handlers, Express and Station Employees, AFL-CIO in U.S., Congress, *Northeast Rail Transportation*, pp. 483-484.

5. Union Pacific Railroad Company, "A Brief Survey of Railroads of Selected Industrial Countries," New York: mimeo, 1973, p. v.

6. Kimon A. Doukas, *The French Railroads and the State* (New York: Columbia University Press, 1945).

7. G.R. Stevens, *History of the Canadian National Railways* (New York: The Macmillan Co., 1973); J. Lorne McDougall, *Canadian Pacific: A Brief History* (Montreal: McGill University Press, 1968).

8. France, Institut national de la statistique et des etudes economiques, *Les Transports en France 1971-1972*, no. 921 des collections de l'I. N. S. E. E., serie C, no. 27, p. 14.

9. A.W.J. Thompson and L.C. Hunter, *The Nationalized Transport Industries* (London: Heineman Educational Books, 1973), p. 154.

10. U.S., Bureau of the Census, *Statistical Abstract of the United States 1974*, 95th edition, (Washington, D.C.: U.S. Government Printing Office, 1974), p. 568.

11. J.H. Chapulut, Jean Frebault, and Jacques Pellegrin, *Le marche des transports* (Paris: Seuil, 1970), p. 69.

12. Federal Republic of Germany, Bundesverkehrsministerium, *Transport Policy Report 1970* (Bonn: Bonner Universtäts Buchdruckerei, 1970).

13. United States Railway Association, *Preliminary System Plan for Restructuring Railroads in the Northeast and Midwest Region*, 2 vols. (Washington, D.C.: U.S.R.A., 1975), p. 13.

14. "Emergency Rail Employment Bill Reported," *Congressional Quarterly Weekly Reports* 33, 39 (September 27, 1975): 2088-2089.

15. Prudence Crewdson, "Ford Presses Deregulation as Alternative to Proposed Consumer Advocacy Agency," *Congressional Quarterly Weekly Reports* 33, 19 (May 10, 1975): 988-989.

13 The Impact of Representation for Diffuse Interests: Lessons from Patent Policy

Lawrence A. Baum

In the analysis of interest-group politics, a useful distinction can be made between specific and diffuse interests.[1] Specific interests are those strongly felt by relatively small groups of people. Diffuse interests, in contrast, are distributed over a broad public to whose members they have relatively little importance. Specific interests are exemplified by the interests of producers, while diffuse interests are exemplified by those of consumers.[2]

Specific and diffuse interests tend to play very different roles in the political process. The divergence in their roles is due largely to the fact that specific interests are more easily organized to take political action. This advantage has at least two bases. First, persons with specific interests are more likely to be aware of those interests than are persons with diffuse interests. Second, the large size and small stake of groups with diffuse interests limit their members' incentives to organize and to take concerted political action.[3] Groups with diffuse interests sometimes can overcome their disadvantages to achieve effective political organization, but in most instances they fare poorly at organization in comparison with groups that have specific interests.

Differences in organization generally translate into differences in representation before policymakers. The well-organized group may have representatives continually in contact with agencies whose decisions affect its interests. A poorly organized group, in contrast, is likely to obtain only an irregular and limited presence before policymakers. For this reason, government decisionmakers hear much more from those with specific interests than from those with diffuse interests.

The extent of an interest's representation is only one determinant of its success in the policy-making process, so that an interest with weaker representation than its opponents is not doomed to failure. But extreme differences in representation between competing interests may virtually ensure victory for the side heard more clearly. Thus a diffuse interest in conflict with a specific interest tends to suffer unfavorable policy outcomes.

Nowhere is the relative weakness of diffuse interests more clearly manifested than in the field of economic regulation. Regulatory agencies frequently decide questions on which the immediate interests of producer groups and of their consumers conflict, issues such as the setting of minimum rates for services and the limitation of entry into a regulated industry. Producers generally are well represented before regulatory agencies in formal and informal proceedings, while the consumer interest usually lacks regular representation because of limited organization and agency procedures. This condition facilitates the much-lamented process by which regulators develop lines of policy favorable to the industries they regulate, policy frequently unfavorable to consumers.[4]

If poor representation helps to explain the adoption of policies which harm consumers and other groups with diffuse interests, one obvious remedy is to provide mechanisms of representatation for these interests. Thus E.E. Schattschneider advocated that political parties be strengthened as vehicles to represent broadly shared interests in society.[5] With the same goal, Ralph Nader and others seek to mobilize consumers to support their own interests on important policy questions.[6]

The current proposal to establish a Consumer Advocacy Agency within the federal government derives in large part from the same motivation as the Schattschneider and Nader programs.[7] A major function of the proposed agency would be to act as representative of consumer interests before regulatory agencies and other policymakers. In effect, the proposal is intended to remedy the difficulty of mobilizing consumers by providing an institutional surrogate to support their interests. The result, its proponents hope, would be to induce agency policies more favorable to consumer interests than those of the present. Indeed, people on both sides of the debate over the proposed agency seem to assume that it would be effective in reshaping the policies of agencies with which it interacted.[8]

Whether a Consumer Advocacy Agency would have the impact desired by its advocates is a complex question. The essence of the question, however, concerns the assumed linkage between improved representation and improved policy outcomes. Limited representation is an important weakness of consumer interests in regulatory agencies, but even well-representated consumers may enjoy little success because of other disadvantages. To evaluate attempts to improve representation for diffuse interests, we need to understand more fully the impact of representation as a variable on the outcome of conflicts between interests.

Efforts to determine the effect of group representation on policy outcomes face the same difficulties that have plagued efforts to measure interest-group influence generally.[9] Precise measurement of influence or of representation as a means of influence is impossible. However, it is possible to gain some insight into the effect of group representation by examining a policy area in which the representation of interests varies among agencies while the issues involved are similar. In such an area, the impact of interest representation may be discerned in general terms. This chapter will take that approach to analyze the linkage between representation of diffuse interests and the policies of government agencies.

Representation and Outputs in Patent Policy

The field of patent policy is well suited to the kind of analysis that has been proposed. The central issue in patent policy is one on which specific and diffuse interests conflict, and policymakers in all three branches of the federal government deal with this issue in comparable form. The diffuse interest is well represented in proceedings in some agencies, but not in others. The policy-making process in each agency may be examined to reach some conclusions about the effect of representation for the diffuse interest on patterns of patent policy.[10]

The central issue in patent policy concerns the standard of patentability. The patent grant is a form of bargain, in which the federal government allows the inventor a limited monopoly over his invention in exchange for its public disclosure. The "standard of patentability," the severity of the requisites for inventors to receive patents, constitutes the key term of the bargain.

The patent statute enacted by Congress contains requirements for the receipt of patents, and these requirements help to shape the standard of patentability in the Patent Office and in the courts.[11] But the statutory language is necessarily general in form, so that administrators and judges must exercise considerable discretion in its interpretation. In effect each agency establishes its own operative standard of patentability, and standards inevitably vary among agencies.

The attorneys who apply for patents on behalf of corporate and individual clients constitute a specific interest which benefits from relatively low standards of patentability. The lower the standards, the surer and easier is the task of obtaining patents for clients. Accordingly, patent attorneys have a strongly felt interest in the establishment of lenient standards. Organizations of the "patent bar" act as advocates for this interest in Congress, in the Patent Office, and in federal courts.[a] In the legislative arena they are aided by manufacturing and commercial interests that benefit from ownership of patents.

There is no specific interest which favors high standards of patentability. Those businesses which suffer from competitors' ownership of patents comprise a large and vaguely defined group. Consumers suffer in the short run and probably in the long run from the establishment of low standards,

[a]The most inclusive and important of these organizations is the American Patent Law Association, with a membership of approximately 4,000.

which allow monopoly prices for inventions of relatively limited benefit; their interest is particularly diffuse, an interest of a group whose members are almost totally unaware of their stake in questions of patent policy.[12]

The Patent Office

The agency whose standard of patentability has the greatest impact is the Patent Office, a bureau within the Department of Commerce which passes on each application for patent.[b] Patent Office rules of procedure insure a monopoly of representation for the patent bar and its interest. The Office's policies effectively are made in thousands of individual decisions to accept or reject patent applications. These proceedings are *ex parte*, with the patent examiner faced only by the attorney who represents the patent applicant.

The Patent Office consistently has take a lenient attitude toward the requisites for patentability. In the past decade nearly 70 percent of all applicants have been granted patents, the result of a standard generally considered to be quite low.[13] Thus the Office's policies are favorable to the interest of the patent bar. Moreover, the Patent Office frequently acts as ally of the patent bar in the bar's efforts to obtain favorable legislation.

Patent Office policies that support the patent bar's interest are a product of several factors, including the policy preferences of the agency's officials and its administrative problems. These administrative problems stem from the backlog of patent applications to be processed. The backlog produces pressure for speedy handling of applications. This pressure in turn favors the awarding of patents, chiefly because it limits the patent examiner's search of existing inventions that might anticipate the invention for which a patent is sought. The inequality of representation afforded competing interests plays one important part in the process that leads to lenient standards. Continual interaction between patent examiners and patent attorneys gives the bar some opportunity to shape examiners' attitudes toward patentability, and the arguments of patent lawyers for particular clients constitute a subtle pressure in favor of accepting applications. Most important, the absence of representation for those who favor high standards means that no advocate searches for evidence which would contradict the applicant's claims. The significance of this factor is suggested by the frequency with which courts invalidate issued patents on the basis of evidence that was not possessed by the examiner who allowed these patents.[14]

Even if there were equal representation for the two interests in Patent Office proceedings, other factors probably would impel the Office to adopt relatively lenient standards of patentability. However, the absence of

[b] As of January 1975, the official name of the Patent Office has been changed to the Patent and Trademark Office. The shorter name will be used in this chapter.

representation for those in disagreement with the patent bar seems to have an important marginal effect on Office standards, such that many applications are allowed patents that otherwise would be denied. Hence the case of the Patent Office suggests the significance of inequality of representation for competing interests.

The CCPA

The Court of Customs and Patent Appeals (CCPA) hears appeals by applicants whom the Patent Office has denied patents or has granted patents narrower than desired.[15] Each disappointed applicant is opposed by a representative from the legal staff of the Patent Office; whatever the Office's orientation in its own decisions, it opposes these appeals wholeheartedly. Accordingly, there is full representation for both sides before the CCPA.

During the first quarter-century of its patent jurisdiction, from 1929 to 1956, the CCPA adopted a high standard of patentability. In line with this standard, the court overturned Patent Office decisions infrequently. The role of the Office as representative for the diffuse interest in high standards played an important part in the CCPA's adoption of these standards. The court's judges, inexperienced in patent questions, gave great deference to Patent Office expertise. If the arguments of patent lawyers have been uncontested, this deference probably would have gone instead to the bar and to its position.

Since 1956, the position of the CCPA has changed dramatically. The court has become the leading judicial advocate of lenient standards of patentability, and it overturns Patent Office decisions nearly twice as frequently as it did prior to 1956. (The proportion of appealed Patent Office decisions modified or reversed by the CCPA prior to 1956 was 22 percent; the proportion since that time has been 40 percent.) This policy change is not a product of interest representation or influence. Rather, it stems from the appointment to the court of several patent attorneys who share the bar's stand on patentability. Their strong personal preferences relegate to insignifance other factors, including the representation of competing interests.

Congress

Congressional policy on patents is made chiefly in subcommittees of the Judiciary Committees. For several decades these subcommittees and their predecessors have taken little action on patent policy, even when interest groups demanded change in the law. This inaction has given Congress a record inclining toward neither interest in patent policy.[16]

If legislative stalemate can be seen as a partial victory for the diffuse interest in patent policy, this success may be ascribed largely to the work of the Department of Justice. Because of the roles of its Antitrust and Civil Divisions in patent law, the Department has taken a position strongly supporting high standards of patentability, and it acts as a vigorous advocate for this position in Congress and elsewhere in government.[17] Though legislation never was enacted with such a purpose, the Justice Department to a considerable degree provides the kind of surrogate representation for the diffuse interest in patent policy that a Consumer Advocacy Agency might provide in other policy areas.

If the patent bar were a very powerful group, the representation provided by the Justice Department might not be sufficient to produce legislative stalemate. But the bar is relatively weak and ineffective in legislative lobbying, and its corporate allies have too little interest in patent policy to expend much of the leverage they possess. Faced with competing interests, neither sufficiently powerful to coerce favorable action, congressmen tend to divide ideologically on patent questions. Conservatives, responsive to what they perceive as business interests, generally support the patent bar. Liberals, fearful of private monopolies, provide a base of support for the Justice Department.[c] Because patent policy is of little interest to Congress, this divergence of opinion results in a deadlock that seldom is overcome.

The "Generalist" Courts

The federal district courts hear suits for the infringement of patents, in which the validity of patents held by the plaintiff usually is challenged. District-court decisions in patent cases are appealed to the courts of appeals at a high rate. These two sets of "generalist" courts also hear antitrust suits involving the alleged use of patents for illegal anticompetitive purposes.[18]

In patent infringement cases, both patent owner and accused infringer are usually well represented by attorneys. By instituting suit, patent owners in effect give their defendants an incentive to support the interest in high standards of patentability. The Justice Department is occasionally a party to patent-antitrust litigation, supporting the diffuse interest by stressing the anticompetitive potential of patents. Thus, as in the CCPA, both sides of the dispute over standards of patentability are well represented in the generalist courts.

Judges vary considerably in their positions, but the courts generally

---

[c] In one of the few floor votes on patent legislation in recent years, the Senate in 1962 rejected an amendment opposed by the patent bar, 28-53. Northern Democrats favored the amendment, 23-7, while Southern Democrats and Republicans opposed it, 5-46.

have adopted high standards of patentability. This position is indicated by the high proportion of patents that the courts invalidate for failure to meet their standards. The courts' high standards are a product chiefly of their concern about patents as monopolies and about the leniency of Patent Office standards. Both concerns exist in large part because of the effectiveness of the Justice Department and of attorneys for accused infringers as communicators and advocates. The presence of these two groups in court proceedings plays a powerful role in shaping the policies of the generalist courts.

Discussion

The pattern of federal policy on patents provides some support for those who advocate the creation of mechanisms to represent diffuse interests. Precise measurement of the effect of interest representation on policy outputs was not possible, but this variable appears to exert an important influence on the shape of patent policy. The existence of representation for the diffuse interest in high standards of patentability has had considerable effect on the policies of Congress and of the federal courts. The absence of such representation contributes to Patent Office policies which favor the specific interest in low standards.

At the same time, it must be recalled that the strength of interest groups depends on more than their ability to obtain representation before policymakers. Representation for the interest in high standards of patentability is effective in part because the patent bar is not particularly powerful as a group. Many of the specific interests in the regulatory arena, such as airlines and telephone companies, are considerably more powerful than this segment of the bar. An opponent of these interests might have little chance to equal their influence even if it obtained an equal presence before policymakers.

Moreover, patent policies like other policies are heavily influenced by factors other than interest-group activities. The position of the current Court of Customs and Patent Appeals, for instance, is based chiefly on its members' policy preferences. That example is particularly relevant to the independent regulatory agencies, whose officials often hold views highly favorable to regulated interests. Such views could not easily be overcome simply through the provision of representation for interests opposed to those of regulatees. Similarly, administrative pressures like those faced by the Patent Office may do much to dictate agency policies whatever the configuration of interests on the issues with which the agency deals.

The conclusions from this study, then, must be mixed. The findings suggest that those who wish to strengthen the position of diffuse interests like those of consumers are correct in seeking to provide representation for those interests; representation can make a considerable difference in some situations. Yet interest representation is only one variable helping to determine government policy, and the effect of other variables may be to limit the impact of a Consumer Advocacy Agency. Thus the success of such an agency in changing regulatory policy should be seen not as inevitable but only as a possibility. Diffuse interests are likely to benefit from the provision of improved representation, as the case of patent policy indicates. Whether they will benefit significantly in a particular arena is a more complex question. To answer this question, both reformers and those who pass on the merits of proposed reforms need to take a broad view of the policy-making process in which a mechanism of representation for diffuse interests would operate.

Notes

1. Several scholars have dichotomized interests in ways somewhat similar to the specific-diffuse dichotomy. These include distinctions between special-interest and public-interest groups (Schattschneider), between specific-tangible and general-intangible interests (Cohen), and between privileged and latent groups (Olson). See, respectively, E.E. Schattschneider, *The Semisovereign People* (New York: Holt, Rinehart and Winston, 1960), Chap. 2; Bernard C. Cohen, "Political Communication on the Japanese Peace Settlement," *Public Opinion Quarterly* 20 (Spring 1956): 27-38; and Mancur Olson, *The Logic of Collective Action* (Cambridge: Harvard University Press, 1965), Chap. 1.

2. On consumers, see Mark V. Nadel, *The Politics of Consumer Protection* (New York: Bobbs-Merrill, 1971), esp. Chap. 7.

3. On the effects of size, see Olson, *Logic of Collective Action*, chaps. 1-2.

4. Marver Bernstein, *Regulating Business by Independent Commission* (Princeton: Princeton University Press, 1955); Louis M. Kohlmeier, Jr., *The Regulators: Watchdog Agencies and the Public Interest* (New York: Harper & Row, 1969); Emmette S. Redford, *The Regulatory Process* (Austin: University of Texas Press, 1969).

5. E.E. Schattschneider, *The Struggle for Party Government* (College Park, Md.: University of Maryland, 1948).

6. Nadel, *Politics of Consumer Protection,* Chap. 5.

7. In the 94th Congress this proposal is embodied in S. 200. In its earlier versions, the proposed agency was called the "Consumer Protection Agency."

8. U.S., Congress, House, Subcommittee of the Committee on Government Operations, *To Establish a Consumer Protection Agency*, 93rd Cong., 1st sess., 1973.

9. See Lewis A. Froman, Jr., "Some Effects of Interest Groups in State Politics," *American Political Science Review* 60 (December 1966): 952-62.

10. The short examination of patent policy-making in this chapter necessarily ignores some important features of this subject and oversimplifies others. This examination is based on analysis of quantitative policy-output data, interviews with policymakers, and other data collected by the author. Output data presented in the chapter were gathered by the author. Other aspects of this research are reported in Baum, "The Federal Courts and Patent Validity: An Analysis of the Record," *Journal of the Patent Office Society* 56 (December 1974): 758-87; and idem, "Decision-Making in a Specialized Court: The Court of Customs and Patent Appeals" (Paper delivered at meetings of the Midwest Political Science Association, Chicago, Ill.,May 1-3, 1975). There is an excellent discussion of patent policy-making, with emphasis on the role of the Supreme Court, in Martin Shapiro, *The Supreme Court and Administrative Agencies* (New York: The Free Press, 1968), Chap. 3.

11. U.S., *Code*, vol. 35, secs. 100-12 (1970).

12. Proponents of low standards would argue that consumers ultimately benefit from such standards, because they maximize the incentive to produce useful inventions. The ultimate effects of high and low standards are impossible to determine with certainty, but the weight of opinion from outside the patent bar is that low standards work against the consumer interest. See, for instance, Carl Kaysen and Donald F. Turner, *Antitrust Policy: An Economic and Legal Analysis* (Cambridge: Harvard University Press, 1959), pp. 162-78.

13. Edwin L. Reynolds, "The Standard of Invention in the Patent Office," in *Dynamics of the Patent System*, ed. William B. Ball (New York: Central Book Co., 1960), pp. 5-9.

14. U.S., Congress, Senate, Committee on the Judiciary, *Court Decisions as Guides to Patent Office,* 86th Cong., 2nd sess., 1970, Study No. 25, p. 6. In any suit for patent infringement, the alleged infringer can claim as a defense that the patent involved is invalid for failure to meet the statutory criteria. In effect, the court is asked to find that the Patent Office erred in issuing the patent.

15. On the CCPA, see Baum, "Decision-Making in a Specialized Court."

16. Only one truly major piece of patent legislation has been enacted in the past half-century, the Patent Act of 1952. This Act, favorable to the

patent bar's position, was the product of unusual circumstances. Shapiro, *Supreme Court and Administrative Agencies*, pp. 204-213.

17. Marcus A. Hollabaugh, "The Scott Amendments v. The Second Patent Crusade," *Antitrust Law Journal* 39 (1970): 780-90.

18. On the role of the "generalist" courts, see Baum, "Federal Courts and Patent Validity"; and Abe Fortas, "The Patent System in Distress," *Idea* 14 (Winter 1971): 571-79.

**Part VI
Critiques**

14 Federal Regulation of Economic Activity: Failures and Reforms

George Daly and David W. Brady

Background

Economic regulation refers, in its broadest sense, to any governmental intervention into market processes. So defined, the term encompasses taxes and subsidies of all sorts as well as administrative control over prices, entry, profits and other facets of economic activity. Such regulation has become a pervasive phenomenon in our society and is practiced in one form or another by all levels of government.

Recently, a number of individuals representing a broad and diverse group of economic interests—consumers, businesses, some members of Congress, and the White House—have come to seriously question the wisdom and consequences of regulation by various federal regulatory agencies to the extent that regulatory reform has become an important public and political issue. Among the charges made against regulation are that it encourages inefficiency in a variety of ways, contributes to inflation, serves as a vehicle to protect special rather than public interests, and seriously harms the economy. Defenders of present forms of regulation accuse such critics of oversimplifying reality and argue that while regulation may be an imperfect tool, it is clearly preferable to the conditions—monopoly or "cut-throat competition," for example—that would prevail in its absence. While regulation has always had its opponents and supporters, the movement for reform appears stronger now than it has been since the 1930s.

The Rationales of Regulation

The rationale for economic regulation presumes the existence of circumstances such that regulation will improve the working of the market system. Economists generally refer to such circumstances as "market failure"; i.e., instances in which the workings of the free market are or appear to be inconsistent with economic efficiency. In addition, observation of the actual pattern of regulation in this nation and elsewhere suggests that other purposes such as "fairness" and political and/or economic power also underlie its existence. This chapter outlines the rationales for and methods of regulation, discusses the failures of regulation and sketches the thrust behind different types of regulatory reform. In the concluding section an analysis of the future of such reform is put forward. In the first section both political and economic rationales for regulation and the major methods of regulation are summarized. In the second section some of the failings of regulation are examined from both a political and economic standpoint. In the third section the major regulatory reform alternatives are given, and in the final section the prospects for reform are examined.

Rationales for Regulation: Economic Efficiency

Natural Monopolies. There are certain types of production which are inherently inconsistent with a competitive market structure; e.g., the provision of telephone services in a particular locality. For example, the existence of fifty competing railroads (and roadbeds) serving a particular route or the dual distribution of natural gas to a city would involve wasteful duplication of fixed facilities. Therefore, monopoly (the sale of a good or service by a single firm) is the only rational alternative. This, in turn, suggests the need for regulation because monopolists freed of the discipline of competition will not produce at quantities and prices consistent with maximum social welfare. In the United States such monopolies have generally been regulated by government while in Europe they have typically been nationalized.

Public Goods. Some types of commodities, termed public goods, must be supplied to everyone if they are to be supplied to anyone. Recognizing this, rational consumers would never voluntarily pay for such services. Thus, they must be produced by the government and financed by involuntary taxes. The prime example of a public good is national defense. Other more mundane examples are mosquito abatement, disease control, and police protection.

Third-Party Effects. The production and/or consumption of some commodities involve spillovers that influence the welfare (either positively or negatively) of other individuals. When this is so, private interest and public welfare do not coincide and a rationale for government intervention into the relevant market may be presumed to exist. Specifically, it is desirable that those activities (such as education) which exert indirect benefits to third parties be subsidized while those (such as pollution) which inflict harm be taxed or otherwise restricted.

The Absence of Competition. The ability of the marketplace to produce efficiently presupposes that a reasonable degree of competition prevail within it. Where this is lacking the government may, through antitrust actions, attempt to restore it. The Rockefeller oil monopoly in the early twentieth century or more recently the monopoly in aluminum are good examples of markets controlled by a single producer. And in each case through antitrust action the government sought to restore competition.

Informational Deficiencies. The efficient workings of the market mechanism also requires that the market participants be fully aware of the nature of commodities and services sold and their prices. Where such information is difficult for individual consumers to learn (as in drug purity, for example) economic regulation can enhance market efficiency by producing such information through labeling, testing, standard setting, or other methods.

Inefficient Extraction of Natural Resources. In some situations markets may be inefficient with regard to the use of natural resources. Until the invention of seamless pipes allowed natural gas to be safely and efficiently pumped to markets across the country, billions of cubic feet of natural gas were flared (burned off) in U.S. oil fields each day. The useless burning of natural gas not only wasted this resource but also reduced the amount of crude oil that could be taken from oil fields. In such circumstances the government may act through regulation to prevent the inefficient use of resources.

Non-Efficiency Rationales

The above rationales for government regulation represent the basic "case" for intervention into market processes *insofar as economic efficiency* (roughly defined as maximum production for minimum cost) is concerned. However, even the most casual perusal of economic regulation in the United States indicates that much of these activities are not justified on this basis alone. The most important of these "noneconomic efficiency" rationales can be generalized and grouped below. As we shall see, these factors, singly or in combination, are fundamental to much of U.S. regulatory policy.

"Correcting" the Distribution of Income. Some economic regulation represents a deliberate attempt to alter the distribution of income within society. Farm price supports, for example, cannot be justified on any of the efficiency grounds listed above. Rather they may reflect, among other things, public concern with the plight of the farmer. Other programs such as welfare payments to mothers of dependent children and minimum wage policy are partially justified on the grounds of income redistribution.

Political and Economic Power. Some types of economic regulation appear to be clear reflections of political or economic power. For example, the Interstate Commerce Commission (ICC) was formed in 1887 largely in response to the political power of certain railroads who were being economically damaged by competitors. Often economic groups will try to shift economic risks to the government through legislation such as the Robinson-Patman Act. Tariff policy in the United States and the pro-rationing of oil production are good examples of groups shifting economic risks to the government. Tariffs which protect U.S. business from foreign market competitors by charging such competitors high import duties clearly shifts economic cost from the manufacturer to the public. Minimum wage laws are largely a reflection of powerful unions who in this way eliminate potential low wage competition.

The Reduction of Uncertainty and Preservation of the Status Quo. Sudden changes in the ways commodities and services are produced and consumed can have profound effects upon the distribution of wealth in society. The possibility of such sudden changes and the enormous uncertainty involved in them may be abhorred by many individuals. It would appear that one of the explicit goals of regulation is to reduce such uncertainty in the belief that much of the uncertainty associated with the workings of the free market have serious societal costs; costs which may justify some sacrifices of efficiency within the allocative system.

Methods of Regulation

Reflecting the diversity of phenomena regulated and the apparent differences in the objectives of much of the regulation, a wide variety of regulatory techniques have evolved. The principal methods along with specific examples of each are listed below.

Price Regulation. One form of market intervention used by regulatory bodies is that of setting prices. Examples of this type of regulation as used by federal regulatory agencies include: establishment of ceiling prices for domestic "old" and "new" crude oil as set by Federal Energy Agency (FEA) and of the well-head price of natural gas by the Federal Power

Commission (FPC), the determination of airline and rail and motor transport fares by the Civil Aeronautics Board (CAB) and the Interstate Commerce Commission (ICC), respectively, and the determination of maximum interest rates payable to depositors by the Federal Reserve and the Federal Home Loan Bank Board (FHLB).

Franchise Awarding and Licensing. A second frequently used method of regulation is the awarding of franchises (and thus the prohibition of entry into the industry by would-be competitors). Prime examples of this are found in the activities of the Federal Communications Commission (FCC) in awarding broadcasting licenses, the CAB in awarding airline routes, the Federal Maritime Commission (FMC) in allowing shipping privileges, the Federal Reserve and FHLB in granting bank charters and the National Labor Relations Board (NLRB) in conferring exclusive bargaining privileges (after elections) on labor unions. In cases where competition is impossible, such as the distribution of natural gas to markets, the government will award exclusive franchises.

Standard-Setting. In many areas regulation involves the definition and enforcement of standards of various types, such as minimum standards—industrial safety, grain grades, etc. As was argued above, such standards (if well chosen) are defensible on grounds of economic efficiency alone when there is substantial ignorances in the marketplace. Examples of this type of regulation include: the definition of emission indices and fuel characteristics by the Environmental Protection Agency (EPA); construction characteristics of eligible homes by the Federal Housing Authority (FHA); standards of drug quality as defined by the Food and Drug Administration (FDA); portfolio and public disclosure policies as required by the Federal Reserve, the FHLB, (and associated deposit insuring institutions, the FDIC and FSLIC) and the Securities and Exchange Commission (SEC); and work condition standards as set by the Occupational Safety and Health Administration (OSHA). Frequently, it is this particular type of regulation which most deeply involves the respective regulatory body in the affairs of the industry concerned.

The Direct Allocation of Resources. In a number of instances regulatory or quasi-regulatory agencies have become directly involved in the determination of the allocation of goods and services among individuals and regions. For example, much of the nuclear research formerly done under the Atomic Energy Commission (AEC) and now handled by the Energy Research and Development Agency (ERDA) is directly under government control. Similarly, the Bureau of Mines of the Interior Department directly leases oil shale properties and participates in their development. Most dramatically, perhaps, has been the activity of the FEA in allocating gasoline and fuel oil products among regions of the country.

Operating Subsidies and Taxes. Another common form of intervention by federal regulatory agencies has been through the provision of operating subsidies. For example, the CAB has for years directly subsidized the air transport industry and, indirectly, the ICC and the Highway Trust Fund have subsidized the trucking industry as well. Similarly, the FMC has subsidized the construction and operation of American flag vessels for a substantial period and the Department of Agriculture has long provided direct subsidies (price supports and soil bank programs) and indirect benefits (extension services) to American farmers. Also, there are a wide range of subsidies and tax laws designed to encourage or discourage businesses from certain kinds of activity. In fact, most American businesses dealing in raw products receive a depletion allowance similar to the now extinct 27-1/2 percent oil depletion allowance.

Promoting Competition. Several federal regulatory agencies, particularly the FTC and the Anti-Trust Division Of the Justice Department, attempt to produce workable competition through administrative orders and decrees (FTC) and by civil and criminal action in domestic courts (Justice).

The Failings of Regulation: Economic Arguments

The methods of regulation described above have come under increasing criticism and, concomittantly, have generated increasing numbers of proposals for reform of the regulatory process. The criticisms and their associated reform alternatives seem to reflect two differing views of the problem. One, associated largely with many academic economists and increasingly reflected by the Ford Administration, is that interference with the market mechanism on as grand a scale as is practiced in the United States is, by its very nature, likely to lead to significant inefficiencies or inequities. A clear implication of this view is that the degree and diversity of economic regulation should diminish. A second view, implied in the positions taken by groups as diverse as the Ash Council on reform of regulatory agencies and Ralph Nader is that regulation is not necessarily bad but that it has, in its present form, led to serious but correctable problems. Their proposed reforms, therefore, typically involve reorganization and rationalization of existing structures rather than any necessarily reduced role for regulation.

In the remainder of this section specific failures of the regulatory methods and bodies outlined in the previous section will be examined. It should also be pointed out, however, that certain groups and, in particular, certain regulated industries and regulators, are strong defenders of present forms of regulation. For example, motor carriers strongly defend the ICC regulation of routes and entry into the market.

The Distortion of Market Signals: Price Regulation and Direct Allocation. In a smoothly functioning, competitive market the price system signals the existence of shortages and surpluses and reallocates resources in order to eliminate them. Suppose that consumers, for whatever reason, decide they wish to consume more of a particular commodity. The immediate effect of this change in their desires will produce a shortage of the commodity at its existing price. This shortage will, of course, cause this price to rise. This price increase will eliminate the shortage by (a) inducing consumers of the good to consume less of the commodity, substituting cheaper commodities in its place, and (b) inducing producers in search of profit to produce more of the commodity. Needless to say, this price increase, even if temporary, may produce budgetary hardships on those consumers who consume a great deal of it and may increase, at least temporarily, the welfare of those who produce it. Nonetheless, the original desire for more of the commodity will have, in fact, been satisfied and society will, therefore, be better off.

Any governmental regulation which, however well motivated, fixes any price accordingly robs the market mechanism of its basic means of allocating resources and thus of eliminating shortages or surpluses. Thus, we find that where such regulations exist they are frequently associated with such phenomena. FPC regulations on the well-head price of natural gas for interstate shipments have, by enforcing less than market clearing prices, produced shortages of this fuel, by encouraging the consumption of it while simultaneously reducing exploration for it and increasing our dependence on imported petroleum. "Parity" prices for many agricultural commodities have often produced agricultural surpluses which have generated storage costs and discouraged the movement of marginal farmers to other pursuits. Subsidized FHA and VA mortgages have encouraged patterns of urban development which have proven very costly both in terms of the energy requirements they have and in the financial starvation of many central cities. Similarly, limitations placed on interest rates payable on time accounts at commercial banks and savings and loans has prevented competition, limited the ability of small savers to cope with inflation, and added significant instability to domestic housing markets. In short, many attempts by the government to directly influence or set prices appear to have resulted in serious distortions and inefficiencies within the economy.

A second area in which federal regulatory agencies have created serious problems via price regulation has been in their efforts at "cross-subsidization''; i.e., the use of high profit activities to subsidize low profit ones in the transportation industry. This has been particularly true in the areas of air and rail transport where highly unprofitable routes (usually involving low density air travel markets in the case of air and passenger traffic in general in the case of rail transport). While protecting a few customers these practices have produced significant costs for the firms involved, discouraged the development of alternative transport for the subsidized routes, discouraged (through artificially high prices) the use of the efficient form of transport on the nonsubsidized routes, and have been an important element in the financial troubles faced by most air and rail transport.

The Distortion of Market Signals: Subsidization. Related but different from direct intervention with the price mechanism are allocative inefficiencies produced via subsidies given particular industries. For example, both air and truck transport have been heavily subsidized, with the effect that they can underprice more efficient rail transport. This has not only encouraged the waste of scarce resources (particularly energy) but it has also heavily contributed to the financial plight of the domestic railroad industry.

The Restriction of Competition. As was noted earlier, one of the primary economic rationales for government intervention into market processes is the absence of competition in the chosen industry. In spite of this, however, one of the unfortunate side effects of some regulation has been the reduction of competition within markets and the benefits such a process brings.

A number of examples of this phenomenon come readily to mind. For instance, the restriction of entry into banking and thrift institutions and interest rate limitations by both federal (FRB and FHLB, respectively) and state governments (for state chartered institutions) by requiring charters. Such restrictions are justified by a desire to protect depositors and, through them, the country's financial structure. However, both of these goals are assured by deposit insurance and regulation of banking practices. Entry restrictions can only be justified, therefore, by the protection they afford stockholders, not the public. As we have also noted, the interest rate ceilings on time accounts and the legal prohibition of interest payments on checking accounts precludes price competition in this area as well. Similarly, the awarding of exclusive franchises to domestic airlines, radio and television stations and the prohibition of price competition by the CAB and ICC are clearly anticompetitive in effect if not intent and undoubtedly benefit stockholders at the expense of consumers. In short, there are many areas in which regulation has helped produce for an industry what the industry could not produce for itself—cartelization and the attendant inefficiencies.

Reduction of Technological Progress. On a number of occasions regulatory bodies, apparently in an effort to preserve the status quo, have adopted policies which have had the effect of seriously impeding technological progress and the benefits it confers. The most prominent occurrences of this have been in the area of transportation. For example, the adoption of the most efficient form of piggyback flat cars for the long distance rail hauling of tractor-trailers was held up for many years for a variety of reasons, including the allegation that they would provide "unfair" competition. Similarly, the adoption and spread of cable television and the substitution of satellites for oceanic cable transmission have been delayed by apparent efforts to protect various firms' investments in competitive and/or obsolete equipment.

Reduction in the Diversity of Products. Where there are significant deficiencies of knowledge and when an activity exerts harmful effects on others (e.g., environmental degradation) it may be necessary for the purposes of allocative efficiency to impose certain standards on products or on consumption or production processes. Purity standards for drugs, truth in packaging legislation, OSHA regulations on industrial safety and amenities all fall in this category. Even where some standard is justified, it is still crucial to select a reasonable one in the sense that its benefits outweigh its costs. Unless this is done, allocative efficiency may not be attained.

Unfortunately, some of the standards selected by regulatory agencies appear to be inefficient. EPA emission indices for automobiles appear to have been, in retrospect, overly restrictive in terms of the costs for the added equipment and energy costs they have imposed on society compared to the environmental benefits obtained. Similarly, the coal industry's influence on the FPC sometimes prevented the supply of natural gas and petroleum products for home use where such products would have been cheaper and more efficient than coal.

The Failings of Regulation: Political/Economic

The shortcomings of regulation discussed in the preceeding sections were essentially economic in nature and were measured in terms of the degree to which they misallocated scarce resources and, thus, reduced the output of the economy for what it would have been in their absence. Another and perhaps more fundamental set of criticisms of regulatory policy are more political and administrative in nature. Essentially, they suggest that even if regulators were economically well-intentioned and aware of the likely allocative consequences of their actions, resource misallocation would result.

Capture by Special Interests. A group of people with opinions as divergent as those of the conservative economist Milton Friedman and consumer advocate Ralph Nader would argue that regulators are almost certain to be dominated by the industry they are intended to regulate. Such critics contend that such a development is inevitable because while each member of the public has a small interest in regulatory policy, the industry or group regulated has a substantial and very concentrated one. Thus, economic self-interest will motivate the industry to dominate the regulatory process while individual citizens, whose collective interest may be greater, will not be so motivated. In addition, it is only natural for relationships and perhaps shared values to develop between regulator and regulated. Indeed, the knowledge required may be present only among individuals who have either been in the industry or are likely to join it. Some political scientists have argued that there is a regulatory cycle in which during the first years of its existence the government regulators do ''regulate,'' but that over time they are ''captured'' and regulate in the interests of the regulated. In an interesting variant of this capture theory, it is argued that the industries are captured by the regulators. Specifically, since the business of the agency is to regulate, they proclaim policies which are designed to keep them in business. Such theories cannot explain all regulatory malfunctions. Few, for example, would argue that the actions of the FPC have been in the interest of producers of natural gas or that some of the stringent OSHA regulations are likely in the long run to be to the benefit of workers or employers. Yet, it is also clear that surely, if not inevitably, some regulatory agencies have come to protect the regulated rather than the public and, in some instances, it has always been so; e.g., the formation of the ICC to protect several inefficient railroads.

The Absence of Coordination: The Lack of Universal Standards. Another alleged failing of regulation is that because its responsibilities are spread among a number of agencies, particular types often work at cross purposes. Both the Department of Agriculture and the Pure Food and Drug Administration regulate various and sometimes overlapping areas of food industries. Under such conditions, it is not surprising that regulatory policy is ambiguous at best and contradictory at worst. Another variant of this theme is that government regulatory actors do not set clear standards for the regulated industry. Thus, regulation occurs on a case-by-case basis and the public interest is not served. For example, the Nuclear Regulatory Commission does not have clear standards for what constitutes a statistically significant loss of fissile material (indicating that a possible theft of nuclear materials has taken place). Thus, a fabricating plant in New England has one standard, while a plant in Illinois has another.

Administrative Lags. In a number of agencies, such as the FPC and the ICC, some administrative procedures have become so complicated that only legal specialists can fully understand the issues involved. This and other factors have made certain regulatory bodies extremely slow in responding to what may be very vital needs. For example, the filing of environmental impact statements and/or the certification of safety requirements have had a clear and negative impact on this nation's attempt to achieve increased energy self-sufficiency. This is particularly true of the Alaskan pipeline construction, the suspension of virtually all offshore drilling following the Santa Barbara oil spill and, perhaps most importantly, the ten-year period required for the completion of nuclear reactors in this nation (compared to much shorter periods in other nations). Perhaps the most dramatic and tragic case of this appeared in the recent demise of the Rock Island Railroad in which its request for regulatory relief took a decade during which time it fell into bankruptcy, thus ultimately making the issue moot.

Corrupting Influences on the Political Process. Many critics contend that regulatory policy can be used for purposes of political blackmail. The granting of an exclusive franchise, the awarding of an air route or an import license can have significant wealth effects. Indeed, at least at the municipal level, such economic rewards have long been an integral part of political affairs. The recent disclosures of Watergate in which illegal campaign contributions from heavily regulated industries and the threatened use of FCC license renewals to attempt to influence broadcast journalism were observed to serve as stark reminders of the potential influences economic regulation may generate for the political process.

Ignorance and Bad Judgment. Finally, there is perhaps the single and most fundamental problem facing regulatory policy today: the wealth of information and intelligence required to make equitable and efficient decisions. Quite apart from the difficulties facing those who must set some price or some standard, in the real world such individuals are compelled to select a particular price or standard. An important criticism of regulatory policy, therefore, is that even the best intentioned and undominated board simply does not and cannot have the informational and intellectual resources to make such judgments.

Of course, this is not to imply that the market mechanism has better or more abundant information and, thus, can make better judgments. However, once a regulation is enacted, vested interests develop which tend to perpetuate its existence. Thus, regulations which have far outlived their usefulness (e.g., the prevention of entry into banking, FPC limits of the well-head price of natural gas) continue mistakes that may have been cured by the market.

Major Reform Alternatives

As has already been noted there are two basic positions taken by the critics of the federal regulatory apparatus. The first is that regulatory involvement to the degree presently practiced will inevitably lead to resource misallocations of the types discussed earlier. Such views naturally suggest deregulation of the economy along a broad front. A second viewpoint, not necessarily fully incompatible with the first, is that present procedures are what lead to inefficient regulation and that what is needed are improvements and sometimes radical changes in those procedures rather than simple deregulation. Some of the proposals of those groups are presented here.

General Deregulation

This as noted is the solution advocated by those who feel that involved regulation is inherently inefficient. Such views are prominent among large groups of academic economists. More importantly, the President's Council of Economic Advisors (CEA) in its 1975 report called for such actions and President Ford has announced a legislative program that would substantially deregulate the transportation industry by removing restrictions on rate competition and entry in the alternative transport modes. In addition, the Ford Administration has long backed (as have four of the five FPC Commissioners) freeing the price of interstate natural gas and the removal of the price ceiling on "old" oil. However, both of the actions require congressional approval and/or support which has not thus far been forthcoming.

On the other hand, it should be noted that while deregulation has been put forth in general, only in transportation and energy have there been specific proposals for deregulation. In short, general deregulation may be for some a rallying point, but in fact such deregulation is not likely to be seriously proposed over a wide range of interests.

Increased Coordination Among Regulatory Bodies

A number of study groups have, noting the fact that many regulatory policies appear to work at cross purposes, suggested reforms aimed at increasing the coordination and consistency of policies. A report prepared for President-elect Kennedy in 1960 (the Landis Report) suggested that a member of the White House Staff be given authority to oversee regulatory agencies. More recently, the Ash Council on regulatory reform, in a report prepared for President Nixon in 1971 decried the absence of coordination, especially in the transportation area. In particular, they recommended that the major federal agencies responsible for transport policy (the ICC, CAB, and FMC) be combined under a single head.

Such proposals do not appear to have significant public or congressional support at this time. The major reasons for this are that some individuals feel that the proposals simply would not work and, more importantly, that other more basic reforms would obviate the need for them.

Making Regulators More Responsive

The Consumer Protection Agency. Underlying much of the economic case against regulation is that it creates inefficiencies by advancing private interests at the expense of larger public interests. A reform proposal heavily supported by consumer groups has been to increase the representation of the "disenfranchised" consumer through the institution of a federal Consumer Protection Agency. In its present form, the legislation establishing this Agency would allow it to intervene in behalf of consumer interest in virtually all federal regulatory proceedings. In each of the last two sessions of Congress such legislation has been defeated by Senate filibuster. Recent changes in the composition of the Senate, however, make it appear likely that such legislation will be passed this session, perhaps even over a presidential veto.

Reducing Excessive "Legalism." A principal point raised by the Ash Commission was that: "The judicial cost of agency review proceedings places too great an emphasis on legal perspectives to the detriment of economic, financial, technical, and social perspectives." Among the suggestions put forward by the Commission was the appointment of a single head of such an agency to replace the present collegial form of existing regulatory commmmissions, that people with technical, social and economic expertise become relatively more important (and lawyers relatively less) in the affairs of most regulatory commissions, and that review procedures be greatly simplified. Little support for such a reform has developed, however.

Increased Public Representation in Regulatory Proceedings. Apart from the Consumer Protection Agency mentioned above, a number of consumer groups have recommended that the interests of consumers be represented either directly on commissions or indirectly in testimony before them. It has been pointed out, for example, that in hearings before the Consumer Product Safety Commission, individual consumers are unable to afford to appear. Again, the need for this reform would be largely obviated by the existence of the CPA.

Decreased Independence of Regulatory Agencies

In many instances, regulatory commissions are substantially independent of both the president and Congress thanks to their semi-independent status and the length of the terms of their administrators. Some and, in particular, the Ash Council, have argued that this independence has had the effect of shielding the agencies from public opinion and the economic changes that are occurring in society and should be reduced. The resulting lack of accountability, it is held, has in many instances had the effect of significantly reducing the flexibility and responsiveness of the agencies.

Basic Structure Changes in Regulatory Proceedings

Some individuals, particularly those like Ralph Nader, argue that regulation per se is not bad and that what we suffer from is rather *bad* regulation and, in many instances, from too little regulation. Ralph Nader, for example, favors stronger control over many industries, particularly the automobile industry, and he feels that the public interest is so greatly influenced by the behavior of large corporations that the public should be represented on their Boards of Trustees. In addition, he would argue for federal support of "cooperative centers" and other new economic institutions that would hopefully reduce the power of industries, particularly regulated ones. Critics may find it ironic indeed that the proposed cure for damages done by regulation is still more regulation.

De facto government ownership of regulated industries represents another alternative to economic regulation. This has already taken place to a substantial degree in rail passenger service and has been proposed for oil importing activities.

Conclusions

While it is clear that the reform of federal regulatory agencies and policies has become an issue of greater political and economic importance than in the past, it must be remembered that the economic activities presently regulated are diverse and complex and that the same is true of those groups who seek reform. For this reason, while many can agree that present forms of regulation have caused significant economic problems, there is no clear consensus among them regarding what, if anything, can or should be done to correct the situation.

Among the contending parties, at least three distinct groups and attitudes are discernible:

1. The Ford Administration and many academic economists who feel that many forms of regulation have produced economic distortions of varying degrees of severity, most of which have had the effect of reducing economic efficiency. In general, this groups favors deregulation along a broad front with greater reliance placed on the market as an allocative tool.

2. The regulatory agencies themselves and those sectors of the economy; e.g., the trucking industry, who clearly benefit from present regulatory practices. While acknowledging some deficiencies in present regulations, these groups would suggest the present system is perhaps the best of a set of imperfect alternatives, that disorder would prevail in its absence and that any sudden changes in regulatory formats would be likely to produce severe economic dislocation. In particular, these individuals would argue that general deregulation and reliance on the market naively presumes that the market behaves like the economists competitive model.

3. Individuals, best typified by Ralph Nader, who effectively straddle the two previous positions. They have little faith in the ability of free markets in our present corporate environment but at the same time believe present regulatory practices to be essentially corrupt. Their solution is to drastically overhaul both the power of corporations and the nature of regulatory procedures with particular emphasis on greater representation of and responsibility towards the "public interest."

A consequence of the division of opinion outlined above is that no clear consensus exists with regard to regulatory policy and that this, in turn, reduces the likelihood of meaningful reform. For example, President Ford has made regulatory reform a "number one" priority of his administration while Ralph Nader has asserted that no meaningful reform can take place as long as Ford occupies the White House. Thus reform clearly means different things to different people.

As a result, fundamental regulatory reform is unlikely in the near term future. Moreover, those changes which do take place are likely to be as fragmented as the views of regulation's critics rather than forming a consistent pattern. Among the most significant of these changes that we are likely to observe will be:

1. The Ford proposals for substantially deregulating the transport sector (ICC, CAB,and FMC).
2. The removal of the ceiling on the well-head price of natural gas shipped to interstate markets, a move favored by the Ford Administration as well as four of the five FPC Commissions.
3. The formation of a Consumer Protection Agency as outlined above pending the ability of Congress to overide a likely presidential veto.
4. The eventual decontrol of prices of "new" crude oil.

While sweeping regulatory reforms thus appear unlikely, events of the near future may greatly influence its scope and form. The public stances taken by the Ford Administration in favor of general deregulation makes the prospects of such policies heavily dependent on that Administration's political success. Should it succeed, greater reliance on market processes would appear to be an inevitable result. Should it fail politically, greater, if altered, government intervention into the economy would appear likely. In any case, however, regulatory reform will likely be a gradual process.

15 Economic Regulation, the Free Market, and Public Ownership

Alan Stone

Periodically since the Civil War this nation has seen bursts of literature critical of big business and its performance. Governmental response to the scandals brought to the public's attention usually consists of new reform legislation purportedly designed to cure the problems, after which the storm subsides—until the next cycle. The early years of the twentieth century and the late nineteen thirties are instances of early reform waves. Polemics like Upton Sinclair's *The Jungle* and the 1935 *Partners in Plunder* by J.B. Matthews and R.E. Shallcross typify early reform literature. The current reform wave began, after a long period of quiescence, with the publication of Ralph Nader's *Unsafe at Any Speed* in 1965 and has lasted through a decade.

Subsequent to 1965 a veritable avalanche of popular literature critical of both business performance and the failure of regulation has been published. While most of these studies are of individual industries or regulatory agencies—and many employ anecdotes for unjustified generalizations—they still add up to a damning indictment that the private enterprise system is satisfying neither the individual consumer not public economic goals. Nor has regulation been able to improve performance, except at unacceptable cost. Virtually every major industry was shown to have failed the public in crucial ways: dangerous cars from the automobile industry, pollution from the paper and pulp industry, questionable additives from the food industry, inadequate refining capacity from the petroleum industry, excessive profits and incredible executive compensation across the board, price gouging of especially vulnerable consumers such as the aged by the pharmaceutical and nursing home industries, etc.

Yet the Naderites and prior generations of reformers persist in their faith that new regulatory reforms will be *the* answer to the failings of past regulation, forgetting that prior generations of reformers had the same misplaced hope. The reformers have never questioned the process of business regulation itself, which—to their credit—the free market school has done in a continuing series of penetrating critiques contained in the *Journal of Law and Economics* and the *Bell Journal of Economics*. Those who place their faith in "bigger and better" regulation as the answer to the problem of deficient corporate performance might be, in Milton Friedman's phrase, expecting cats to bark.[1]

The Shortcomings of Regulation

Let us first look at some of the intrinsic deficiencies of regulation. In so doing we will do no more than briefly mention the political failures of regulation. Agencies are, as McConnell and others have shown, frequently "captured" by the very interest they are supposed to regulate. Further, it is quite clear as the Naderites have shown that reglatory bodies are sometimes staffed by incompetents from top to bottom. Even when competent, many regulators are more sympathetic to industries they are supposed to regulate than they are to their purported mission. Finally, as former Senator Fred Harris has observed, day-by-day lobbying activities for which only corporations have the requisite resources, the promise to public officials of future lucrative jobs in industry, and sometimes outright bribery may sometimes aid business interests in procuring agency outputs to their advantage.[2]

While instances of each of these charges undoubtedly occur, there are deeper reasons for economic regulation's failure which operate irrespective of agency personnel or outside influences and are intrinsic to the nature of regulation itself. In examining this problem, let us focus on the experience of the Federal Trade Commission which enforces both highly general statutes, like the FTC act outlawing "unfair methods of competition and unfair or deceptive acts or practices," and extremely explicit statutes such as the Fur Products Labeling Act and the Truth-in-Lending Act. Moreover, the agency has used both traditional regulatory techniques such as issuing cease-and-desist orders against transgressors and, more recently, has employed innovative techniques such as trade regulation rules, corrective orders, and affirmative disclosures. In short, it has recently stretched regulatory techniques to novel lengths.

Yet according to the most recent study of the agency, its performance is still woeful in the control of consumer fraud.[3] Anyone doubting this conclusion is invited to pick-up at random a mass circulation magazine directed to gullible consumers (movie magazines, etc.) and count the great number of questionable advertisements in each. Further, its antitrust regulation (which the FTC shares with the Justice Department) generally has had as little effect on structure as on conduct. The leading study of changes in American industrial structure in the twentieth century concludes: "Governmental policies appear to have had even less effect on the development of the large firm or the overall structure of industry than have had individual entrepreneurs. . . . Clearly the needs and requirements of changing technologies and markets rather than antitrust policies have played the major role in determining changes in concentration in American industries."[4]

Why is it, then, that regulation has failed to have the desired impact in the instances of both specific statutes and the more general statutes? Why has failure occurred both in instances of weak remedies like cease-and-desist orders as well as more stringent remedies like injunction, divestiture, penalties, and seizure? Finally, why has it equally failed when discovery techniques have been reasonably good as in the case of inspection under the Fur Act or when inadequate discovery techniques have led to a system of relying on the very persons regulated to supply information on transgressions?

Let us first look at some of the traditional reasons given for regulation's failure. In the first place, there is usually a limited amount of resources—both time and money—to carry out effectively the designated tasks, and the amounts of each required to police effectively the subject areas are many times what can ever be reasonably expected to be appropriated. Consider, tor example, the manpower which the FTC would need just to examine all questionable advertising or all instances of parallel pricing to see whether collusion exists. The problem is compounded when one realizes that not only must resources be allocated to discovering violations—which firms do their best to conceal—but to obtain compliance with orders and rules already entered. The problem, too, has a political dimension for vastly increasing a policing presence raises, in the judgment of many, grave civil liberties questions. Short of vast increases, the incremental increases appropriated to the FTC, Antitrust Divison, and similar enforcement agencies are not likely to allow these agencies to cope with their problems. Steady increases in the number of policemen have not reduced the number of serious crimes or their solutions. Indeed crime rates appear to rise as the number of police rise. (Better reporting may account for part of the "increase" in crime rates.) Short of totalitarian measures, regulation is not apt to be effective as long as strong incentives exist to violate the law.

Secondly, business regulation's defects also stem from the fact that it has been modeled on the system of private litigation. This means, in the first place, that there is apt to be a significant delay between the time when the undesirable event took place and its discovery by the enforcement agency. Secondly, additional time lapses before the agency's enforcement arm has mustered and ordered the facts sufficiently well to issue a complaint or propose a rule. Thirdly, the respondent must be given a reasonable amount of time in which to answer and prepare its case. Next, the time for pre-trial procedures designed to reduce the number of issues affords additional time for delay. In this process respondents are afforded ample time to skillfully raise procedural side issues. Then the case goes before an administrative judge for trial, often of lengthy duration as both sides present and quarrel over the admissability and relevance of witnesses and exhibits. The administrative judge must then spend time in reflecting on the evidence and arguments presented by both sides and write a decision explaining the reasons for it. But we are not through yet, for appeals and arguments before the full administrative agency, the Courts of Appeal and sometimes the Supreme Court follow before an order is made effective. Given the enormous time span inherent in litigation processes, a great deal of harm—sometimes irreversible—may occur.

The trade regulation rule procedure under the new Magnuson-Moss Act only marginally meets the great problem of delay. What difference does the new statute make? Under the new rule-making procedures set forth in Section 202 of the Magnuson-Moss Act, the Federal Trade Commission must still discover the alleged wrong which calls for the promulgation of the rule and must still investigate the activities to determine whether they constitute wrongdoing. If satisfied that wrongdoing on a scale broad enough to justify a rule exists, the agency must next publish a notice of proposed rule-making, stating with particularity the reasons for the proposed rule. It must then allow sufficient time for interested persons (not simply affected persons) to submit written data, views, and arguments. Then it must provide opportunity for an "informal" hearing in which time must be allowed for oral presentations, some cross-examination, and some rebuttal. Parenthetically, there is ample opportunity for any interested party to raise procedural issues in this respect on whether it was denied ample opportunity for cross-examination and other issues, allowing further delay. Next, the agency must review all of this material and promulgate a final rule. Again, appeals are permissable. Whether the new procedure will be more time consuming than the case-by-case method (which still will exist in less general practices) remains to be seen. But, in any event, it is obvious that the new procedure still allows enormous time to elapse between the occasion of the presumed wrong and the entry of public relief.

Nor would it appear that the time gap problem can be significantly alleviated within such constitutional requirements of due process as notice and a fair opportunity to be heard. Only an injunction proceeding offers any hope of significantly reducing the time between transgression and relief. But even here the event must first be discovered, and this can occur long after great harm has been done. In addition, an agency must still prepare its case and muster facts and argument sufficiently well to persuade a court that continuation of the practice will probably result in such harm to the "public interest" as to outweigh a respondent's interest in continuing the activity in question. Only in a few cases is such a showing likely to persuade a court that relief should be entered before full trial, and even then considerable time between the institution of a practice and injunctive relief is bound to have elapsed.

If business regulation is apt not to reach a practice until long after it took place, can the forbidden practice be deterred in advance through effective sanctions? Virtually all agree that the cease-and-desist order has been an ineffective sanction. The Magnuson-Moss Act adds to this the right of the FTC to bring an action on behalf of consumers against a respondent after entry of a cease-and-desist order or after a rule has been violated. The relief in such cases may include damages, money refunds, and return of property. In order to sustain the action, the Commission must show that a "reasonable man" would have known under the circumstances that the practice was dishonest or fraudulent. Mere deception, in other words, is insufficient. Nor does the provision apply to practices that are encompassed under the antimonopoly aegis. In brief, then, these new provisions would appear to be aimed at the activities of the multitude of small fly-by-night con men.

Yet outright criminal penalties imposed on their activities by various state laws have apparently not reduced such activities. In an era when the effectiveness of deterrence to the commission of proscribed acts is increasingly questioned in the criminal law area, those concerned with trade regulation still cling to a simplistic set of notions. Yet, the con man is very likely to reasonably calculate that he can still get away with prohibited actions. Justice, he knows, will not be swift and sure; there is an excellent likelihood that his acts will escape the purview of the FTC. And besides, if he is caught, he will only be required to give back what he defrauded under the Magnuson-Moss Act and will not be subjected to criminal penalties. Finally, in business, regulation, unlike most criminal conduct, a defrauder may hide behind the facade of the corporate form with its limited liability for individual shareholders. All things considered, it may be well worth the effort of the unscrupulous to deceive.

The Problem of Private Discretion

There is one additional and crucial defect of regulation not usually considered, and it is embraced within the concept of discretion. But the discretion we focus on is not the discretion of the statute or administrative agency, but the discretion which remains within the interest which is to be regulated. Put very simply, for example, Professor Chandler's conclusion, based upon meticulous research, that antitrust policies have meant very little in shaping either industrial structure, conduct or performance, is more explicable on the basis of the wide discretion open to firms, even after regulation, than any other factors. Moreover, regulating one firm or even industry still allows considerable discretion in the hands of rival firms or industries selling close substitutes.

Let us look more closely at this notion. If one limits discretion in cigarette firms by requiring warnings on packets, or banning television advertising, there are still a sufficient number of ways for the message to get through. Moreover, when one examines a total cigarette advertising message for cigarettes, the warning plays a very small part in it. The ingenuity of producing a message attractive to consumers—psychologically, subliminally and otherwise—is focused on those parts of the message over which the firm exercises a high degree of autonomy. Again, the disclosure requirements of the truth-in-lending law are fairly overwhelmed, in the case of the ghetto merchant selling to a customer, by the attractiveness of the product, appeals related to it, his ability to shift what might have been interest charges to the selling price, etc. Truth-in-lending has not, in a word, come close to stopping price gouging of a particularly vulnerable group of consumers. Nor does truth-in-lending face up to the problem that extremely hard to discover oral representations by sellers can completely defeat the written word.

Not all regulations, of course, can be so defeated, particularly those concerned with the attainment of minimum standards. Yet while this is true, the public can be defeated in other ways stemming from the firm's discretion in imposing costs or penalties in other areas. The most obvious case is passing on costs. But there are, in addition, less obvious ones. For example, since 1962 the new food and drug Amendments have imposed stringent requirements on pharmaceutical firms to demonstrate the safety and efficacy of newly marketed drugs. Yet the costs of testing and documenting have risen so sharply for the constrained firms that there has been a sharp drop off in the number of new drugs marketed, and the decline has been particularly noticeable among smaller firms.[5] While drug firm spokesmen and the "free market" proponents of deregulation claim that the 1962 Amendments "forced" the drug firms into adopting this conduct, it is clear that these firms were not "forced" at all; rather, they collectively, although probably not collusively, exercised their discretion in shifting their behavior.

In similar fashion, the allegedly overzealous regulation of natural gas rates by the Federal Power Commission led to similar distortions. The FPC tended to sharply restrain prices during inflationary periods leading the regulated industry to curtail exploration for natural gas which, in turn, led to the severe natural gas shortages of the mid-nineteen seventies.[6] Important here again is the fact that firms were not, strictly speaking, forced to stop exploring for natural gas, but chose to do so in the light of their commitment to enhance or at least maintain their profit and growth positions above any other social values.[7] In addition, where regulation limits discretion to the point where a firm's or an industry's profitability is impaired, it may be denied the capital to either furnish or improve the service or good it is expected to provide. In this case the costs or penalties can be imposed by the exercise of discretion by firms and industries with which the regulated one must interact, here capital-raising and lending institutions.

To summarize this line of argument, the impact of regulation may often be nullified through the wide area of discretion left to the firm, or if stringently enforced, the regulation may lead to undesirable costs or penalties imposed upon the public purportedly served. Under this hypothesis, the critical variable is not so much the discretion vested in a regulatory agency by the operating statute, but rather the discretion remaining within the firm.

Meanwhile, regulation is a very costly process to the consumer. Public expenditures alone are estimated to be approximately $2 billion per year. But far more insidious are the costs to firms which are passed on to consumers. While the writer has never encountered a convincingly calculated estimate of total regulatory costs passed on to consumers, "guesstimates" are frighteningly high. For example, the Goodyear Tire and Rubber Company has announced that it expended $30 million in 1974 to comply with federal and state regulations. If we assume that the ratio of regulatory costs to volume of sales is the same for the top 500 manufacturing firms as it is for Goodyear (0.0057), total regulatory costs for this group of firms alone were in excess of $4,753 million per annum.[8] While there is no simple way of telling what proportion of this sum is passed on to consumers, probably most is. Thus, while this sum is clearly suspect as an accurate calculation of the private sector costs of regulation to consumers, it indicates that the total amount is quite substantial and raises quite clearly the questions of: (1) whether the purported benefits from regulation are worth the direct costs, and (2) if they are worth the direct costs, whether the process of regulation can realize these benefits. Our conclusion, based upon the foregoing, is that the kind of business regulation we now have, on balance, is not and can not be an effective instrument for promoting public values.

What Values Should a Politico-economic System Promote?

Several alternative models to the standard regulatory ones can be postulated. But before so doing, let us back up and try to pinpoint what values regulation, and for that matter, competition are supposed to protect and enhance. It is sometimes forgotten that competition and regulation are not ends in themselves, but are expected to serve human well-being. Adam Smith, for example, considered himself not a technocratic economist but a moral philosopher and argued for free and unrestrained competition in his famous "invisible hand" passage, on the ground that each individual pursuing his own selfish interest would most effectually promote society's interest. While most persons today no longer have the same faith in the free market solution, and many values have changed since the writing of *The Wealth of Nations*, there is still a rather surprisingly high degree of concurrence on a core of values which a politico-economic system should promote. Let us now try to list some of these, before asking how the alternative models would meet them.

The first two values are safety and health. Consumers have a right to expect that products and services offered to them will be reasonably health-giving and safe for anticipated use. Obviously, this does not mean that products will be safe and healthy under all circumstances, but that they will be so under reasonable conditions of use. No matter how automobiles, for example, are constructed, unreasonable use can result in the destruction of driver and car. But within reasonable cost-of-production ranges, they should be as safe as possible.

There is, however, a caveat to these values which leads to the third major value. The consumer may decide to forego safety and health in order to satisfy other gratifications. Put another way, the history of mankind teaches that we often cannot be saved from our follies. We may decide to consume cigarettes, notwithstanding full understanding of the proven risks, or we may decide to purchase aluminum siding, notwithstanding our inability to afford it. Under these circumstances we expect to be told the truth about a product and not deceived. This means, first, that we are entitled to all of the important information about a product. Secondly, it means that misinformation will not be given to us, and thirdly it means that we will not be psychologically manipulated to acquire.

The latter point is the most troublesome of all. It requires no demonstration to show that the amount of relevant and impartial information conveyed in advertising is small compared to the sum total of statements of a psychological, subliminal or just simply nonrational nature contained in the mass of advertisements with which the consumer is bombarded. Moreover, although this is far from certain, the nonrational parts of the message may effectively nullify the portions which convey information in their impact upon the consumer.[9] Consumers are not "free" to choose cigarette smoking. They are essentially manipulated to choose this activity. Consumer sovereignty, premised upon the ability of consumers to choose rationally, is the central premise of FTC advertising regulation, yet the assumption has become increasingly questionable, which the FTC implicitly recognizes in the bait-and-switch cases. The competing alternative models to regulation, then, must face the enormous problem of truth, a crucial underpinning of the theory of consumer sovereignty.

At first blush the above values bear no integral relationship to the set of values more narrowly focused within the economic realm. This latter set has been articulated in a number of post-Wold War II documents, as well as some prior to this era. However, the most notable is the Employment Act of 1946. One of the most important of these values is simply that services and goods should be adequately provided by enterprises. Obviously the notion is elastic and equally obvious, the importance of services and goods vary from nation to nation. American expectations are among the highest, for the American consumer demands the provision not only of railroad transportation, energy and pharmaceuticals, but also the provision of lamps, television sets, door locks, etc., beyond the immediate dreams of the inhabitants of most of the world. When the provision of such services and goods becomes inadequate, we perceive performance as inadequate. We also anticipate that the range of prices for most goods and services should be within the purchasing power of most consumers; not everyone will be able to purchase a Cadillac or even a new car, but virtually everyone should be able to acquire a used car with reasonable performance characteristics.

These considerations lead to additional values. While profits are certainly permissible, they should not be "excessive," reflecting prices higher than need be. For price levels to be low, however, requires innovativeness and progressiveness leading to cost cutting, and hence, price cutting. The value of innovativeness or progressiveness also relates to a demand for increasing the quality of goods and services. Passenger railroad transportation in this country, for example, is generally perceived as both too expensive and of low quality. "Reasonable" price levels and innovativeness also lead to another set of values somewhat harder to define. We demand that a firm's prices should not reflect a commitment to waste—frills and unproductive expenditures. The pharmaceutical industry, for example, has been sharply criticized for pushing up the prices of drugs beyond reasonable bounds because of its employment of a veritable army of detail men who do not convey much accurate information anyway.[10] Soap and cleanser manufacturers have been criticized for spending approximately 10 percent of their sales on advertising, which tell almost nothing about the products, while automobile manufacturers have been called to task for the waste inherent in annual model changes.

The final set of values we will mention are far less consensual, especially in application, than the foregoing ones. These values concern what economists term externalities—the intended, unintended or incidental byproduct of some otherwise legitimate activity.[11] The most important of such externalities are air and water pollution caused by firms, as well as by high levels of consumption. While it is difficult to set forth a consensual public value on undesirable externalities, it is probably fair to state that most of us wish to balance them against the benefits which will be lost by reducing or altering the actitivy leading to the undesirable externality. Thus, most of us object to air pollution emanating from steel mills. But we are not willing to forego steel production entirely. Rather, we are groping for a balancing strategy allowing steel production to take place either at a lowered rate or at greater costs necessary to reduce air pollution through installation of control devices, or through yet other strategies.

Alternatives to Regulation

This compendium of public values is by no means intended to be exhaustive, even in the economic sphere. Rather, it is intended to be a backdrop for evaluating alternative models designed to achieve these values. If economic regulation is insufficient, what will do? The alternatives to regulation include: (1) atomistic restructuring of industry, (2) restructuring of industry at lower levels of oligopoly, (3) the free market solution advanced by the "Chicago School," (4) the full-scale public utility model in which a firm's discretion is gravely reduced and shifted to public institutions, and (5) public ownership. Models (1) and (2) may be employed in conjunction with either regulation or the free market. Because space limitations preclude a thoroughgoing discussion of each alternative model, we can do no more than point to some difficulties and benefits of each model.

The Free Market Model

Ultimately, the "free market" model depends upon the thesis that the free market will best satisfy public values through the instrumentality of the "invisible hand." Yet the evidence is simply overwhelming that public values and the goals of firms diverge sharply. Cigarette firms, for example, felt no responsibility to warn customers of their products' danger. Nor did auto manufacturers voluntarily make cars safer. Indeed, the enormous volume of fraud which the FTC and various federal, state and local bodies have uncovered point conclusively to the fact that when profit and sales goals conflict with public values, the latter must yield in business calculations. Nor, to cite still another example, do firms attempt on their own to balance externalities in the manner previously suggested.

The reasons for corporate inattentiveness to public goals have been well stated by Professor Neil Chamberlain:

Even in these limited exercises in social responsibility the individual corporation must recognize two constraints. First, it must show a profit that compares favorably with the profit positions of other major corporations. This is necessary for several reasons. The legal framework vests ultimate corporate authority in a board of directors nominally elected by the stockholders, and incumbent managements must perform well enough to forestall a challenge to their position. . . . Further, although internally generated funds provide much of the capital needed by large corporations, it is occasionally necessary to resort to the capital markets for new financing. Whether in the form of equity issues or long-term loans, the terms on which that capital can be secured depend on the price at which the corporation's stock is selling, which in turn reflects its present and prospective profit position. Moreover, a strong profit position is necessary to discourage an attempted takeover by a less socially conscious corporate raider who sees a return on assets that is not being fully realized by a management that may have followed its 'corporate conscience' with excessive zeal.

Second, a corporation must maintain a size (preferably a rate of growth) that permits it to continue those facilitating activities—advertising, research and development, personnel policies, public relations—on at least the scale that has brought it to its present position. A decline in size, even a declining rate of growth, creates problems of holding onto and recruiting high-quality talent and of finding places for or dismissing older employees. . . .

Such a fixation on profit and size does not arise because these are necessarily the most desirable objectives that can be imagined . . . but because the firm is driven to them by the requirements of its position.[12]

In summary then, corporations follow the path of profit and growth above all other values. If their discretion is further enlarged through the operation of the free market principle we may expect at that in some areas their derilections might expand correspondingly, even though some market distortions attributable to regulation might disappear; natural gas would flow again and new drugs will be produced again. But the costs of the free market approach might very well outweigh the benefits.

The Atomistic Model

Let us now examine the atomistic model advocated by a string of romantic liberals, of whom former Senator Fred Harris and the late Senator Estes Kefauver are conspicuous examples. In general, the advocates of the atomistic approach point to the increasing helplessness of the individual confronted with modern large-scale business, labor, and governmental institutions. To these advocates, smallness is goodness. Yet the notion that smallness is goodness is belied by the innumerable orders entered by the FTC against small firms, many of which involve vicious frauds. Further, greatly enlarging the number of enterprises renders regulation ever so much more difficult. Finally, as Robert Heilbronner succinctly stated in answer to the proposals for atomization, industries characterized by small units:

. . . have also been the models of industrial backwardness, characterized by low research and development, low wages and long hours, antiunionism, company towns, etc. I see no reason to believe than an IBM cut down to size would spend its fragmented profits in a more socially beneficial manner than its master company. . . . The power of the corporation to work social good or evil would not be lessened by fragmenting it. It would only be made less visible and hence, in the end, less accountable or controllable than by bringing it out into the open at the top.[13]

Lower Levels of Oligopoly

If atomizing the structure of American industry appears to be a fruitless policy, what of policies creating less concentrated oligopolies as embodied in the Hart Bill? Implicit in such proposals is the assumption that performance by smaller firms and less concentrated oligopolies is superior to performance by larger firms and more concentrated oligopolies. While early studies, particularly one by economist Joe Bain, found a positive correlation between profits and industrial concentration, later studies have seriously undermined these. For example, Yale Brozen, who carried forward into later years Bain's study and enlarged the number of industries sampled, found that the alleged relationship between concentration and profit did not exist. He found that rates of return in highly concentrated industries moved toward the average rate in later years.[14] Further, another recent study also tends to show that variations in profit rates are not associated with concentration or are only weakly associated. Rather, "most of the explained variation in profit rates comes from economies of scale in production, changes in industry demand and changes in firm demand."[15]

The best evidence to date shows that "most if not all of the positive correlations between profit rates and concentration uncovered by some earlier studies can be attributed to variations in the size of firms, not the degree to which markets are concentrated."[16] Thus, the higher profit rates of high concentration industries are due to the greater proportion of very large firms in such industries. These firms tend to produce more efficiently and at lower average cost than their smaller competitors.[17] Large firms benefit from plant economies of scale, capital raising economies, procurement economies, etc., while multi-plant large firms benefit from economies of coordination, research, and distribution.[18] Thus, a move to deconcentrate industries by breaking up large firms is very likely to increase, not decrease, costs and prices.

This conclusion tends to be confirmed by a study of price increases over the 1947-1971 period which shows that the prices of products produced by large oligopolistic corporations have displayed a generally slower rate of increase than have "market determined" prices.[19] A deconcentration policy might very likely have the effects of raising costs and prices, advancing the rate of inflation and retarding economic development by sharply reducing profits which could be employed for expansion, cost reduction or innovation. Nor is there convincing evidence that any compensating public benefits would accrue from such a policy.

Public Utility and Public Ownership Models

Finally, we reach the full-scale public utility and public ownership models. In the former model almost all of a firm's discretion is transferred to a public authority which effectively makes every major decision for a firm.

But why, one may ask, should private ownership be continued in such circumstances if all justification for the entrepreneurial function is removed? In any event, as a firm's discretion is more and more removed and as profit considerations are made subsidiary to other "public interest" considerations, it is only reasonable to believe that needed capital would not gravitate toward such industries from lending institutions. Rather capital would gravitate toward industries and nations which do not impose such fetters on the profit motive. The government would then have to become the principal source of funds. The full public utility model, then, tends to lead to the final model—public ownership—the great merit of which is that conflict between public goals and corporate profit maximizing goals *could* disappear since there is *theoretically* no further role for the latter. This is not to say by any means that accounting disappears, but rather that turning a profit becomes only one of several enterprise goals. But public enterprise raises the question of whether an alternative system of effective incentives can replace the pecuniary system of incentives under capitalism. For public ownership is not necessarily a panacea as the examples of the United States Post Office and the French match book industry, among others, illustrate. Moreover, public ownership has been associated with enough repressive regimes to raise the question of whether public ownership and totalitarianism are inexorably linked, as Hayek and others argue. We need not belabor the dangers of concentrating economic and political power in a few hands; several nations dramatically illustrate them.

The writer, frankly, recognizes that these constitute grave questions. Yet the attractiveness of a solution which appeals to mankind's finer instincts rather than to his baser ones is too great to throw away simply because of a number of bad examples. Why did the Soviet Union, China, etc., become totalitarian? Is it not plausible that their underdeveloped status, rather than their economic systems, is the root cause? Could not widespread public ownership in the United States or any other developed society operate within a democratic framework?

Obviously, space precludes any detailed analyses of these questions, but the questions of: (1) how public ownership can be instituted without the repressive apparatus with which so-called Socialist regimes have so frequently been saddled, and (2) the substitution of new incentives for profit maximization constitute far more fruitful lines of inquiry than the old saw of how to improve regulation.

Notes

1. See the discussion in Milton Friedman, "Barking Cats," *Newsweek*, February 19, 1973, p. 70.

2. On the capture thesis, the class is Grant McConnell, *Private Power*

and American Democracy (New York: Alfred A. Knopf, 1967). The leading case study is Samuel P. Huntington, "The Marasmus of the I.C.C.," *Yale Law Journal* (April 1952). A typical Naderite study of regulation is Edward C. Cox, Robert C. Fellmeth, and John E. Schulz, *The 'Nader Report' on the Federal Trade Commission* (New York: Richard E. Baron, 1969). The theme of closeness between regulators and regulated and corruption is developed in Bernard Schwartz, *The Professor and the Commissions* (New York: Alfred A. Knopf, 1959). See also Fred R. Harris, "The Politics of Corporate Power," in Ralph Nader and Mark Green, *Corporate Power in America* (New York: Grossman, 1973), pp. 25-42.

3. See U.S., Congress, House, Subcommittee on Commerce and Finance, Committee on Interstate and Foreign Commerce, *The Federal Trade Commission–1974*, Staff Report, 1974. See also Richard A. Posner, *Regulation of Advertising By The F.T.C.* (Washington: American Enterprise Institute, 1973); and Alan Stone, "The F.T.C. and Advertising Regulation," *Public Policy* 21 (1973): 203-234.

4. Alfred D. Chandler, Jr., "The Structure of American Industry in the Twentieth Century: A Historical Overview," *Business History Review* 43 (Autumn 1969): 280.

5. See Sam Peltzman, "An Evaluation of Consumer Protection Legislation: The 1962 Drug Amendments," *Journal of Political Economy* (September-October 1973): 1049-1091; and J.M. Jadlow, "Price Competition and the Efficacy of Prescription Drugs," *Nebraska Journal of Economics and Business* (Autumn 1972): 121-133. That technological development in highly regulated industries falls far short of the ideal and even of a reasonable target for public policy is the burden of William M. Capron (ed.), *Technological Change in Regulated Industries* (Washington: The Brookings Institution, 1971).

6. Paul MacAvoy, "The Effectiveness of the Federal Power Commission," *Bell Journal of Economics and Management Science* (Spring 1970): 113-128; and Paul MacAvoy, "The Regulation Induced Shortage of Natural Gas," *Journal of Law and Economics* (April 1971): 167-199.

7. That these are the overriding goals of business firms is empirically verified in James S. Earley, "Marginal Policies of Excellently Managed Firms," *American Economic Review* (March 1956): 44-71; and James S. Early in *American Economic Review: Papers and Proceedings* 47 (1957): pp. 333-335.

8. "Goodyear Chief Hits Regulation." *New York Times*, November 11, 1975, p. 45; and "*Fortune*'s Directory of the 500 Largest Industrial Corporations," *Fortune*, May 1975, pp. 208-238.

9. See. E.J. Mishan, *The Costs of Economic Growth* (London: Penguin Books, 1967), pp. 147-151.

10. For details see the long series of hearings and reports of the Senate Subcommittee on Antitrust and Monopoly collectively entitled *Administered Prices: Drugs*.

11. A superb essay summarizing the literature on externalities is E.J. Mishan, "The Post War Literature on Externalities: An Interpretative Essay," *Journal of Economic Literature* (March 1971): pp. 1-28.

12. Neil W. Chamberlain, *The Limits of Corporate Responsibility* (New York: Basic Books, 1973), pp. 5, 6. See also Christopher D. Stone, *Where the Law Ends* (New York: Harper Row, 1975), pp. 88-92.

13. Robert Heilbronner et al., *In the Name of Profits* (New York: Doubleday, 1972), p. 210.

14. Compare Yale Brozen, "Bain's Concentration and Rates of Return Revisited," *Journals of Law and Economics* (October 1971): 366; Yale Brozen, "The Antitrust Task Force Deconcentration Recommendation," *Journal of Law and Economics* (October 1970): 279-292; Yale Brozen and Joe S. Bain, "Relation of Profit Rate to Industry Concentration: American Manufacturing, 1936-1940," *Quarterly Journal of Economics* (August 1951): 293-324.

15. Stanley Ornstein, "Concentration and Profits," in J. Fred Weston and Stanley I. Ornstein, *The Impact of Large Firms on the U.S. Economy* (Lexington, Mass.: Lexington Books, D.C. Heath and Company, 1973), p. 101.

16. Harold Demsetz, "Two Systems of Belief About Monopoly," in Harvey J. Goldschmid et al., *Industrial Concentration: The New Learning* (Boston: Little-Brown, 1974), p. 179.

17. Harold Demsetz, "Industry Structure, Market Rivalry and Public Policy," in Goldschmid, pp. 80, 81. Yale Brozen, "Concentration and Profits: Does Concentration Matter?" in Goldschmid, *Industrial Concentration*, pp. 69, 70; and Betty Bock and Jack Farkas, *Concentration and Productivity* (New York: The Conference Board, 1969), pp. 4, 5.

18. See, for example, Charles E. Edwards, *Dynamics of the United States Automobile Industry* (Columbia, S.C.: University of South Carolina Press, 1965); and John S. McGee, "Economies of Size in Auto Body Manufacture," *Journal of Law and Economics* (October 1973): 239-274.

19. A.A. Thompson, "Absolute Firm Size, Administered Prices and Inflation," *Economic Inquiry* (June 1974): 240-254. See also the findings of Professor Ralph Beals, Reported in "Are Some Key Industries Pushing Up Inflation?" *Business Week* (October 6, 1975): 48.

Index

203

About the Contributors

Lawrence Baum is an assistant professor of political science at Ohio State University, with interests in judicial politics and in the policy-making process. His present research is on court screening of litigation and on relationships among courts in the federal judicial system.

David W. Brady received the Ph.D. in political science from the University of Iowa in 1970. He is the author of *Congressional Voting in a Partisan Era* and articles in the *American Political Science Review, Journal of Politics, American Journal of Political Science* and other professional journals. He is a professor of political science at the University of Houston.

Charles Bulmer is an assistant professor of political science at the University of Alabama in Birmingham. His teaching interests include American government and public policy, political theory, and international relations. He holds the Ph.D. degree from the University of Tennessee. Dr. Bulmer is engaged in research on equal employment opportunity policies in state agencies and is coauthor of "The War Powers Resolution: A Limitation on Presidential Power?" in the fall 1975 issue of the *Georgia Political Science Association Journal*.

John L. Carmichael, Jr. is an assistant professor of political science at the University of Alabama in Birmingham where his teaching interests include public policy, constitutional law and American foreign policy. He holds the J.D. degree from George Washington University and the Ph.D. degree from the University of Alabama. He is engaged in research on the constitutional and legal issues in congressional investigations. He is the author of "Land-Use Controls and the Right to Travel," in the winter 1976 issue of the *Cumberland-Samford Law Review* and, with Charles Bulmer, of "The War Powers Resolution: A Limitation on Presidential Power?" in the fall 1975 issue of the *Georgia Political Science Association Journal*.

George Daly is Professor and Chairman of the Department of Economics at the University of Houston. His specialty is public choice theory and his work has appeared in a number of professional journals including *The American Economic Review*.

Daniel J. Fiorino is an instructor in political science at Middlebury College. He received an M.A. from Johns Hopkins University in 1973, and is a Ph.D. candidate at Johns Hopkins. From 1973-75, he was a research

213

assistant at the Brookings Institution. His principal areas of interest include the judicial process, administrative behavior, and regulatory agencies.

Richard Fraenkel has been teaching at the University of Minnesota. He is now working at Purdue University on local participation in rural development activities.

John R. Gist received the Ph.D. from Washington University (St. Louis) and is an assistant professor of political science at the University of Georgia. His teaching and research interests are in the areas of American politics and the budgetary process. He has published articles on the budgetary process.

Don F. Hadwiger is a professor of political science at Iowa State University in Ames, Iowa. His research field is policies administered through the U.S. Department of Agriculture. He has written *Federal Wheat Commodity Legislation* (Iowa State Press, 1969), coauthored *Pressures and Protests: The Policy Process in American Agriculture* (Chandler, 1968).

Charles B. Hagan is Professor Emeritus of Political Science at the University of Houston. Previously he taught at the University of Illinois and Duke University where he received the Ph.D. He has published numerous articles on American politics and public policy.

William Jenkins, Jr., received the Ph.D. from the University of Wisconsin-Madison and is an assistant professor of political science at Wayne State University. His research interests include the judicial process and the role of the courts in the formation of economic regulatory policy.

Lloyd D. Musolf is Professor of Political Science and Director of the Institute of Governmental Affairs, University of California, Davis. His main books include: *Mixed Enterprise: A Developmental Perspective* (1972); *Legislatures in Developmental Perspective*, with Allen Kornberg (1970); *Promoting the General Welfare* (1965); *Public Ownership and Accountability: The Canadian Experience* (1959); and *Federal Examiners and the Conflict of Law and Administration* (1953).

Mark V. Nadel is the author of *The Politics of Consumer Protection* and a forthcoming book, *Corporation and Political Accountability*. He was an assistant professor of government at Cornell when this article was written and is now with the Office of the Assistant Secretary for International Affairs, U.S. Department of the Treasury.

Markley Roberts is an economist with the AFL-CIO in Washington, D.C. He has worked at the Washington Star Newspaper and in the office of Senator Hubert H. Humphrey and has been involved in national and local political activity.

Alan Stone, an assistant professor of political science at Rutgers University, was a trial attorney with the Federal Trade Commission. He is coauthor of *The Ruling Elites* and author of a forthcoming study of the politics of trade regulation as well as articles on business-government relations and political sociology.

Norman C. Thomas is Professor and Head of the Department of Political Science at the University of Cincinnati. Previously he taught at the University of Michigan and at Duke University. His recent work has included studies of national educational policy-making and the presidency.

Garth Youngberg is an assistant professor of political science at Southwest Missouri State University. He received the Ph.D. from the University of Illinois. His teaching interests are in the area of American politics and his research has focused on agricultural policy, including the farmer committee system.

About the Editor

James E. Anderson is Professor and Chairman of the Political Science Department at the University of Houston. His books include *Public Policy-Making* (1975), *Texas Politics: An Introduction* (1971), *Political and Economic Policy Making (1970), and Politics and the Economy* (1966). He has been an officer in the Southern and the Southwestern political science associations.